MW00981738

_40_ _of 200 copies,_

limited first printing, December 2014

www.voicesofhumanism.com

place under Non-Fiction;
Religion & Atheism;
Politics, Civil & Human Rights;
Science & Cultural Studies

FIRST EDITION, LIMITED TO 200 COPIES
ISBN 978-0-9877987-1-8

Contact the Editor, Gary Bauslaugh, at *gary@voicesofhumanism.com*.
Contact the Designer & Publisher, Emrys Miller, at *emrys@voicesofhumanism.com*.

Copyright © 2014 by Rocketday Arts, the contributing writers and illustrators.
All rights are reserved, but several parts of this book are available to under a Creative
Commons licence, free of charge. Contact *emrys@voicesofhumanism.com* for further
information on the availability of specific articles.

Library & Archives Canada Cataloguing in Publication info available upon request.

Rocketday Arts, Publishers
140 Moss Street, Victoria, BC, Canada, v8v 4M3
www.rocketday.com

Voices
of Humanism

an anthology of 35 articles by 15 humanists

FOR THEO MEIJER

WRITERS & ILLUSTRATORS

THANK YOU

ROCKETDAY ARTS

INTRODUCTION

What is humanism? Is it only about contesting the beliefs of the religious, as so often it may seem?

On the contrary, humanism is a multidimensional worldview that entails a deep respect for the seemingly conflicting, but actually complementary, ideas of personal autonomy and commitment to community. Personal autonomy, and the freedom of thought it entails, is not the enemy of civilized and respectful human relationships; rather, it is the means by which we can overcome the ignorance and prejudice that are so corrosive to such relationships. Humanists believe that independence of thought, not dictated or directed by any arbitrary authority, can best lead to the rationality and justice that are at the heart of building more tolerant and compassionate human communities.

We are all autonomous individuals but, as philosopher Joseph Tussman writes in the opening essay in this collection, we are not independent of those who live around us. We cannot simply be unbridled individualists, free of obligations to community, unconcerned about being our brother's or our sister's keeper. Of such people Tussman writes:

> *They have forgotten that we did not create, nourish, sustain or develop ourselves; that we did not invent our mother tongue and the mind or consciousness so dependent on it; nor the arts and skills embodied in the habits that constitute our character and culture ... Each of us is an individual person but we are all group generated, group shaped, group sustained, group dependent.*

Following from these two core beliefs — personal autonomy and allegiance to community — humanism asserts a number of positive and life-affirming ideas. In 1952 the International Humanist and Ethical Union (IHEU), with 90 member organizations from around the world, formulated a statement describing in some detail the full meaning of humanism in the modern world. At the 50th anniversary of the organization in Amsterdam in 2002 the statement was reformulated, with seven fundamental principles, as reprinted here:

1 — *Humanism is ethical.* It affirms the worth, dignity and autonomy of the individual and the right of every human being to the greatest possible freedom compatible with the rights of others. Humanists have a duty of care to all of humanity including future generations. Humanists believe that morality is an intrinsic part of human nature based on understanding and a concern for others, needing no external sanction.

2 — *Humanism is rational.* It seeks to use science creatively, not destructively. Humanists believe that the solutions to the world's problems lie in human thought and action rather than divine intervention. Humanism advocates the application of the methods of science and free inquiry to the problems of human welfare. But humanists also believe that the application of science and technology must be tempered by human values. Science gives us the means but human values must propose the ends.

3 — *Humanism supports democracy and human rights.* Humanism aims at the fullest possible development of every human being. It holds that democracy and human development are matters of right. The principles of democracy and human rights can be applied to many human relationships and are not restricted to methods of government.

4 — *Humanism insists that personal liberty must be combined with social responsibility.* Humanism ventures to build a world on the idea of the free person responsible to society, and recognizes our dependence on

and responsibility for the natural world. Humanism is undogmatic, imposing no creed upon its adherents. It is thus committed to education free from indoctrination.

5 — *Humanism is a response to the widespread demand for an alternative to dogmatic religion.* The world's major religions claim to be based on revelations fixed for all time, and many seek to impose their world-views on all of humanity. Humanism recognizes that reliable knowledge of the world and ourselves arises through a continuing process of observation, evaluation and revision.

6 — *Humanism values artistic creativity and imagination and recognizes the transforming power of art.* Humanism affirms the importance of literature, music, and the visual and performing arts for personal development and fulfillment.

7 — *Humanism is a life stance aiming at the maximum possible fulfillment through the cultivation of ethical and creative living and offers an ethical and rational means of addressing the challenges of our times.* Humanism can be a way of life for everyone everywhere.

How does a humanist's perspective influence thinking about social issues? *Voices of Humanism* gives some answers to this question by providing commentaries by humanists on a wide range of issues of human importance. These essays show how humanistic thinking leads to rational, thoughtful, evidence-based and sometimes even humorous approaches to social issues — not to say that humanists are the only people in society doing this, but to show that they, with their particular beliefs, are in the vanguard of progressive thinking.

What does a humanist have to say about morality or education or politics or metaphorical expression? We find that their views on such topics are far from being monolithic: as expressed in this book, they are varied and sometimes conflicting. The complex difficulties of building a better human society, along with the idea of freedom of thought that is prized by all humanists, ensures that many different perspectives on social issues will exist in the humanist movement. What these perspectives have in common is not uniformity in conclusions but consistency in approach; all are infused with the reason and compassion that lies at the heart of humanism.

Most of these essays were originally published in the Canadian magazine *Humanist Perspectives* during the five years (2003 to 2008) when I was Editor, and Emrys Miller (of Rocketday Arts) was the Designer. The essays, chosen to explore the seven fundamentals of humanism as expressed by the IHEU, show how humanistic thinking can help lead us toward a more rational, just and compassionate world.

Thank you for joining us on this exploration. ❧

Gary Bauslaugh, Editor

PART 1

HUMANISM & ETHICS

Humanism is ethical. It affirms the worth, dignity and autonomy of the individual and the right of every human being to the greatest possible freedom compatible with the rights of others. Humanists have a duty of care to all of humanity including future generations. Humanists believe that morality is an intrinsic part of human nature based on understanding and a concern for others, needing no external sanction.

MORALITY
WITHOUT RELIGION

by Joseph Tussman

SPEECH GIVEN AT KOSMOS CLUB
BERKELEY, SEPTEMBER 2002

I was thrilled when, as a teenager, I encountered Ivan Karamazov's "If there is no God, everything is permitted." But Ivan is no longer one of my heroes. I retain some sympathy for Dostoyevski's old Czarist General who, overhearing some atheistic chatter in his club finally jumps to his feet exclaiming "If there is no God, how can I be a General?" I was not there to assure him that he could, in any case, keep his rank.

But I am here now and I am tired of hearing from a parade of TV sages that without God there can be no morality. It is not merely that they are mistaken, but that they go — are permitted to go — unchallenged. In a charitable mood I take the "no God = no morality" pronouncement as a simple confession that the speaker cannot imagine why anyone would act *morally* except in obedience to the commands of a great Lawgiver who will detect and punish all disobedience. No great Lawgiver, no great commandments, no moral law, no morality, no reason to act morally except the hope of reward or fear of punishment.

Morality, in short, as simply a higher sort of *legality* with God as the Sovereign-enactor, Judge, punisher and rewarder. And thus, no God, no morality.

The trouble is, that while there are Kingdoms (or polities) in the world, the world is not — may not be — a Kingdom. I love Genesis as I love Homer; I believe Genesis about as I believe in the Iliad. I also believe in the existence and importance of morality and I am tired of being told that unless I share some version of the Kingdom view I can't have morality. So I will now explain very simply the universal secular basis of morality.

The Human Unit is a group. It is only necessary to remind us of this obvious fact in a culture infected by the delusions of individualism. The *individualist* heresy is a topic in its own right and I will content myself here with a few passing insults. Individualists are persons afflicted by some combination of amnesia and ingratitude. They have forgotten that we did not create, nourish, sustain, or develop ourselves; that we did not invent our mother tongue and the mind or consciousness so dependent on it; nor the arts and skills embodied in the habits that constitute our character and culture; that 'growing up' is essentially 'growing into' ways of life waiting hospitably to receive us. Each of us is an individual person but we are all group generated, group shaped, group sustained, group dependent. This is beautifully expressed in the great Platonic parable about our two-stage marsupial birth, about how after we emerge from a brief time in the first womb we are popped into our great marsupial pouch, the Polis, in which we complete our development into human beings, equipped with language, mind, character and culture.

I pause to note that as members of groups we are involved in a division of labour, a variety of tasks, a differentiation of function. And that we experience cycles of dependence, interdependence and relative independence.

But I linger over a crucial implication of being 'group' creatures. It seems utterly clear to me that group creatures must have a psychological make-up suitable for that condition. They must have innate, deep-seated drives, cravings, impulses that serve the interests, well-being and preservation of the group, including the sporadic pleasure of self-sacrifice.

This is so obvious that I am puzzled by how reluctant people are to admit it. The dominating metaphysical assumption — really counter-intuitive — is that we are individuals constructed so as to always seek and promote our own personal interests.

We seek to explain 'altruism' away as really selfishness after all or, if that fails, a sort of insane aberration. An old philosophy professor of mine invented a lovely fallacy — "the fallacy of the suppressed cor-relative." Put simply: we make the obvious distinction between selfish and unselfish acts. Then, in a mood of cynicism or disillusionment we deny the distinction — suppress the correlative — all acts, including the 'unselfish' act, are selfish after all. My individualistic friends are always doing that. All acts are selfish, they insist, even as they proceed to trample on their private interests for the sake of children, colleagues, friends, lovers, and even country. But as I once said, "Nothing is as irresistible as an error whose time has come." It is an error dear to our age of individualism.

Morality is deeply concerned with the relations of members of groups to one another. The language in which the demands of morality are expressed is the language of obligation — of should, ought, of what one is supposed to do, ought to do, is obliged to do or, in a grimmer mode, has a duty to do. Being moral involves doing the right thing in the domain of obligation.

Everyone growing up in any culture will experience something like a chore. To be a functioning part of a group is to have a part to play, to share in the division of labour. In a simple childish way it is to have a chore that is yours to perform. It is an early lesson in responsibility, a significant initiation, a step away from mere dependence towards the dignity of interdependence.

You cannot describe a chore (or a task or a function) without using the language of morality. Whether it is bringing in the morning news-paper, or keeping the dog's water dish full, there is something you are supposed to do, ought to do, should do. It is a step beyond doing merely what you want to do or feel like doing. You may feel honoured to be assigned the task, and you may feel like doing it, of course, but you are obliged to do it whether you feel like doing it or not. A child grasp-ing the demands of a chore is learning about the duties of office, about obligations, about the priority of obligation over desire, and, alas, about the dereliction of duty. The chore is a primitive paradigm of morality. Understanding it is a step in growing up and every normal person — in any society — comes to grasp the force of this fundamental aspect of social consciousness, to share the intuition of obligation.

Now, beyond chores or functions, consider games. A game is a kind of social activity, present in every culture and especially familiar in a gaming culture like ours. A game is constituted by explicit and implicit rules defining what you are supposed to do and how you are to do it. Winning a game is doing something within the rules. Cheating is trying to win while violating the rules, and everyone knows that you are not supposed to cheat. Everyone who plays or watches games knows the difference between a sportsmanlike respect for the rules and the spirit of the game, a dubious habit of stretching the rules, and a deplorable tendency to try to get away with breaking the rules. The lessons of morality are inescapably deployed by the life of games, and a child may find that if he won't play by the rules they won't play with him, that he may suffer exile.

Finally, in this short list, consider promises. Every child knows, even if bitterly disillusioned, that a promise is something you are supposed to keep, to fulfill. If I promise to read two chapters tomorrow to make up for missing one tonight, I am supposed to do so, ought to do so, have an obligation to do so. Children grasp promises as they grasp chores and games. "But you promised!" is an indignant recognition and step into the complex world of commitments, covenants, agreements, contracts. Even a child understands that we are supposed to keep promises, fulfill agreements. It is a moral intuition that is part of the necessary, inherent equipment of a social animal.

Chores, games and promises (among other things) inescapably exercise and develop the moral sense of every member of any group or family or community and become part of the habitual structure of one's character. In growing up we learn to be 'moral,' we acquire the habits of morality, long before it occurs to us to ask — as we inevitably will — *why be moral?* Why should I do what I am supposed to do, play by the rules, honour my commitments when I could gain by not doing so? What is the point of being moral, when the wicked flourish at the expense of the righteous? Habit, as we know, becomes subject to reflection, and every generation poses the *why be moral?* question, although seldom as deeply as in the Book of Job and Plato's Republic.

The familiar *why be moral?* crisis is really better stated as *why should I continue to be moral?* It arises in a moral context, in a functioning world of roles and agreements, conditions that are prior to the possibility of immorality. It is, after all, only in a world in which debt-honouring is a habit, that it is possible to borrow, to acquire the debt that it is then possible to not honour. Morality is prior to, presupposed by immorality. Or, to put it another way, immorality is parasitic upon existing morality. 'Cheating' depends upon others not cheating; it lives on, depends on the existence of a system of rules sustained by general observance; it takes advantage of those who play by the rules.

I stress the parasitic quality of such immorality to express my contempt for the silly glorification of the rampant young lion who breaks free of the chains of conventional morality, the strong who are unrestrained by the conspiracy of the slavish or mediocre weak, the exceptional hero to whom the rules do not apply, and all that stirring urchin 'philosophy' that disguises the pathetic parasitism of great or petty scoundrels.

Nevertheless, the *why be moral* crisis — always arising, always recurring — must be dealt with. Argument must be marshalled to support conventional habit. How does the argument go?

I assume that the *if everyone did that* argument, although basically true, won't work because the questioner assumes that the others, generally, will continue to play by the rules, making it possible to gain by taking advantage of them. The heart of immorality is treating oneself as an exception to the rules. It is the gleaming profitability of that *that* is so appealing, overcoming, in the case of incipient sociopaths, the sense of righteous belonging. So we must, sadly, move beyond reminding the tempted that the contemplated behaviour is wrong or immoral or, more starkly, evil. It appears profitable.

So we argue the consequences and move in two directions. First, you will be detected, found out, caught, and suffer punishment — disapproval, exclusion, fines, imprisonment or other concrete material sanctions. This is countered by the claim that detection will be avoided or that the punishment will be mild compared to the gains. I spare you the pain of pursuing this weary argument.

Second, even if undetected you will suffer the internal pangs of conscience, of guilt and shame. You will, in this way, punish yourself. The familiar response is to claim or develop a calloused conscience, to minimize the significance of guilt and shame or to seek, with the aid of a school of advisors, to exorcise these archaic emotions. Unfortunately, they are not merely archaic. They are, for a social being, a group animal, what thirst is for a biological creature — a reminder, like a red light on a car's dashboard, that something vital is being neglected. In the case of guilt, that you are harming the sustaining context of significant human life, including your own. Shoving us all, in your feeble way, to a condition described by Hobbes in which life is "solitary, poor, nasty, brutish and short." A sane person heeds the warning. But it is hard to deal with a miserable sociopath who may suffer from the delusion — and a delusion it is — that, in his crooked way, he is happy.

Being moral is, I repeat, doing the right thing in the domain of obligation. Awareness of and responsiveness to the claims of morality is part of the habitual equipment of a normal human being. The sociopath lacks the insights and convictions of a normal human being. He lacks the intuitions of obligation. He does not suffer the torments of an insulted conscience. What can we do about him? How can we make him 'moral'? I'm sorry, but I have no new cure for forms of moral idiocy. But I note that this idiocy is marginal. The fate of morality does not rest on what can convince or convert the sociopath; anymore than the fate of rationality or logic turns on finding arguments that can convince the irrational.

It is sometimes claimed that a religious conversion or 'getting religion' can do the trick. I hope so, although I suspect that the religion embraced by a sociopath would be a sociopathic version of religion. I do have some respect for the interesting 'born again' experience. Every human being has had the experience, however deeply buried in the layers of the mind, of being thrust from the womb, helpless in a cold world, and saved from extinction by acts of unearned love. This 'saved by unearned love' is simply a universal fact of life and its sudden recollection or realization may well transform an ungrateful life. It is, for me, a secular experience common to every human being in any community, or any religion or of no religion at all. It is not an exclusively Mediterranean insight.

But what might cure the sociopath is not why normal people behave morally. If we would treat others as we would like to be treated, if we modestly decline to treat ourselves as exceptions, it is not because of commands, of punishments and rewards. It is because of the human sympathetic imagination that is part of the nature of human social beings. They do not have to be scared into morality. Morality is a necessary human habit.

Let me end as I began, with poor silly Ivan Karamazov. He had returned from the University in the grip of an idea that created havoc in his family and friends, his home town and the local church: "If there is no God, everything is permitted!" Who, I would like to know, what non-tenure-track teaching assistant, had taught him that? What reading had he been assigned? I suppose it was the subject of Ivan's term paper, and I bet it even got an A. Not, let me assure you, a grade he would have received in my freshman philosophy class at Berkeley. In one of my grimmer moods I might have simply scrawled "Incomplete. See me!" In the gentler Socratic mood that I sometimes tried to achieve, I might have written:

Dear Ivan — Do you really think that, if there is no God, you are permitted to ignore the red traffic lights on Telegraph and Bancroft? Please explain. And I assume you don't mean anything as foolish as that if you escape detection and punishment you are permitted to do what you are not permitted to do.

Morality is, in short, a natural and necessary feature of the human situation. We are group creatures and we develop the language of desire and the language of obligation, of pleasure and of morality. We do not need to be reminded that where there is morality there is, of course, immorality as well, and that life involves us in the familiar struggle between them. Between right and wrong, good and evil. The spectacle of that struggle can be ugly and disheartening, full of cruelty and betrayal. It sometimes depresses me. I cheer myself up with two sayings that I share with you, in case you need comforting. Auden once wrote of the Governess in the dead of night giving the Universe an 'F' for behaviour.

My more charitable grade — I was rather a soft grader — "For Angels, terrible; for animals, not bad." And finally, "Always remember that we deserve the glory of having created the great ideals that we betray."

To sum up — Morality is too important to be made to depend upon anything else. Not on philosophy or metaphysics, not on a variety of religious beliefs, not on power or coercion. We are, as I have repeatedly said, group beings or, as the Greeks said, political animals, and the fundamental principles of morality are necessarily and universally imbedded in the human scene. 🦋

EDITOR'S NOTE

I knew Joe Tussman — not well but through mutual friends. He kindly gave me permission to publish this essay, which I first did in the summer of 2006 in the magazine *Humanist Perspectives*. I saw Joe for the last time in Berkeley in September of 2005, where he and some friends met for lunch every week in a small restaurant. My friend Bob Rowan, former Philosophy professor at UBC, had been Tussman's student and they had remained close friends ever since. Bob invited me to the lunch, where he, Joe and three or four others talked about ideas and expressed their often strong opinions. It was an extraordinary experience, and pleasure, to be there with them.

I was in Berkeley, with Bob, investigating the American electronic voter fraud, and Joe and others talked about some of the things we had discovered. Some comments were made about the hopelessness of it all — how democracy was being so seriously compromised, how human nature seemed so fatally flawed. Joe didn't say much about this, but he listened closely — he always listened closely.

Finally, after all the others present had commented on how bad things are, Joe said:

"I was out walking the other day, and stopped to rest on a bench near the Society of Friends Hall [in Berkeley]. I was wearing my old clothes and, tired from the effort, leaned forward to rest my head on my cane. A woman came and sat down beside me — I didn't even notice her at first. She had come there to have her lunch. After a short while she turned to me and said, 'Are you hungry? Would you like something to eat?' She thought I was a derelict. I found this extraordinarily touching. This is still a world where such things happen. There is much kindness in humans."

Joe's friends, and there are many, were devastated by his death, though it was not unexpected. He had been frail and had been having heart trouble for some time. The world may not be such a bad place, but it certainly became a poorer place with his passing.

WHAT IS CONSCIENCE?

by Trudy Govier

"Let conscience be your guide."

But what *is* 'conscience?' We often think of it as a kind of a voice in the head, telling us what's right or wrong — a 'better self' within, representing the claims of morality. Each person is assumed to have an individual conscience, urging moral action or restraint. But what voice speaks to us as the voice of conscience? What is the source of its authority?

For religious believers, ready answers seem to be available: conscience is the voice of God and its teachings are divinely certified — hence their authority. Such a conception raises problems even within a theological frame of reference — and it is clearly not available for non-believers. Humanists who use the notion of conscience face the challenge of making sense of it in some other way.

We tend to think of conscience as though each person has within a kind of inner moral authority that articulates sound principles and applies them appropriately to the situations at hand. When conscience tells us something, this oracle within makes itself known, speaking out on relevant occasions to urge action or restraint, satisfaction or guilt. Is conscience, then, a special faculty of the mind, functioning to represent moral knowledge within us? That can't be quite right. For one thing, given variations and differences between cultures and individuals, the idea that we possess clear knowledge on moral matters is open to challenge. For another, the idea of a part of the brain organized to generate moral insight is scientifically implausible.

When we describe ourselves as feeling twinges of conscience, or the promptings of conscience, feelings seem to be involved. Is conscience, perhaps, a matter of feeling? An inner expression of such emotions as guilt, remorse, satisfaction or pride? This must be part of the story. But it can't be the whole account of conscience because these feelings are not simple sensations. They are based on beliefs about the rights and wrongs of situations and actions. If we feel guilty about what we've done, that sense of guilt presumes first that we did something wrong and second that we were responsible for doing it. A notion of conscience as feeling and feeling only will not allow us to account for these presumptions, which are cognitive in nature.

Perhaps the so-called 'voice' comes from social teachings and what we call conscience is the product of social learning. We have been taught in our families and communities what is right and wrong and when we feel promptings of conscience, we are recalling those teachings as though there is a voice speaking inside us. Being naturalistic, this theory may be attractive to many humanists. But it cannot account for many fascinating cases in which people have been inspired by 'conscience' to act in defiance of social norms in such contexts as apartheid, corporate corruption, and abuse of animals. Conscience is felt as something particular and individual: in striking cases highly motivated people may experience its voice as one that urges resistance to the teachings of communities and families.

Is the notion of conscience so embedded in faith and theology that it needs to be eliminated from a scientific world view? I find this solution unattractive, being convinced that the notion of conscience is a highly useful one. 'Conscience' is our way of describing the plain fact that many people are concerned with the humanitarian implications of their practices and actions.

When people think about conscience in relation to science, they consider ethical challenges to scientific research and its practices. A scientist whose 'conscience' troubles him when he is doing weapons research will reflect on whether the discoveries are likely to cause human suffering and death; these are concerns about consequences of the scientific work for human wellbeing and the wellbeing of other sentient creatures. Sometimes presumed attitudes of respect or disrespect are the central concern of such ethical deliberations. Central to conceptions of human rights is the conviction that humanity is something with dignity and intrinsic worth. Critics of research into genetic manipulation argue that its implications of manipulable human material threaten treasured, and ethically fundamental, conceptions of humanity and nature.

Should humanists relinquish the notion of conscience? Would relinquishing this notion entail giving up on ethics entirely? Few serious humanists would welcome those implications — as is immediately apparent when we examine articulations of humanist principles. If the humanitarian dimension of human thought were eliminated due to philosophical skepticism about the foundations of ethics, the loss would be terrible.

My own modest proposal is that we think of 'conscience' in terms of moral beliefs rather than moral knowledge. The shift from knowledge to belief acknowledges human fallibility and uncertainty — and, as their corollary, the fallibility and uncertainty of human conscience. The idea of 'conscience' as a shorthand way of referring to moral beliefs allows for a realm of moral reflection and direction. At the same time, it renders intelligible skepticism and disagreement on moral questions. To think of conscience as a voice within is a useful metaphor, but to think of it as the definitive authority is to lapse into error.

Conscientious people reflect on moral matters and care about the impact of their actions on those other than themselves. Being aware of the significant effects that our actions can have on others and on our fragile and interdependent environment, conscientious people — including humanists — seek to act with consideration and respect that transcends self-interest. We reason that, by consistency, if we are worth something and if our personal wellbeing counts because we can suffer and care what happens to us, the same will hold true for others. They are beings with dignity and worth; their wellbeing matters.

If I talk about "what my conscience tells me to do," I'm referring to "what I think I ought to do, all things considered." What we call the 'dictates of conscience' come from our thinking, reasoning and deliberating. The notion of conscience provides a shorthand way of referring to moral beliefs. The 'voice of conscience' is something we have constructed for ourselves, taking into account personal experience, feelings, social teaching, scientific findings and relevant religious teachings. A humanist notion of conscience allows for its individuality by stressing the thought and deliberation that construct conclusions from these varied sources. For humanists there will be no inconsistency in using all of them, provided that none is presumed to provide the last, definitive word.

The voice of conscience is not divinely inspired, according to this account. It is no more transcendent than the everyday voice that reminds us to carry an umbrella or take out the garbage. And yet conscience dares to pronounce on matters of morality, often highly serious matters with profound implications. That voice comes from within our very human selves: it has been constructed by our own deliberation and reasoning. It should never be ignored, although it is human, fallible and utterly mundane. ❧

A PROBLEM
OF ACKNOWLEDGEMENT

by Trudy Govier

Victims of past wrongs such as slavery, apartheid or colonialism can receive acknowledgement only if those responsible for the wrongs sincerely admit their responsibility. Victims may request public apologies, legal judgments, inquiries, truth commissions, monetary compensation, revision of curricula and textbooks, or public commemoration in the form of museums, statues, artwork or memorial days. For acknowledgement to be granted, accused perpetrators must agree that what was allegedly done was *actually done*, what is claimed to be wrong *was actually wrong*, and they, the alleged agents, *were actually responsible for the acts in question.* The language of acknowledgement is passive in a way that can be highly misleading. Urging 'acknowledgement' and waxing eloquent about its reconciliatory value, it's too easy to ignore the fact that while victims want to receive it, those from whom it is requested will rarely be enthusiastic about responding.

In a culture saturated with therapy, the notion of denial is likely to be more familiar than that of acknowledgement. We can think of acknowledgement as an opposite of denial. In a personal context, acknowledgement of a problem means admitting that you have it — spelling it out to yourself and accepting it as part of who you are. Acknowledgement of a problem implies acceptance of some commitment to do something to address it. In individual cases, the person who needs to acknowledge his problem is the same one who can be expected to benefit from acknowledgement. That is not true in most political situations. There, benefits are anticipated by one group, while costs must be paid by another. Those asked to acknowledge rarely expect to benefit from doing so. If we seek to understand why acknowledgement is valuable, we have to contextualize the question and ask "valuable for whom?"

In political contexts, why is acknowledgement important? This one question turns into three. First, why is moral acknowledgement important for victims? Second, why is it important for community and society? Third, why is it important for perpetrator groups? A crucial problem about acknowledgement is that although the first two questions are relatively easy to answer, the third is not.

From the victim perspective, acknowledgement of past wrongs articulates, publicly, a recognition of moral worth. The clear implication of moral acknowledgement is that victims did not deserve the harmful treatment they received. A clear and all-important implication is that these wrongs should never be repeated. This conveyed commitment offers reassurance to victims and a basis for renewed trust and cooperative capacity — elements crucial in any context of reconciliation between previously opposed groups.

From the societal perspective, the value of moral acknowledgement is also clear. However it is expressed, an official public acknowledgement that certain policies and actions were wrong stands as a credible and durable obstacle to subsequent denial. These forms of acknowledgement are public expressions of more humane values — durable, almost tangible expressions of the principle that basic rights belong to all human beings.

From the perpetrator perspective, acknowledgement has costs and its benefits are less obvious. That's the problem: at this point there's a gap in the theory of acknowledgement. This difficulty tends to receive little attention, because discussions of redress and reconciliation usually focus on the needs and interests of victims. We rather naturally tend to empathize and identify with victims and will far more easily regard ourselves as allied with them than as associates of perpetrators.

In the wake of the Good Friday Agreement (1998) setting out arrangements for ceasefire and political compromise in Northern Ireland, people who committed acts of violence are often referred to as ex-combatants. Many such persons served long prison terms; by many, they are regarded as ex-criminals, or even criminals. Persons more comfortably removed from the conflict often criticize the proposed political arrangements on the grounds that we are going to have "criminals are in government" or "terrorists are running around on the streets."

On a short visit to Belfast, I had the opportunity to discuss acknowledgement with a graduate class on Reconciliation. I pointed to the gap in theories of acknowledgement so far as perpetrators were concerned and asked those present for suggestions. Suppose, for instance, that someone had been an on-the-ground combatant in Northern Ireland's 'Troubles.' Suppose that there were considerable pressure on him, and on groups to which he belongs, to acknowledge having caused harm and suffering and to express remorse for having done so. Should ex-combatants do this? If victims and society stand to gain from such acknowledgement, they will have to receive it from ex-combatants, and if acknowledgement is valuable in contexts of reconciliation, then ex-combatants, and they alone, can make a crucial contribution to it. But what is in it for them?

Various responses were offered. Several people said, well if militants had brought harm and suffering to others due to their actions in the Troubles, then they should admit it; they should attempt, as individuals or through relevant community groups, to make practical amends for the damage, to the extent that that was possible. Ex-combatants who could acknowledge such wrongdoing to themselves and express it in some public form would be offering reassurance and a basis for trust to victim groups and to the public at large, which would clearly be a good thing. By their admissions, such persons would be making a crucial contribution to reconciliation processes and to avoiding a resumption of the political violence. Through such acknowledgement, ex-combatants would be cooperating in processes that would prevent further victimization. The moral argument for acknowledgement strikes me as cogent, but it makes no specific appeal to the interests of ex-militants themselves. The benefits accrue elsewhere.

I asked again. From the point of view of ex-combatants: what would be in it for them? Well, a person who had seriously harmed others could express his remorse, several people said. And if he did that, he might relieve his burden of guilt and come to feel better about himself. Expressing his guilt might help him develop a positive conception of himself — especially if, as a result of an apology or acts of restitution, he was forgiven by victims or their representatives. Relieving guilt would be a reason for a perpetrator to acknowledge wrongdoing — and that would be a reason based on his own self-interest.

This answer has some plausibility, but it also has its limitations. The alleged benefits for perpetrators come only on the assumption that they believe that they did something wrong. People who don't believe that have no burden of guilt to be relieved and no remorse they need to express. They feel no need to be forgiven — if someone were to forgive them, would feel it as patronizing and insulting. In Northern Ireland, acts of violence were committed over a thirty year period by people who thought they were fighting for a just cause — on both sides. And the same will be true of other violent political struggles — whether we are talking about the Basques, the Serbs, the Croats, the Tamil Tigers, the Palestinians and even the Taliban. Some who assault, threaten, maim and kill are criminal types — but many others are people who conscientiously think they are fighting a just war in order to protect and preserve their community. They may have served long jail terms for acts defined by others as illegal, but they see themselves as political agents and combatants — not as criminals or murderers. Did they act wrongly? Are they 'perpetrators' who have an obligation to acknowledge the wrongs they committed? They will not think so; they see themselves as brave fighters for a just cause.

In a context where a ceasefire is reasonably secure and the terms of a political settlement are gaining credibility, people who supported the conflict and shared responsibility for the violence may begin to change their minds about the conflict. They may come — as have the mainstream Nationalist and Unionist groups in Northern Ireland — to believe that it can be conducted by nonviolent means. Political arrangements will be revised and in their wake, reconciliation processes will begin. In this context, there is often a tendency to reinterpret the violent conflict and to isolate, criminalize, and scapegoat those who fought within it. Many people conveniently ignore their own role in supporting enmity and violence.

In such a context, putting pressure on ex-combatants in particular to acknowledge wrongdoing is problematic to say the least. In Northern Ireland, many such persons regard themselves not as wrongdoers but as brave combatants in a just war. Their role as fighters has been a central part of their identity; for many, it defined their role in the world. They saw themselves — and in many cases continue to see themselves — as taking brave risks to defend their community and sacrificing comfort and safety to do that. Several ex-combatants said categorically that the present situation in Northern Ireland is different, but as for their actions in the Troubles, if similar circumstances arose again, they would do it all over again. In that sense they have no regrets. These men don't think of themselves as having acted wrongly, so they don't accept responsibility for wrongdoing. Given these facts, they are in no position to offer sincere acknowledgement of wrongdoing. They aren't sorry for committing wrongs because they don't regard themselves as having done that. The gap in understanding acknowledgement seems very real.

As individuals and groups, people may come under considerable pressure to acknowledge. But coerced acknowledgement has no value for reconciliation and the restoration of trust.

In Belfast, several people spoke of a 'divided society.' The phrase captures the fact that there's no moral consensus on who was right in the Troubles. Perhaps no one; perhaps everyone. Perhaps the very concept of being right makes no sense in such contexts — though that interpretation would leave most victims desperately unsatisfied. Ian White, former head of the Glencree Reconciliation Center near Dublin, said sadly that in the Irish struggles, "We can only say that we have harmed one another greatly." Though wise in its implication of mutuality and shared responsibility, this comment does not fill the gap in our understanding of acknowledgement. Moral acknowledgement presupposes some fundamental level of agreement about who was responsible for doing what to whom, and whether the actions in question amounted to wrongdoing.

When your sense of identity and purpose have been tied to a political struggle conducted in a violent campaign, there are going to be enormous disincentives to renounce your sense of rightness in the interests of reconciliation. This is not to argue impossibility, but only to recognize a central difficulty. Any argument that you should relinquish your sense of justification and purpose because somebody else will benefit from your acknowledgement of wrongdoing is unlikely to carry the day.

For acknowledgement to be received it must be granted. Victims seek acknowledgement and for them to receive it, perpetrators and their affiliates must grant it, which brings us to the 'ex-combatant' role. My discussions in Northern Ireland helped me to understand how central this role is in any context seeking political reconciliation. In the wake of a violent political struggle there are, as a matter of necessity, many persons who have lived through that struggle, taken part in it, and made sacrifices for it. Many such people have been trained in the use of weapons and the perpetration of violence. An enormous challenge for rebuilding and moving towards a civil society characterized by the rule of law and sustainable peace is to reabsorb these people. They have to give up the ways of violence and find places in society where they can lead meaningful lives doing other things. I don't pretend to know how to achieve this sort of reintegration. But I do think I know a little bit about how not to do it: stigmatizing, scapegoating, and criminalization are not going to help.

My own sense is that people involved in threats, maiming, bombings, abductions and killing have committed wrongs — even granting that the context was one of a political struggle. But then, I'm generally more skeptical about political violence than many others and would be less ready to call in a just war to address issues of justification. I'm convinced violent action is needed far more rarely than most people suppose. And I'm very skeptical about claims that violence is a method of resolving conflicts — political or otherwise. Typically, people resort to violence in a political struggle because they believe it, and it alone, will bring them the result they want. The assumptions underlying this reasoning are many, and they're highly contestable. A common problem is that people make predictions on the basis of a narrative that ends too early. They ignore the physical and emotional messiness of the aftermath. ("We'll march triumphantly into Baghdad, destroy the dictatorial regime, be welcomed as liberators and get out." Right?) A physical victory does not eliminate a problem, even if 'bad guys' are killed, and the aftermath of political violence includes not only devastated infrastructure and physical injuries, but deep emotional wounds.

In Belfast, one ex-combatant, told me about the aftermath of his own involvement. As a young man, this person (we'll call him 'Paul') had been recruited to a Loyalist paramilitary and had killed someone. Paul had served a long jail term during which he received a university degree. Later he involved himself in reconciliation processes and ended up holding workshops and activities for ex-combatants on both sides of the struggles. Paul was a highly successful organizer and facilitator — so much so that he had gone to Bosnia and Kosovo several times to conduct workshops aimed at creating understanding between Croats, Muslims and Serbs. Those workshops were based on participants sharing stories about what they had gone through in the wars, and they had been well received.

Paul attended the Reconciliation seminar and said he appreciated my comments about the gap in standard accounts of acknowledgement. I said well, yes, I had written about this topic, but I later realized — from an entirely theoretical perspective — that the problem of acknowledgement by ex-combatants was not addressed in my account. Paul agreed, going on to say that it struck him the problem arose not only in my reflections but in other theories and, more significantly, in his own real experience. In divided societies — and that means most societies in the wake of a violent political struggle — people do not agree about what was right and wrong. Those called 'ex-combatants' or 'terrorists' or 'perpetrators' do not see themselves as wrongdoers and are thus not willing to acknowledge wrongdoing. If, when attending reconciliation workshops or conferences, they are pressed by victims or others to acknowledge guilt or express remorse, they will resist it. They will feel they have been scapegoated, and made victims themselves.

Paul told me sadly that there was another aspect of his reflections, one that might fill the gap so far as acknowledgement is concerned. He knew that actions he had taken as a young man had cost others their lives and all future happiness. Some days, he said, he would feel the warmth of the sun and take pleasure in the beauty of this world. He would begin to feel happy. But then he would reflect that there was someone else who could never enjoy such things. Actions of his had denied this person life and joy — and there was no way to bring those things back. Thinking more about what he had done and lived through, he recognized an ambivalence in himself, one that had been present even during his active days in the struggle. Though he had believed himself justified in fighting for his people, Paul was also aware that killing was something inhumane. He said that by killing another human being, he had destroyed something in himself, something he could never replace. There was a level at which he felt profound guilt about what he done and regarded it as fundamentally wrong — even though, in the 'just war,' it seemed right and still does.

Paul's work as a counselor and facilitator has given him considerable experience with other ex-combatants. He believes that most others have similar ambivalent feelings. These men believe they were right and justified; they resist pressure to express guilt and remorse. But somehow, deep down, they also sense that killing or harming other human beings was wrong. Many ex-combatants are involved in alcohol or drug abuse, broken relationships, or family violence. To Paul, these features of their lives show that they have been deeply hurt by their involvement in political violence. They are suffering deeply, but in ways they do not acknowledge, even to themselves. It is not only the questionable nature of their acts that they fail to acknowledge; it is the effect of those acts on themselves. "You have to be able to live with yourself," Paul said — and he told me sadly that he finds it difficult.

Moved by Paul's honesty and openness, I asked him whether it could help such people to be forgiven by victims. He didn't think so. The guilt was so deep, they would not be able to accept forgiveness even if it was offered to them. I asked about self-forgiveness, to be able to "live with yourself." He shook his head sadly.

Paul's conviction that many ex-combatants have deep guilt and pain suggests that the gap of acknowledgement might be filled. If these men carry a burden of guilt, then — at least potentially — there is something to be relieved through acknowledgement and reconciliation. I find myself hoping that ex-combatants really do suffer as a result of killing and wounding other people. If it's true, then they hurt too, and need to heal. Reconciliation processes can offer something to them as well as to victims. There is some prospect of a gain for ex-combatants — and the gap of acknowledgement would be addressed.

Under the circumstances — we were in a coffee shop — my conversation with Paul could go no further. But I'm still thinking about him and what he told me — and the many thousands of former fighters who might feel the same way. ✣

VISITING
UNINHABITED ISLANDS

by Trudy Govier

F rom the standpoint of the history of ideas, the Galapagos are the most famous islands in the world. One thousand miles from the South American continent, isolated, uninhabited by mammals, they struck early observers as puzzling. Within the eighteenth century framework of a design theology, the islands seemed highly anomalous. If God created the world and created it for the use and enjoyment of human beings, why would He have created these remote islands? Black with broken lava rock, occupied by strange and ugly creatures, they seemed to be of no use. When he visited the islands in 1835, Charles Darwin found them puzzling too. In addition to such fascinating creatures as iguanas and giant tortoises, there was the matter of the many species of finches. If God had created the world, what would have been his purposes in making these different species, to inhabit neighbouring islands? This apparently unanswerable question led Darwin away from design theology: it was not that God had mysteriously created species ideally suited for the lava archipelago; rather, chance arrivals had evolved to fit there. This reasoning inspired Darwin's evolutionary theory, establishing for the Galapagos Islands a firm place in the history of ideas. Darwin said that the Galapagos Islands brought us nearer to the mystery of mysteries — the first appearance of new beings on this earth.

I traveled in the Galapagos with my family in 2003. We were eco-tourists, with a group and a guide on a small boat. Carefully, we walked on monitored trails, sight-seeing, and wondering at the unique and almost uniquely tame animal species. We were warned not to touch the animals and that warning was not irrelevant — they were, in fact, tame enough to touch. These animals had never been hunted and seemed to have no fear of humans. We could swim with sea lions and giant tortoises. One woman said, "it's so wonderful to see animals without feeling guilty." Working on a book about political reconciliation at the time, I wondered whether our eco-tourism amounted to an effort toward reconciliation — reconciliation with nature.

From the point of view of deep ecology, we would want to value, love, and treasure the unusual species of the Galapagos — as people indeed do. We would want to value the biodiversity in this ecosystem, and preserve its integrity. Deep ecology teaches that the flourishing of non-human life and ecosystems is valuable in its own right and does not depend on its usefulness for human purposes. On this view, we should not value nature as a resource and source of commodities for ourselves. Rather, we should appreciate and understand that the flourishing and self-realization of every creature has value.

Interestingly, conservation itself often cannot proceed on the basis of this assumption. Its efforts point to new mysteries and anomalies, because considerable intervention is needed to keep a natural ecosystem, with its species diversity, viable in today's mobile world. In the Galapagos, many of the conservation and preservation efforts are aimed at keeping non-indigenous species out. The problem is, unique species of the islands, including iguanas and giant tortoises, are threatened by invasive species introduced (mostly since the early nineteenth century) by human beings. Goats, rats, cats, dogs, pigs, and over four hundred species of non-indigenous plants threaten the ecosystem that Darwin found in the Galapagos. The blackberry is said to be an especially aggressive and persistent plant. In the early 1800s there were four goats on The Islands; there are now estimated to be some 100,000. Goats compete with indigenous species for the sometimes-scarce vegetation and so they are culled. To preserve the ecosystem and protect the tortoises and iguana, every effort is made to kill off goats.

It is beautiful, even somewhat mystical, to reflect that all nature's creatures have intrinsic value and merit respect as forms of life. The problem is, this viewpoint, central to Deep Ecology, provides little guidance for policy and practice. It is surely not the background value theory of conservation efforts on the Galapagos. It was clear even on a short visit that animals living in the Galapagos do not all have the same value status. Threatened species like the giant tortoises are treasured and may be protected by captive breeding and rearing programs. In one breeding program for tortoises, a mate was found in the San Diego zoo. Lonesome George, believed to be the last survivor of his species, was valued as an individual; he was a poster subject. Sadly, he died in 2012. The land iguanas on the island of Santa Cruz bounced back after cats and dogs on the island were eradicated. These, then, are species — even individuals — that are protected and cultivated. Status one. There are also species that are left alone. These species are judged neither to be threatened nor to be threatening. Sea lions provide an example. (There are two different species on the Galapagos.) With these species, individual animals that are injured or ill are left to die. When we saw an orphaned sea lion pup lying on the beach looking sickly, with flies buzzing around it, no one sought to intervene. The animal would be left to die. "The mothers know they are ill," the naturalist guide told me. "A hawk will get it." The species is not in jeopardy. Status Two. As for the threatening non-indigenous invaders — goats and others — killing them is an act of conservation. Status Three.

For conservation of this ecosystem, human visitors and human settlement on the islands need to be limited. Status? Don't ask. Eco-tourism has supported conservation efforts, financially, and has provided jobs for some Ecuadorians. Visitors must restrict themselves to marked trails, garbage is kept to a minimum, and the park fee is large. (Eco-tourists tend to be reasonably affluent.) Philosophically, I found it fascinating to reflect that these efforts to preserve a unique ecosystem located the integrity and identity of that system with respect to a very human reference point — the state of the islands when Darwin visited in 1835.

What is Nature? A common response to this question is to

understand Nature as things in the world as the world would be if there were no human intervention. When this assumption is made, the accompanying assumption is usually that human intervention is a bad thing. But in the Galapagos — as in many other contexts — energetic human intervention is needed in efforts to keep an ecosystem viable and natural. To preserve marine ecosystems, fishing has to be restricted. Sea cucumbers and lobsters have been harvested to dangerous levels. To preserve land ecosystems, immigration from Ecuador has to be restricted. Without culling, goats would eliminate tortoises and land iguanas. Without weeding, non-indigenous plants would overwhelm native vegetation. Without restrictions, tourists would virtually invade, leave litter and garbage and demand consumer goods, food, and accommodation. A 'natural' market response would result in luxury condos and large hotels, inspiring a deluge of immigration by poor Ecuadorian citizens looking for work.

The Galapagos Islands have been declared by UNESCO to be a World Heritage Site. In June, 2007, less gloriously, the islands were listed as a World Heritage *In Danger* Site. Though eco-tourism has in many ways benefited the islands, it seems the main threat to the integrity of this ecosystem is *people*. There is contamination from boat paint and engines, oil spills and over-used sites, drains on fresh water supplies, and — despite strenuous efforts — introduction of plant and animal species from the mainland.

Human beings have made great efforts to preserve the ecosystem of these islands, which is so significant in the development of our understanding of adaptation and evolution. We hope that our efforts will continue and the distinct marvels of the Galapagos will survive. But there are still threats. And the final irony? In the end, the greatest threat may be us — the particularly and peculiarly invasive species of *human beings.* 🌢

LIVE FREEGAN OR DIE

by Jonny Diamond

We are driving across the 59th Street Bridge, from Manhattan to Queens, in the hour before dusk on Canadian Thanksgiving. It is a humid 30 degrees Celsius and traffic is at a near standstill. Looking south from the bridge, out over a broad stretch of the East River — neverending Brooklyn to the left, jagged, abrupt Manhattan to the right — a sallow red haze dominates the horizon, obscuring downtown's skyscrapers. It's like a postcard from the apocalypse. My wife, an Upper East Sider born and bred, witness to a thousand New York sunsets, is startled: "I've never seen a sky like that. It's like an entirely different part of the world."

This is the reality of global warming: in the gallery of contemporary fears, from the shadowy threat of terrorism to the erosion of civil rights, it is the most visible, the easiest to internalize. But, paradoxically, global warming is the most banal — it's just the weather, after all. So while it is widely accepted as a commonplace problem of modern life, for most Americans, solutions to climate change are largely symbolic, gestures of magical thinking that alleviate guilt but do little to alleviate waste. So fully developed are western habits of consumption that the changes — in both infrastructure and behaviour — needed to forestall environmental collapse seem beyond us as a society.

Even in liberal New York, one is daily confronted with the twin furies of environmental calamity: waste and consumption. Walking along my block in Brooklyn, the night before garbage pick-up, and the street is piled high with old TVs, stereos, dinettes, baby strollers, VCRs, and dozens of plastic toys, all cresting into a great wave of cheap, made-in-China flotsam. As I pick my way among the rats and ordure, a giant luxury SUV — which appears to be nearly three cars high and is tricked out with two internal flat screen TVs, a studio-quality stereo and some kind of hydraulic suspension system — pulls up as the driver asks me how to find the Brooklyn Bridge. I tell him where to go. I turn the corner onto a busy commercial avenue and an older man in a dirty shirt asks me for change in front of a shop selling $300 face cream; next door, an upscale diner offers a $13 hamburger; a few storefronts down, outside a bagel place that has just closed, I poke my toe at one of the many garbage bags — it is full of bagels, ready for the dump. Anger comes easily in New York on nights like this, followed quickly by despair.

But as I have learned over the last decade, slowly and sometimes painfully, New York is a city of extremes, and just when the indifference of rich and poor alike to the common good seems too much to reconcile with a thoughtful humanism, along come examples that redeem our small hopes for a better world. Action is often the only course for redemption in the face of despair, and that's what the Freegans of New York have been taking over the last fifteen years.

For those unfamiliar with the term, 'freegan' is a play on the word 'vegan' (people who don't eat or use animals or animal byproducts) and has come to stand for a philosophically fluid group of people who resist waste wherever possible, striving to exist outside the capitalist system of commodity and exchange by only consuming and using things they find (essentially, free things). While this includes collecting old furniture, bicycles and even computer equipment and repairing it for reuse, freegans are probably most renowned (or notorious, depending on your squeamishness level) for surviving on nothing but free food, most of which is foraged from the city's dumpsters and garbage bags.

For many, the idea of squirreling through the trash and eating whatever you find is thoroughly unappetizing, and I'll admit it was the same for me — until my wife, an environmental writer and long-time refurbisher of lost causes, took the freegan plunge and spent a night wandering around lower Manhattan looking for discarded food. Perhaps 'wandering' isn't the right word. The Freegans of New York are an organized bunch, thanks largely to the work of Adam Weissman, the de facto face of NYC freeganism. Mr Weissman, originally from New Jersey, is in his late twenties and is the founder of the website *www.freegan.info*, which among other things, provides weekly itineraries of the best spots for food — actual schedules of which stores discard what kinds of food, when. For example, a very popular stop on the New York freegan's pick-up route is a certain fancy organic health food store which makes its buffet salad bar available to the freegan who comes prepared with containers, along with plentiful stacks of organic salad greens in pre-wrapped packaging; also on the list is high-end grocery Dean & Doluca, which periodically discards hundreds of three-dollar pastries (some baked that day) around 10 PM on Thursdays.

Returning home at 1 AM after that first night of freegan'ing (apparently it can serve as noun, verb, or adjective) my wife, flushed with excitement and adrenaline, spent a solid hour showing and telling me all about her night's 'catch' as she called it: on top of the aforementioned hundreds of pastries (croissants, scones, muffins, danishes, etc) and the bags of spinach, romaine, and arugula, she'd acquired two cases of tangerines, three litres of premium organic yogurt (sealed, *three days* before the sell-by date), six loaves of multigrain bread, four-dozen bagels, 40 pounds of Idaho red potatoes, and lastly, nearly $80 worth of free-range chicken and grass-fed beef. This last find — meat from the trash — might seem like pushing it a bit, especially as we're vegetarians, but my wife took half an hour to cook up the meat as a stew and we've been able to feed our own dog, a friend's dog and even given some of the local shelter dogs a treat. As the two of us stood in awe at the freegan bounty before us, it quickly became apparent there was too much food for two people to consume without most of it going to waste. After freezing as much as we could (imposing on our neighbour's relatively spacious freezer), we put together three large bags of groceries and distributed them to some lower-income families on the block that we've become friendly with — it was that simple, from waste to bounty.

Granted, salvaging a box of coffee éclairs from a garbage bag on Spring Street is not going to reduce carbon levels in the atmosphere, but in a society (and a city) that fetishizes convenience and choice to the extent that, according to a 2004 University of Arizona study, nearly half of all edible food in the United States goes to waste, one must begin to make the personal political. No doubt, the view from the 59th Street Bridge will continue to amaze and disturb us as we idle behind gargantuan suvs, but through personal decisions about consumption and public resistance to waste, maybe we too can begin to serve as examples to others, as New York's freegans have been to us. ❧

PART 2

HUMANISM & REASON

*Humanism is rational. It seeks to use science creatively,
not destructively. Humanists believe that the solutions
to the world's problems lie in human thought and action
rather than divine intervention. Humanism advocates the
application of the methods of science and free inquiry to
the problems of human welfare. But Humanists also believe
that the application of science and technology must be
tempered by human values. Science gives us the means but
human values must propose the ends.*

THINKING CRITICALLY

by James Alcock

For every complex problem,
there is a solution which is simple, neat and wrong.

—H L Mencken

Who amongst us admits to being an uncritical thinker? "If I were you, I wouldn't waste my time getting a flu shot this winter. Of course, please remember that I am an uncritical thinker." "I'm totally opposed to the Kyoto Accord—but bear in mind that I don't think critically." While such admissions might be refreshing, we never hear them. No one wants to be thought of as being of uncritical mind. More importantly, we rarely are aware that we have not been thinking critically.

What is 'critical thinking'? While the definition is somewhat arbitrary, critical thinking is essentially a disciplined process of evaluation of a proposition or argument, a process that involves seeking out all available evidence, both supportive and contrary; weighing the value of that evidence while taking into account past experience; logically analyzing that evidence; and (most important) monitoring our thought processes as we go along, looking for possible weaknesses and errors and biases in our reasoning. This self-monitoring is a vital component of critical thinking, for we are all very vulnerable to error. For example, if you are a skeptic about paranormal or supernatural claims, do you judge putative evidence fairly, or do you fail to give it its proper due because you do not believe that such phenomena exist? Or if you are against gay marriage, is your reasoning sound, or did you first react emotionally and then muster arguments to support your position?

How does one become a critical thinker? Do our brains automatically go into critical thinking mode whenever we deem it necessary? Hardly! Just as speech develops automatically, and yet we have to study grammar and composition in order to become good speakers and writers, so too does thinking develop automatically, but we have to study logic and critical analysis if we are to become good thinkers. However, while the need for years of language instruction is well-recognized by society, the need for thinking instruction — that is, in the ability to think critically — generally is not.

And just as our linguistic history is a very long one, so too is our intellectual history. The ability to think critically has evolved over centuries. Until the ancient Greeks put their minds to it, no one had conceived of deductive logic, whereby precise conclusions follow automatically from explicitly stated axioms. Yet, it may be surprising that despite their advances in logic, those same Ancient Greeks did not possess the mathematical concept of zero, nor did the Romans (there is no zero in Roman numerals). While zero is a concept every schoolchild now takes for granted, it was not discovered until Indian mathematicians did so in the 6th century. We take for granted the notions of basic probability — "What are the odds of winning a lottery?" — but although gambling was common at the dawn of recorded history, an understanding of even very simple probabilities, 'the odds,' did not begin to take shape until the 17th century.

The point of all this is that no individual is ever going to be able to develop the skills necessary for careful rational analysis, involving ideas that took our civilization millennia to develop, on his or her own. We have to learn to think critically; we have to learn to apply logic, to find flaws in arguments, and to know what data is needed in order to come to a proper evaluation of a particular argument or claim. The wise amongst us will avail ourselves of the intellectual tools that have been developed and accumulated across the millennia.

There are many specific concepts that we need to learn from our intellectual forebears in order to become good critical thinkers. Consider the control group. The idea of the control group came into science about only about a century ago. For example, it is not enough to know that research shows that 80% of headaches go away in 30 minutes after taking Oil of Bergamot. We also need to know the percentage of headaches that go away after 30 minutes if one takes nothing (control group), and the percentage of headaches that go away when people think they are taking Oil of Bergamot but are actually given an inactive substance (placebo control group). In other words, we have to look at the base rate for recovery from headaches when there is no treatment.

Ignoring base rates cripples critical enquiry. Suppose ten people were arrested for sexual assault after having watched pornographic movies. What does that tell us about the effect of pornographic movies on sexual assault propensity? While it might seem to suggest a link, in fact, it tells us nothing at all. We can only evaluate any relationship between viewing pornography and sexual assault if we also know how many people watch pornographic movies and do not commit sexual assault, and what proportion of people who do not watch pornographic movies nonetheless commit sexual assault. To the non-critical thinker, the ten accused may provide strong evidence of the dangers of pornography, and yet, taken alone, the presumed correlation is illusory.

FALLACIES

As well as learning about control groups and placebos and the like, we need to learn about how to recognize and avoid various logical fallacies that have a significant presence in human discourse, fallacies such as these:

petitio principii, or *Begging the Question*. This fallacy involves circular reasoning, in which one assumes what one is trying to prove. (For example, the evidence for God's existence is provided by the all the evidence of intelligent design that is found in the world that He created.)

The False Dilemma (sometimes called the *Fallacy of the Excluded Middle*). Only two options are provided. Belief in the paranormal often draws from this fallacy. (For example, either the psychic was cheating or he was using psychic powers. Since we can find no evidence of cheating, then this 'proves' that he was using psychic power.)

post hoc, ergo propter hoc. It is so easy, and often so appealing, to conclude that because something occurred 'after the fact,' it occurred 'because of the fact.' "He was a heavy marijuana user, and now uses cocaine as well. Thus, this shows that marijuana smoking leads to cocaine addiction." The earlier example of pornography and sexual assault involved this fallacy.

OTHER FACTORS AFFECTING CRITICAL THINKING

Intuition. The untutored human brain is programmed to learn about the world around us, and to associate those things and events that 'go together.' We are born into this world not as logical rationalists, but as magical thinkers, with the capacity for learning automatically about 'what goes with what,' and then later interpreting these associations in terms of 'what causes what.' It is this innate ability to associate events that occur close together in time that underlies not only our intuitive learning about the world, but also superstitious learning — seeing cause and effect relationships when none exist. Rub a potato on a wart at midnight, and when the wart later goes away, we learn that the ritual caused it to do so. Pray to the Sun God when the fields need rain, and any subsequent rainfall tells us that the Sun God has answered our prayers. (Again, these are examples of *post hoc, ergo propter hoc*).

This automatic, intuitive route to learning about the world is gradually supplemented by an intellectual route, whereby we learn to reason, to theorize, to predict events around us based not on intuition but on logic. This intellectual approach is the result in part of personal experience, but depends to a very great degree on social transmission through schooling and literature.

Critical thinking should not ignore intuition, but neither should it accept it outright. Intuition is based on a largely non-conscious evaluation of a present situation in terms of past experience. The carpenter or the mechanic may 'intuit' solutions to problems without being able to tell us precisely how they came to the correct conclusion. However, while intuition can serve us well at times, it can also mislead us terribly.

Cognitive biases. The formidable strength of the human brain comes not from its ability to carry out rapid computations and never make an error — as is the case with a good computer — but from the ability to go beyond the available information, to fill in missing data, to project current trends into the future while taking into account a number of other factors that are not involved at the moment. Yet, cognitive psychologists have discovered a number of systematic biases in our thinking that result from this creativity, biases about which the critical thinker must learn in order to minimize their effects.

Cognitive bias — Emotion. It is generally most difficult to examine propositions in an unbiased and critical manner when emotion plays a significant role. Emotion may trump rationality when considering such hot button issues as, for example, same-sex marriage. We generally feel very uncomfortable when there is a mismatch between our emotionality and our logical conclusion, and if our logical analysis leads us where we do not want to be, we may escape by allowing our emotion to sabotage our reasoning. Pierre Trudeau's personal motto was "Reason over passion"; this is a *sine qua non* of critical thinking.

Cognitive bias — Personal factors. People differ in terms of their abilities to accept ambiguity or uncertainty. While some people can live with the belief that there may or may not be life after death, others who have grown up to be intolerant of ambiguity feel anxious in the absence of simple, concrete answers. Cults and fundamentalist religions typically eliminate ambiguity by giving black and white answers to all important questions.

Premature beliefs — People also differ in terms of their 'primitive beliefs,' beliefs so well-established that they are accepted without question, and are used to screen incoming information. If new information is inconsistent with primitive beliefs, it is likely to be disregarded. The individual who fervently believes in the power of prayer may not even examine research that claims to show that prayer has failed. Another individual who is convinced that the personality does not survive death may reject ghost reports out-of-hand. This of course does not reflect critical thinking.

Cognitive bias — Social factors. As John Donne wrote, "No man is an island, entire of itself…" Our thinking is decidedly influenced by the ideas and beliefs of those around us. There are powerful conformity pressures in any social group that push members of the group to adhere to the majority view. Does it make sense to legalize marijuana? Many people may not even consider the question, for they know that their friends and neighbours and relatives would be aghast were they to conclude that legalization makes sense.

Social influence can contaminate the decision-making process even in groups of highly educated and politically powerful individuals. *Groupthink* is the term used to describe situations where a group of leaders effectively shields itself from information that challenges existing assumptions and beliefs. Through highly selective information gathering, failure to examine other alternatives, failure to critically evaluate each other's arguments, and maintenance of an illusion of unanimity, terribly unwise and irrational decisions are produced. The Bay of Pigs fiasco is but one celebrated example.

These are but some of the factors that serve to distract each one of us from disciplined critical inquiry. No one is capable of being a critical thinker all of the time, of course, and each of us has our pockets of irrationality. Yet, if we are wise, we will not embrace our own conclusions and beliefs too tightly. We should recognize our vulnerability to error, and we should always examine our own reasoning. When was the last time you asked yourself questions such as, "How did I reach this conclusion?" "What are my biases?" "Have I examined all points of view?" "Have I been influenced by my emotions, or by what others want me to think?" It is generally uncomfortable to vet our own thinking in this manner, for it may mean that we will have to revise our conclusions, and if those conclusions satisfy our emotional needs, any revision may make us uncomfortable. However, if we do not, then we will often find ourselves saddled with "simple, neat and wrong solutions" to complex problems.

SELECTIVE SKEPTICISM

by Bryson Brown

*It ain't what you don't know that gets you into trouble.
It's what you know for sure that just ain't so.*

— Mark Twain

D oubts about science are in the air these days. Columnists regularly trumpet the views of global warming skeptics and dismiss the scientific consensus on the effects of carbon dioxide emissions. In a recent poll 50% of respondents did not believe human actions were contributing to climate change. A majority in the United States rejects the evolution of *Homo sapiens* from a common ancestor with the apes. Many North Americans, including high-level politicians within the United States and Canada, prefer a literal reading of Genesis over geology, believing that the Earth is less than 10,000 years old.

Attitudes towards science have become highly politicized in recent decades, as increasing numbers of right-wing politicians have rejected the scientific consensus on a range of issues. The shape of the resulting debates demonstrates both the strength of science and its vulnerability. On one hand, none of these politicians simply rejects science — not the supporters of Ronald Reagan's 'Star Wars' program, not global warming

skeptics, not even young-earth creationists. Scientific methods are recognized as essential to producing reliable knowledge of the natural
world; what's in dispute is always what 'real' or 'sound' or 'biblically
correct' science has to say. On the other hand, scientific issues are often
complex, technical, and poorly understood, which makes it all too easy
to confuse and mislead the public about them.

Creating public doubt about a scientific consensus is quite easy:
some simple public relations strategies will often do the trick. Republican tactician and pollster Frank Luntz famously recommended that,
rather than change its policies to reflect increasing public concern
about the environment, the party should just *repackage* the old policies by giving them environmentally friendly labels. For example, he
proposed the phrase 'healthy forests initiative,' to describe a policy
allowing more extensive logging. On the issue of global warming he
declared, "*the scientific debate remains open.* Voters believe that there is
no consensus about global warming within the scientific community.
Should the public come to believe the scientific issues are settled, their
views about global warming will change accordingly. Therefore, *you
need to continue to make the lack of scientific certainty a primary issue in
the debate.*" Luntz now accepts the scientific consensus that emissions
of greenhouse gases are warming the earth (though he claims the issue
was still open as recently as 2004), but the Frankenstein's monster of
climate change denial that he helped create still lurches on.

As Luntz recommended, it's important to 'defer to scientists and
other experts.' So the first trick is to choose the right experts. There are
almost always 'outliers' in the scientific community — individual scientists who, for one reason or another, reject the consensus on a given
issue. Some are simply contrarian by nature; some have deep-seated
convictions that conflict with the consensus; others can be recruited by
offering research funding. Drawing on carefully selected experts provides fringe views like the ones mentioned at the outset with a veneer
of scientific respectability.

When the consensus is powerful and long-established this trick gets
a bit harder. The claim that the earth is less than 10,000 years old is an
utter absurdity for anyone even slightly acquainted with geology. But
there are still some trained scientists who defend a biblical chronology.

Andrew McIntosh, Professor of Thermodynamics at Leeds University, recently announced his belief that the earth is about six thousand years old. This is an extreme case of an outlier, and the Professor's qualifications lie outside of geology and the physics of nuclear decay used in radiological dating. So his endorsement does little to give legitimate scientific cover. But beggars can't be choosers, and creationists eagerly collect signatures from scientists like Professor McIntosh.

A more recent or less robust consensus is much more vulnerable — for example, the consensus of climatologists that the earth is now warming rapidly and that most of this warming is due to human emissions of greenhouse gases. Two decades ago it was just a hypothesis — though a serious one. But now it is widely accepted, endorsed by the detailed peer-review process of the Intergovernmental Panel on Climate Change (IPCC), by the scientific academies of every G7 country and by a vast majority of professional climatologists. A review by *Science* of nearly 1,000 papers on climatology published between 1993 and 2003 found none that disputed the consensus. However, there are still a number of outliers with recent, perfectly sound credentials in climatology. So those who deny anthropogenic climate change have an easier time finding credible experts to support them.

Still, creating real doubt about a consensus this way requires the public to treat a few experts, selected for their rejection of the consensus, as if they were just as likely to be right as the vast majority of experts in the field. This is obviously a bad bet. For every Galileo or Alfred Wegner who advances a controversial, widely-rejected point of view in science and turns out to have been right, there are dozens if not hundreds of contrarians, cranks and naysayers who are just plain wrong. More importantly, what made Galileo's views on the solar system and *some* of Wegner's on continental drift part of a new consensus was not political forces from outside science, but the development of new evidence within science! Certain tricks are necessary to shore up the chosen contrarian experts.

One such trick is to focus on the mass media. So long as the mass media give more or less equal weight to fringe experts and experts representing the consensus, the public gets the impression that the issue still hangs in the balance. The way journalists tend to treat disputes makes this trick an easy one. 'Objective' journalism requires that roughly equal space be granted to both sides of a disagreement. This is a huge advantage for anyone disputing mainstream science: The public sees a dispute in which each side has interesting things to say. Worse yet, it's very hard to correct any inaccuracies and distortions in the fringe position within the space allowed: mainstream scientists often look doctrinaire and defensive in such reports. The advantage is greater still when some in the audience are dubious about the authority of scientists in general, or about the particular consensus in question. This journalistic approach gives the audience no sense of the weight of evidence on the side of the consensus.

This trick works better if a little supporting research can be placed in the scientific literature. Tobacco companies managed to do this by directly funding researchers and paying a number of experts to write letters to scientific journals disputing a 1992 report on the risks of secondhand smoke. In one survey of the field, the odds that a paper would conclude exposure to secondhand smoke was not a significant risk were found to be 88 times higher if the paper had been funded by the tobacco industry. Worse, in many cases funding sources were not acknowledged. Intelligent design recently received a similar boost when the editor of a journal based in the Smithsonian published a paper supporting that idea. The editor did not have the paper reviewed by any other referees, despite the fact that it was off-topic for the journal and the editor was not an expert on the subject. The editor was, of course, an intelligent-design supporter. Nevertheless, intelligent design supporters have eagerly cited the publication as proof of the scientific bona fides of intelligent design. In the case of climate change, papers by various outliers criticizing the consensus have received huge amounts of attention in the press — even when the papers were published in social science rather than climatology journals.

The third trick is to amplify whatever disagreements remain in the field. Scientific papers almost always focus on the issues that are 'up in the air.' A substantial consensus can be concealed by using present disagreements on details to raise uncertainty about the field in general. After all, if there are disputes about the best statistical methods for analyzing past temperature trends, or apparent discrepancies between satellite measurements and the predictions of climate change models, or disagreements about the relative importance of adaptation and architectural constraints in evolution, then surely these fields are in disarray and their results cannot be trusted! Even as evidence gradually resolves such tensions, disputes can be kept alive in the press for a long time just by repeating the same old claims, and ignoring or rejecting the studies that answer them.

Misdirection is a key to the third trick. Just as a magician cleverly draws our attention to a showy distraction as she performs the crucial move of her trick, our view of science can be distorted by drawing attention to a side-issue which does not make a real difference to the consensus. For instance, Canada's Steven McIntyre and Ross McKitrick — one an economist and the other a statistician and fossil-fuel industry consultant — have published papers criticizing work by Michael Mann and his colleagues, R S Bradley and M K Hughes. The work by Mann et al. produced the 'hockey stick' graph of past temperatures, indicating that temperatures in the northern hemisphere are now higher than at any time in the last 1,000 years. Because this graph was prominently featured in the IPCC report of 2001, it became a prime target for climate change deniers. MacIntyre and McKitrick argued that the shape of the hockey stick graph was an artifact, produced by statistical errors. The National Academy of Science in the US reviewed the issue; it concluded that there were some technical problems with the statistical analysis of Mann et al., which was one of the first attempts to reconstruct such a long-term, fine-grained temperature record. But the errors were not significant, and the Academy confirmed Mann et al.'s overall conclusions.

The focus on this dispute in so many contrarian opinion pieces is a clear example of misdirection. Subsequent work that uses different methods and data continues to confirm the main results, but it is ignored. More importantly, reconstructions of previous climates are not the only, or even the main, evidence for global warming and our part in it. The case for global warming does not turn on this issue, although fans of MacIntyre and McKitrick often write as if it did.

The fourth trick is *poisoning the well*. Degrading the credibility of mainstream science makes any evidence against the consensus seem much stronger. In his novel *State of Fear,* Michael Crichton presents global warming as a hoax and environmentalists as terrorists. Senator James Inhofe and Representative Joe Barton have both claimed that global warming is a scientific fraud. In a speech on global warming, Inhofe declared that human-caused climate change might be the 'greatest hoax ever perpetrated on the American people,' while Barton, who chaired the congressional committee on energy and commerce, demanded details of data and analysis from the Mann paper in order to audit it. Barton also sponsored a report, by E J Wegman, D W Scott and Y H Said, endorsing criticisms of Mann's methods due to McIntyre and McKitrick. Other peer-reviewed papers have rejected these criticisms as wrong in many details, as well as reanalyzing the data to show that different statistical analyses produce the same overall curve. But the Wegman report took a very different turn, suggesting, without any direct evidence, that Mann's connections in the field have biased peer-reviews of his work, thus playing to the conspiracy view of the widespread consensus of climatologists on the reality of human-induced warming.

The fifth and final trick is by far the boldest: the self-indulgent use of throw-away arguments, claims that have no basis in fact or science at all. A few of these appear regularly in the global warming debate. Some ask, if we can't predict the weather five minutes from now, how can we predict the climate decades in the future? This is ridiculous — climate is a kind of average of the weather, from season to season and year to year, and averages can be very predictable even when the data they are averages of are not. Others point out that water vapour is a much more powerful greenhouse gas than CO_2, and suggest that climate models have not taken account of its effects. Again, ridiculous — water vapour levels are determined by temperature, since hotter air quickly evaporates more water from the surface and cooler air quickly loses water in the form of snow or rain. So water vapour does not drive climate change; instead, it amplifies changes driven by more stable causes, like greenhouse gases. This amplification is included in all serious climate models. Lastly, some suggest that climatologists only defend the consensus in order to win larger research grants, or to serve an ideological conspiracy — a cheap, unsubstantiated ad hominem well-suited to distract public attention from the many links between climate change denial and wealthy corporate interests.

The form of these attacks on science is always the same. The result of 'investigation' is specified in advance. What's wanted is not the best supported answer, but support for the predetermined, 'right' answer. The target audience is not experts in the field, but the general public. The aim is to trick the public into a kind of *selective skepticism*. On one hand, no argument for the scientific consensus can be strong enough. Evolution can't be proven, it's said, because no one was there to watch as it took place — as though eye-witness testimony were the only reliable evidence for past events: no matter what the physical evidence shows, no matter that it's often far *more* reliable than testimony, for these skeptics it just can't be good enough. On the other hand, the arguments of selected fringe experts are accepted at face value — and when they become too worn and threadbare, new ones are raised, or the old ones resurrected in new rhetorical forms. Put baldly, this sort of selective skepticism is not very sensible. But the tricks we've described can make it very effective.

Selective skepticism uses familiar, general skeptical arguments, but it aims them only at specific targets. For example, one of the most fundamental arguments for skepticism is the regress: if we demand an explicit, non-circular justification for every belief, and for every premise and every inference used to justify a belief, we can turn every attempt at justification into an infinite regress. But an infinite regress can't ever be completed — so there are really no good justifications for any claim at all.

Radical arguments like this are a challenge for philosophers. Their conclusion is catastrophic — if the regress argument really works, there could be no real justification for any belief on any topic. The most obvious claims about the world couldn't be distinguished from pure nonsense. But our understanding of what we say and do is inextricably linked to how we justify actions and beliefs. An account of justification that breaks this link is a philosophical non-starter. So the philosophical question is not whether radical skepticism should (or even can) be accepted, but where do the arguments for it break down?

From a rhetorical point of view, however, the radical arguments are a rich resource, a never-failing spring of doubt and uncertainty ready to be exploited. They provide a universal recipe for questioning inconvenient truths. With their help, we can undermine any case for any claim, no matter how well supported it really is: OJ Simpson's guilt, the evolution of life from a common ancestor, our role in changing the earth's climate, the list is endless. *Selectively* applying these arguments is easy and comfortable, because we don't notice how corrosive they really are when we apply them to beliefs we don't really use in our lives.

This is a key reason for the huge gaps between public opinion and expert consensus in various scientific fields. Those outside the field have no need to actually use the consensus in their work, while scientists must either accept it or answer the evidence for it convincingly. For many, adjusting their lives to accord with the consensus is downright inconvenient. It may threaten treasured religious convictions, or a perfectly natural desire to continue a familiar and comfortable lifestyle. Many find it far easier to accept the skeptical objections, especially when they are reinforced by clever public relations.

Finding the means to counter these rhetorical tricks is crucial if we are to turn the tide and begin to reduce our impact on the earth's climate. By the time the damage becomes obvious to all, we will be stuck with it, and worse will be on the way. Even if all we can do is slow the process down, the time we gain will help both humans and other life to adjust. Conveying a better appreciation of the evidence supporting a scientific consensus would be a good place to start — but that is a topic for another essay. 🌿

SELF-DECEPTION

by Trudy Govier

Let's say we have good evidence for a scientific hypothesis, but its practical implications threaten our way of life. Protective strategies of thought are possible. We can reject evidence outright, insisting that it does not exist at all — like the man drinking eight beers a day who insists he never has more than two. We can deliberately ignore relevant evidence — like the man who pays no attention to his doctor's admonition that his liver is damaged. We can reinterpret the evidence and argue that it 'really' points to a different conclusion — like the drinker who feels unwell when he's forced to go without his beer, but tells himself his discomfort must come from some other cause. Attacking the messenger and joking also work as strategies of denial.

Some tell jokes about the weather. Maybe global warming is not real after all — after all, we just had some snow in our driveways. And there were strangely cold days in recent years; that could be bad for pine beetles and good for the pines. Hey, could it be that 'Big Al's Glacial Melt' isn't happening? Then too, if there's warmth rather than cold, there might be more lakes and lakeside properties. Real estate values in traditional colder locations could go up. Ha ha.

Peer-reviewed publications by climate scientists indicate a solid consensus that global climate is changing in the direction of temperature elevation and greater turbulence, and these shifts are due largely to the human burning of fossil fuels. Many effects will be negative for human comfort and the integrity of ecosystems. To prevent them we need to change our way of life — radically and fast. It's a threatening scenario.

You don't want to believe it? Try a little self-deception.

The news science brings is not always welcome, and many will want to resist it. To say we would rather not believe in global warming is an understatement. We become accustomed to certain practices and conveniences: we are comfortable, resistant to change, and have a vested interest in life as we live it. There is a great temptation to arrange our beliefs to support our lifestyle, protecting ourselves from uncomfortable conclusions. We deceive ourselves to avoid unwanted conclusions, rationalizing to avoid accepting uncomfortable truths.

And there are supports for all this, outstanding among them the skeptics — sometimes called 'deniers' — and the media outlets that give them a voice. Climate skeptics object to the term 'denial' — which they seem to associate exclusively with Holocaust denial. One commentator, for example, contended that the expression 'global warming denier' reeks of guilt by association, complaining that it's becoming politically incorrect to question global climate change. He claimed that 'thought police' are trying to silence skeptics. If they are, and he himself is one such skeptic, they are doing a mighty poor job: Such commentator often enjoys prominent space in the media.

This commentator quite reasonably calls for careful science, an end to name-calling, and toned-down rhetoric in the climate debate. But along the way he makes stunningly unsound comments about science. He states, for example, that there is no science of the future, only probabilities. But a major function of science is to make careful predictions about the future based on the best-supported descriptive and explanatory theories about our world. If science couldn't do this, he couldn't safely use antihistamines, drive across overpasses, or fly from Toronto to New York.

I agree with the commentator when he calls for well-mannered and careful debate and refraining from name-calling. In this context, as in others, getting rid of insults and hostility would be positive and constructive. But as to the term 'denier', I think he's mistaken. There's a point in calling someone a denier, if the term fits. Not all denial is

Holocaust denial, after all; in fact the Holocaust is a complete red herring in the context. We engage in denial when we fail to acknowledge truths for which we have cogent evidence, evidence whose implications we would accept and act on if we had no special motives for avoidance. And denial is all too human. Against compelling evidence, the heavy drinker may deny his alcoholism; the mother the failures of her child; the perpetrator responsibility for his wrongdoing. And society may deny having a serious problem. In all these contexts, denial is resistance to evidence for unwelcome truths. Denial is tempting because it allows us to continue in relative comfort, believing that things are all right and there is no need to change our familiar customs.

To say that scientific skeptics are deniers, in the context of climate change, is to say that they have good evidence for harmful global warming caused by human-produced carbon emissions and they deny, distort, or twist that evidence so as to protect themselves from the unwelcome truth. The label does fit, and if someone doesn't want to be called a climate denier, he shouldn't practice and advocate denial of global climate change.

Intellectually, a basic problem is that climate change is about trends as distinct from specific events. Extreme winter storms may be expected with warmer global average temperatures — but particular events related to bad weather to cannot be proven to be the result of global climate change.

Personally, we like many aspects of our lifestyle; we don't want to stop driving, living in warm houses, or eating grapes from Chile.

Socially, vested interests — especially oil interests — support institutions and spokespersons who deny climate change. They don't want people to adapt to using less oil and gas — that would be bad for profits. (It's short-term thinking.)

As for media, the fundamental problem lies with the simplistic conception of objectivity as balance. This model is based on the facile assumptions that there are two sides to every question and bias can be avoided by giving a voice to both sides. Accordingly, virtually all coverage of global climate issues incorporates commentary from some sceptic or other. (The scientific status of such persons seems to be diminishing, which may offer some hope.) For example, January 10, 2007, CBC's

The National had a substantial discussion of Canada's strange weather. Peter Mansbridge did the broadcast from Stanley Park, where it was snowing. Dr Andrew Weaver, a prominent climate scientist based at the University of Victoria, was shown lecturing in Victoria. Weaver stated that climate change will be accompanied by extreme storms in winter and droughts in summer. He said firmly, "climate change is here." But of course there had to be another voice for balance. So an 'average citizen' was shown looking at his damaged house, and proclaiming confidently that bad storms happen from time to time: there is no general problem.

The two sides model supports the illusion that there is equally cogent evidence on both sides. It gives the deniers more prominence and credibility than they deserve and perpetuates the profound error that there is disagreement about climate change in responsible scientific circles. That's no longer true.

Sad though it is to say, the truth is less pleasant. ❦

WHEN IGNORANCE
MASQUERADES AS SCIENCE

by James Alcock

Not ignorance, but ignorance of ignorance,
is the death of knowledge.

— Alfred North Whitehead

We live in a highly structured society, and we rely on experts to make it work. A storm has knocked out the electricity? Don't worry; someone will send out crews of electricity experts to repair it. Shopping at the local grocery? Don't worry; government experts make sure that the food is safe to eat. Fell and broke your ankle? Don't worry; people at the local hospital will take over, operate if needed, provide physiotherapy, and get you walking again. It would be difficult to function in this modern world without experts, whether to replace heart valves, repair a television, or collect refuse.

Consider, then, this account of expertise gone wrong, a true story but with minor details changed to protect confidentiality: A few years ago, a woman in Halifax — I'll call her Martha — was told by her husband that, in light of his excellent sales performance, he was being awarded an all-expenses-paid trip for two to a conference in Europe. They had never been to Europe, and he was certain that his wife would be as thrilled as he by this news. Martha was indeed overwhelmed, but not quite in the way that her husband thought. She feigned excitement as best she could, but all that occupied her mind at the time was a troubling secret, her profound fear of flying. Because she had never had the occasion to fly before, there had been no need to discuss the matter, and in any case, she had kept this fear a secret because she viewed her fear as an emotional weakness, and she was certain that her husband would see it that way too.

Thus, rather than admit this weakness to her husband, she decided to seek professional help in the hope that she could rid herself of this problem in the few months that remained before their date with the airline. Her first challenge was to find an 'expert,' a good psychotherapist. How does one do that, she wondered? Because of her wish to keep her secret well-hidden, she could hardly enquire of friends or colleagues to see if they knew a good therapist. In desperation, she turned to advertisements in the Yellow Pages, picked a therapist, and called to make an appointment.

She arrived at the therapist's office at the appointed time with a mixture of excitement and anxiety. She really wanted to rid herself of her fear, but at the same time, the notion of confronting that fear made her uneasy. Little did she know just how justified her apprehension really was, but for reasons that she could never have anticipated.

Once in the hands of the 'expert' — one with credentials on the wall, after all — she was completely forthcoming in her responses to the many questions about her background, her current circumstances, her beliefs and her feelings. That first session just 'flew by,' she later told me, as she let her personal history pour out for the therapist's consideration. Yet, all things considered, hers was an unremarkable story. She had grown up in a loving family. Her father was a now-retired judge who had had a distinguished career. She had always felt very emotionally close to him, but sadly, he had recently been diagnosed with inoperable cancer, and she knew that he did not have long to live. She told the therapist about her many friends, her solid marriage and her wonderful children. She also described her successful and rewarding career. Apart from the longstanding fear of flying, which had no apparent source, her life was very good indeed.

A simple fear of flying in an individual whose history and circumstances are otherwise unremarkable is a straightforward condition to treat, and success is virtually assured if the therapist is competent and the phobic individual is well-motivated to participate in the treatment. However, this therapist, apparently proud of her ability 'to see beneath the surface,' was not persuaded that this was just a matter of a simple phobia, or that Martha's life had been so well-balanced and unremarkable. Unbeknownst to Martha, she considered herself to be an expert in treating the consequences of childhood sexual abuse, and she 'knew' about the diverse symptoms that such abuse could generate in adulthood. She 'knew' that adults often cannot remember sexual abuse that occurred in childhood, even in late childhood, because they unconsciously 'repress' it, pushing it down deep into the 'unconscious mind,' a region closed off to conscious appraisal. This supposed repository of awful memories is then accessible only to a skilful therapist such as herself, who, like a practiced spelunker, crawls ever deeper down the narrow and twisting corridors of the mind to expose the putrid traces of sexual exploitation.

Very early on, this therapist announced that she was quite sure that Martha had been sexually abused as a child, and that the fear of flying was an indirect manifestation of that abuse. Martha was horrified at the suggestion, for she was certain that such a thing had never occurred. However, the therapist then assured her that the very fact that she was horrified by the mention of such abuse was consistent with having been abused, for victims often manage their pain through repression and denial. Doubt about having been abused, she said, is oftentimes part of the denial process, and is actually a further indication that the abuse did occur. Thus, the therapist, in keeping with beliefs associated with the widespread recovered memory movement of the day, began to disengage Martha's reality-testing ability; doubt is not to be trusted — it is a symptom.

The therapist offered further evidence (and I am not making this up!): She instructed the woman to recline on a couch, and then slowly brought her head towards the woman's face. This violation of personal space produced only a little discomfort for Martha. The therapist then moved her head down towards Martha's groin, and when Martha spontaneously covered her groin with her hands, the therapist triumphantly announced that her reaction was precisely that of someone who had been sexually abused! Martha was further shaken by the results of this diagnostic procedure, and the therapist explained again that this shock and surprise was consistent with having been abused.

Having come into therapy for the sole purpose of overcoming her phobia of flying, Martha was now faced with dealing with an emotional can of worms that made the phobia seem unimportant in comparison. Over the next few sessions, the therapist coached her in techniques aimed at revealing the repressed memories. This 'therapy' soon led to the conclusion that it was Martha's father — her loving, distinguished, dying father — who had sexually abused her in childhood. Martha still could not clearly remember any incidents of abuse, but was beginning to have vague notions as to what had occurred of as a result of all the therapeutic 'memory work' involving 'guided imagery,' dream analysis and other techniques that draw on imagination and fantasy. Moreover, again consistent with the dictates of the recovered memory movement, she was told that in order to heal, it was vital that she confront her father about the abuse, and time was short, for he was dying.

The phobia of flying, now relegated to being only a symptom of sexual abuse, was now on the therapeutic back burner, but since Martha still wanted to get to Europe with her husband, her therapist recommended that she see another therapist for treatment of the phobia, while she would continue to work on its underlying cause, the sexual abuse. It was thus that Martha came to see me for treatment of her fear of flying, having this time consulted her family physician for a referral.

Upon our first meeting, she told me about her phobia of course, but also about how crushed she was feeling by the revelation that her father had abused her, and about how she dreaded confronting him on his deathbed. She was now persuaded that the confrontation was necessary, even though she still had no clear memory of what it was that he was supposed to have done to her.

All that I did to effect a dramatic change in Martha was to gently question her basis for believing that her father had abused her, and to encourage her to use her own logic and reality-testing to evaluate what had come out of the therapy sessions. Rather than discouraging critical thinking as the other therapist had explicitly done, I encouraged it. I also explained to her that there is no scientific basis for a belief in 'repressed memories.' I informed her that while many psychotherapists during the 1990s had become part of the recovered memory movement that swept the continent, their belief in repression and the process of memory recovery ran against what experimental psychologists had known for decades about how memory and recall really operate. Finally, I explained that not only is the repression concept ill-conceived, but that the very therapeutic techniques used to 'recover' memory are ideal for generating 'memories' of events that never occurred at all.

Martha is a bright and educated woman. When she turned her own critical thinking back on, it was as though the scales fell from her eyes and she could see clearly again. In our first session, her despondency about what her father had putatively done to her and her need to confront him was transformed into relief, combined with some anger at having been hornswoggled by the ignorant though well-meaning therapist.

The final outcome was a good one. Martha overcame her phobia of flying in time to go to Europe with her husband, and she told me later that she had had a wonderful trip. Quite possibly to this day, he has no knowledge of the fear that brought her into dangerous therapeutic hands. More importantly, she was able to be a loving daughter to her father as he died, and to cherish his memory after he was gone.

Martha's therapist was no doubt well-meaning. As did countless psychotherapists around the world during the 1990s, she had come to believe through workshops and readings that many, if not most, of women's emotional problems are the result of sexual abuse in childhood, abuse that they literally cannot remember. Our courts were filled during those days with such cases for which the only 'evidence' had emerged from lengthy psychotherapy focused on uncovering these supposedly hidden memories. When the recovered memory movement was at its peak, women who went to therapists because they were overweight or wanted to stop smoking or had marital problems or were depressed often became grist for the repressed memory mill, and ended up — still overweight, smoking, depressed, or unhappy in their marriages — with the manufactured conviction that they had been sexually abused in childhood. Because recovered memory therapy provided virtually ideal conditions for creating false memories, many of those women will for the rest of their days have to deal with memories of events that never occurred. Moreover, it is likely that there are still innocent people in Canadian prisons who were convicted only upon the basis of uncorroborated recovered memory. Yet the lives and careers of the therapists, who should have known better, have been by and large unaffected.

This travesty was not caused by simple ignorance. What happened to Martha occurred because an 'expert' truly believed that she was knowledgeable about how memory works, while she was in fact ignorant of her ignorance. She could not distinguish between science and pseudoscience; the recovered memory movement was based in pseudoscience, pure and simple. We need to rely on experts, but such experts ignorant of their ignorance are a threat to us all. Look around at all the certified experts who 'know' that our health is determined by a life force that runs along the spine; who 'know' that all that we need to do to be healthy is to consume the right blend of herbs and spices from the pharmacopium of a naturopath or a 'doctor' of Traditional Chinese Medicine; or who 'know' that magnets worn close to the skin will manage or cure certain ailments. All that will save us from the ignorance of such experts is our own critical thinking and reality-testing ability. That is why it is so important that we both teach critical thinking to our children and hone it and apply it ourselves. Bertrand Russell wrote that "The trouble with the world is that the stupid are cocksure and the intelligent are full of doubt." Unfortunately, he did not get it quite right, for the intelligent can also be cocksure and in error. Doubt based on good critical thinking is our best defence against such folly. ❧

Appealing to
the Natural

by Trudy Govier

Ads based on appeals to the natural are a prominent feature of popular culture. We're urged to restore that natural beauty to our hair, get a treatment to bring out our natural smile, buy a mattress that gives natural support to our sagging back muscles, consume natural foods and wear natural fabrics. These ads exploit the common assumption that what is natural is generally safer and better than what is unnatural.

You don't have to look at ads to see evidence of this assumption. It often comes up in ordinary conversation. Tell people you have a medical problem and many will advise natural supplements as a first recourse. Meet a pregnant woman and she is likely attending classes in the hope of achieving a natural childbirth. Visit an environmental group and you'll find a commitment to restore environments to their natural state.

What's natural is best: it's a common assumption. But questions arise. One problem is obvious: there are some things that are natural and yet harmful to humans — snake venom, for example, and herbal teas that cause miscarriages. At the same time, there are many instances of non-natural things that are beneficial — eye glasses, antihistamines and injectible insulin being conspicuous examples. So one problem with appeals to the natural is that they are insufficient; the fact that something is natural does not prove it desirable or good. Given that something is natural, it remains an open question whether it is right or good or desirable. That was the insight famously articulated by the philosopher G E Moore, who coined the phrase 'the naturalistic fallacy.'

In several prominent religious traditions, it's claimed that homosexual acts are wrong. A major premise in the case is that homosexual acts are unnatural. Interestingly, this premise can be disputed on factual grounds. Homosexual acts occur rather widely in the animal kingdom, so there is a clear sense in which they are not unnatural after all. It's a pretty good rebuttal. But that's not the heart of the matter. The naturalness or unnaturalness of homosexual acts — or any other acts — does not establish their rightness or wrongness. Even if homosexual behaviour were unnatural, that wouldn't prove it wrong.

What about science and the natural? In some areas of science and medicine, we find complex notions of the natural and the normal, supposedly arising from purely biological knowledge. Detailed arguments are found, often based on reasoning about evolution and function. Typically, such arguments raise intricate problems of knowledge, meaning and sufficiency; this is a context deeper than those of advertisement and casual conversation. But questions still arise if we try to prove goodness from naturalness or biological normality. Often social values are subtly incorporated into judgments about the normal, the healthy and the nature. If arguments from 'natural' to 'good' seem to work in such contexts, that's the explanation. We may seem to overcome the naturalistic fallacy, but only because we've incorporated value judgments into our judgments about the 'facts' of the natural.

We so often speak and think of what is 'natural' that one might even say, well, appealing to the natural is something we naturally do. Think of the idea of natural law as a basis for moral systems — the conception is more than two thousand years old. But the same problem surfaces here: even if a line of thought is natural, that doesn't show it's correct.

What do we mean when we say that something is natural? One response is, it occurs in the natural world. Though superficially plausible, this answer turns out to be circular and unhelpful. To make it useful, we have to ask what we mean when we speak of the natural world. We might be contrasting the natural world with some hypothetical super-natural world — meaning that the natural is within space and time and can be empirically observed, while the supernatural is an unreachable, unobservable realm. In this sense of 'natural,' pop-tarts, parking lots and cloned sheep are as much features of the natural world as herbs, grassy meadows and brown eyes. Clearly such a consequence would be unacceptable for many who argue by appealing to the natural.

Here's another line of thought: what's natural, by definition, is what's not artificial. The natural is what exists or occurs without human intervention; the unnatural, by contrast, has been invented and constructed by human beings and so is artificial. In this sense, pop-tarts, parking lots and cloned sheep qualify as unnatural, while herbs, grassy meadows and brown eyes qualify as natural. Herbal concoctions are made of natural products that occur in 'nature' while pharmaceutical products usually have components that did not exist in combination until scientists did their work. So the herbal concoctions are thought to be natural remedies, while pharmaceutical products are not. But puzzles remain. If 'natural' is used to imply a favourable meaning, as is typical in many contexts, then are we presuming that being human-made makes an entity inferior or unsafe? It is, after all, entirely 'natural' for human beings to think, invent and create. To assume that human products are ethically or pragmatically suspect simply because they have been created by us seems unreasonable.

A beautiful forest or meadow may have resulted from clearance or cultivation practices of human beings in the past. If by 'natural' we mean 'not the product of human intervention,' it will be hard to establish that anything is natural. History going back over many years would be difficult to prove. Even if we could establish a history unaltered by human interventions, the problem of sufficiency doesn't disappear. Grant that some entity is not in any sense artificial — it remains an open question whether it is socially valuable. If an area deserves to be preserved or restored, its status should be argued on grounds of its beauty or ecological or economic role. Its naturalness can't prove the point.

People aren't likely to stop arguing from the natural. But when we do it, we should remember two things. In the first place, such appeals should always be supplemented by further considerations: they never suffice to establish conclusions of value. In the second place, we probably don't know what we mean in the first place. ❧

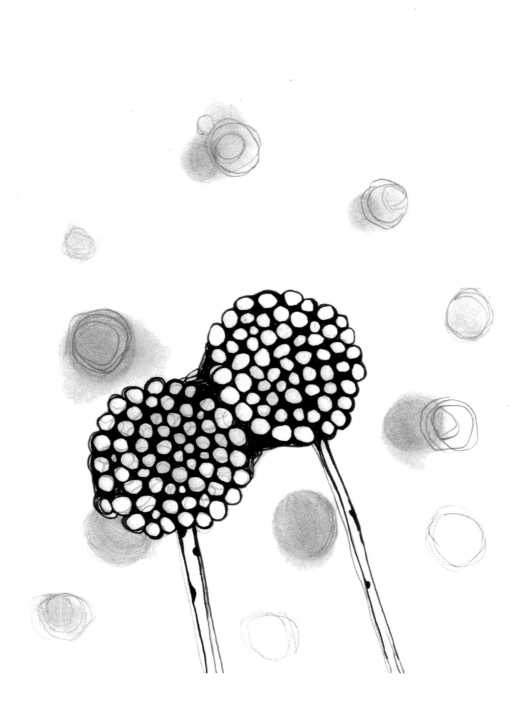

PART 3

Humanism, Democracy & Human Rights

Humanism supports democracy and human rights. Humanism aims at the fullest possible development of every human being. It holds that democracy and human development are matters of right. The principles of democracy and human rights can be applied to many human relationships and are not restricted to methods of government.

MEDIA & THE SHAPING OF REALITY

by James Alcock

Without a free press there can be no free society...
Without a lively sense of responsibility a free press may
readily become a powerful instrument of injustice.

— Justice Felix Frankfurter, US Supreme Court, 1946

The most powerful weapon of ignorance —
the diffusion of printed matter.

— Leo Tolstoy in *War & Peace*

What is your reality? Is it the same as mine? And is there only one reality, or are there many? Is reality, as some post-modernists suggest, whatever you make it to be, so that each of us can construct our own, or is there a real world outside our senses that exists whether we are here to perceive it or not? Unfortunately, the subject of reality is not quite so easy to deal with as it might at first seem. In ancient times, the very existence of a real world was questioned by some early philosophers. For example, the Solipsistic philosophy that seems to have begun with Gorgias (483–375 BCE) posited that there is no reality at all: nothing exists, or if it does, nothing can be known about it. Then in the seventeenth century, Réné Descartes offered his famous Cogito, ergo sum ("I think, therefore I am"), arguing that if nothing else he could be certain of one thing, his own existence. That certainty was based on the argument that in order to have that thought, he must exist to do the thinking.

In modern times, the nature of reality has been put into serious question by Quantum Mechanical Theory, certainly one of the very finest intellectual accomplishments of all time. While Quantum Theory provides astonishingly accurate mathematical descriptions of the way the world works, and has over and over again made very precise predictions that have been borne out by empirical research, it also paints a picture of reality that is very difficult for us mortals to swallow. Most physicists, Einstein being the notable exception, came to accept what is known as the 'orthodox' or 'Copenhagen' interpretation of Quantum Mechanics, promulgated by Danish physicist Niels Bohr and German physicist Werner Heisenberg. Surprising as it may seem to readers unfamiliar with the development of modern physics, this interpretation posits that there is no objective reality at all, but only a phenomenal one, and that nothing exists in the absence of observation. Reality, this suggests, is an illusion. (Yet, it certainly does not feel like an illusion when you stub your toe on the bed!)

Ultimately, we may never be able to clear up the question of what is real, for as Bohr himself said in commenting on quantum reality: "There is no quantum world. There is only an abstract quantum physical description. It is wrong to think that the task of physics is to find out how nature is. Physics concerns what we can say about nature."

Let us leave the question of ultimate reality to theoretical physicists and philosophers, and presume that there is a real world, one that we can perceive with our senses, however inaccurate our perception might be at times. Of course, our beliefs about what is real and what is fantasy are shaped by much more than just direct experience. Parental teaching, formal education, peer influence and the media are amongst the most important influences, and while parents, teachers, peers and the media are generally invaluable sources of knowledge, they are not always sources of uncontaminated truth. They may teach us that the earth is a globe, that drinking methyl alcohol will turn us blind, and that green vegetables are good for our health, but they may also teach us that some races are inferior to others, that capital punishment is a boon to society, and that humans roamed with dinosaurs on this six thousand year old earth.

Our notion of reality is also influenced by the workings of our mind. While we are taught as children that nightmares and dreams are part of a fantasy world, and that their contents do not reflect reality, that lesson may be lost on adults who undergo a so-called near death experience. People often come to believe that these experiences were real, not fantasy, and that they had left their bodies and approached the doors of Kingdom Come. Reality-testing can often break down when we find ourselves in unfamiliar territory.

With regard to reality testing, let me tell you about Richard's reality. Richard came to see me in my clinical practice because he was an exceedingly lonely man. He informed me in a very straightforward and coherent manner that he suffers from schizophrenia, which is controlled by an injection of a powerful anti-psychotic medication at monthly intervals. While he was pleased that the medication suppresses his psychotic symptoms, he wanted help to develop the necessary social skills to build friendships and to integrate into the community around him. This insight into his situation was noteworthy in light of the schizophrenia, and as we chatted, I was impressed by just how well his medication appeared to be working. Then, in the same straightforward manner that he had discussed his loneliness, he inquired about whether I do surgery. Surprised by this comment, I thought at first that he might be confusing psychology and psychiatry, and assuming that I am a physician. Thus, I thought, his question might simply reflect a curiosity about the range of medical activities carried out by a physician who specializes in psychiatry. I explained that a psychiatrist is someone who has first completed regular medical education before specializing in mental disorders, whilst a clinical psychologist's training begins with the study of normal behaviour, followed by specialization in clinical disorders. Thus, I added in the attempt to be responsive to his question, a psychiatrist would have participated in surgery only while a medical student; psychiatrists do not do surgery.

I sensed that I had not fully answered his question, and so I enquired as to why he wanted to know about surgery. He told me that he needed surgery. When I asked for what reason, he replied, without any apparent indication of awareness that this response might strike me as odd, that he needed to have all of his fingers cut off. One question of course led to another, for I then enquired as to why he needed to have his fingers removed, and he told me, again without hesitation: Because of his constant urge to shove them all up his rectum. Once more, a 'Why?' from me. Because, he said, there is a little piano lodged up his rectum, and he has an overwhelming urge to play it. The only solution that had occurred to him was to eliminate those tempted fingers.

While aware that I was running the risk of having him think that I was swimming alongside as he drifted into his vortex of whimsy, I nonetheless asked him why does he not simply have the piano taken out? He responded with obvious excitement at this sensible suggestion, for apparently the idea had never occurred to him. After contemplating this illumination for a moment, he then quietly asked me whether I remove pianos.

Now, let me tell you about Robert's reality, and as with Richard, I shall modify some unimportant details so as to protect his anonymity. Robert, too, was a congenial man with a pleasant, unassuming manner. He worked in the parts department of a large manufacturer, and he was very happy with the sort of work that he was doing. However, he was very unhappy with his workmates, for they teased him relentlessly. It was the stress caused by their torment that had led him to seek my help. He was reluctant at the outset to tell me of the basis for the teasing, but he gradually opened up and explained that coworkers teased him because he is a 'little different.' Indeed, he said, he is different from other people in that he must be in bed every night by midnight in order to fly to the sun to recharge his batteries. If he failed to do so, he said, he would most surely die.

Further enquiry revealed that Robert, too, had been diagnosed with schizophrenia, and as did Richard, Robert believed that his symptoms were totally suppressed by the monthly injections of medication. He asked me, with hope in his voice, whether I believed that he flies to the sun each night. Rather than slapping him in the face with my version of reality, I gently told him that I had no way of knowing for certain, but how would he react if I were to tell him that every night after I go to bed, I am transported to the moon, where I ride my bicycle for half an hour. He laughed out loud, and exclaimed that nobody would believe such silliness. Suddenly, as insight dawned, his grin disappeared and he responded with "Wait a minute..." This was followed by, "I shouldn't be talking to people about flying to the sun — they must think that it is just a silly story like yours!" While I knew that there was no point in trying to free him from his delusion, he now recognized at least that telling people about it at the workplace was not to his advantage. He dealt with this realization in a logical manner, and soon arranged a transfer to another of the company's factories. He was careful not to tell his new workmates about his nocturnal voyages, and since they treated him well, so far as he was concerned, he no longer had a problem. Just as do the rest of us, he knows what is real and what is fantasy, and he knows that he flies to the sun each night.

How can we be so sure that Richard does not have a piano up the Khyber and that Robert does not fly to the sun each night? To each of them, their belief is their reality. To you and me, these beliefs reflect disordered minds, and we rest certain in that opinion without the bother of having to look for the piano or watch for someone flying to the sun (a voyage which, by the way, must first involve a trip half-way round the earth, since he flies at midnight!). We have this certainty because neither claim fits with our view of 'reality,' a view that is shared with the vast majority of people around us. However, in Richard's case, what if we were to talk with a surgeon who had x-rayed him, and who informed us that — who knows how it got there — a small piano is indeed lodged inside the man? Suddenly, based on our trust in the expertise of the surgeon, Richard's piano is no longer delusional; it is reality. Thus, our view of 'reality' is often anchored in a reliance on the pronouncements of accepted authority figures, as it was to an even larger degree when we were children. We came to accept without doubt that the earth is a globe, just as children in centuries long gone came to know that it is actually flat.

We may fervently believe that the Biblical account of creation is a myth, and that our species has evolved from lower creatures, but what about the billions of people who just as fervently believe in their various deities? Their beliefs in Jehovah or Ganesh (the Hindu God with the head of an elephant) or some other supernatural being may make no sense to us, and we might conclude that those believers share a collective delusion. Of course, those folks, solid and comfortable in their beliefs, may well perceive us to be the deluded ones in our denial of a spiritual realm. And no matter what one's view of reality, it is always much more secure when we surround ourselves with others people who share it. Had Robert and Richard described hallucinations of a religious nature, and had they lived in a commune in which religious visions were taken to be a sign of faith, it is quite possible (depending of course on the presence or absence of other symptoms) that they would never have been considered to be mentally ill. Rather, they might be viewed as special people with sacred visions.

The media, of course, play a vital role in filling out our view of what is real, particularly in regard to what is happening in the day-to-day world outside our immediate purview. Were there weapons of mass destruction found in Iraq after the invasion by the 'Coalition of the Willing'? How would we know? We rely on the media, and what our leaders say to the media. It is interesting to note that a Harris poll conducted in October 2004 reported that 38% of Americans believed that Iraq possessed weapons of mass destruction at the time that the US invaded. The same Harris questions, when asked in July 2006, found that, by then, 50% of Americans believed that such weapons existed! Yet, a large majority of Canadians believed all along that Iraq had no such weapons, and now believe that none were ever found. Similarly, while Canadians are very aware that none of the 9/11 terrorists came through Canada, there continues to be a widespread belief in the US that some or all of them did so. This too has been backed up by various polls, but consider this anecdotal example: Just recently, in discussion with an American while visiting in California, he expressed surprise at my wonderment that so many Americans still believe that those terrorists came through Canada. He told me that this was the first time that he had heard anyone even suggest that they had not come from Canada! Does such belief qualify as a delusion?

We necessarily rely on the media to bring us knowledge of what goes on in the world beyond our immediate purview. Is global warming something to be concerned with? Hard to tell, if left to our own devices, and the media play a major role in bringing us information upon which to base a decision. However, if we restrict ourselves to a small range of media, as many people do, we may be seriously misled, deliberately or otherwise. On the other hand, when a majority of media outlets climb on the same bandwagon and promote a common view while failing to examine critically the basis for that view (as was the case with much of the US media following 9/11, and even more so with regard to the invasion of Iraq), or when, as a result of media 'convergence,' an apparent multitude of voices is really only one, then even the judicious media consumer who samples widely may be exposed only to a single message, one not always isomorphic with reality. In consequence, we can come under the spell of a collective delusion based in misinformation and often fuelled by the emotion that that misinformation engenders.

Richard needs a piano mover. Robert flies to the sun. Their powerful delusions emerge from deep inside their troubled brains. The apparent delusions of those who still believe in the existence of weapons of mass destruction in Iraq emerge from deep inside a troubled society, facilitated by a collection of media sources that have failed in their duty to communicate truth. Paraphrasing Justice Frankfurter, without a lively sense of responsibility, even a free press may become a powerful instrument for distorting reality, an instrument that can be wielded by those who seek to deceive rather than to inform. ❧

Beautiful (& Dangerous) Minds

by Shirley Goldberg

I n the late 16th century, Galileo and his scientific theories were contained, more or less, by house arrest. Giordano Bruno, his fellow heliocentrist, was burned at the stake. Ancient history, we say but is it? Scientists today are pressured by government and industry — as never before — to subvert the results of their investigations and to sign their names to studies they know are untrue. The result is what Robert F Kennedy Jr has so aptly labeled 'Junk Science.'

Widespread corruption is one of the dominant signifiers of the decline and fall of empires. And when that corruption engulfs the field of science in an age as technological as ours, the human consequences are potentially catastrophic. The restraints upon Galileo and the tragedy of Bruno didn't appreciably threaten the lives of ordinary citizens. But today, similar muzzling of scientists threatens planetary survival. Pharmaceuticals are rushed to market without adequate testing or despite bad trial results. The Environmental Protection Agency in the US is green-lighting levels of toxins in the air, water, and ground that are known to be pernicious. Denial of climate change has impeded our ability to adapt successfully. Genetic engineering of crops, which irreversibly alters the gene pool, is spinning out of control. Scientists who question its safety lose funding, tenure, and employment.

Perhaps the most corrupted area of research involves weapons. An alarming illustration involves the recent US congressional decision, after decades of debate, to bury all of the nation's nuclear waste in Nevada's Yucca Mountain. The *New York Times* has since reported that the decision may have been based on falsified data.

Many of these examples of junk science must have involved major personal crises for the scientists involved — the stuff of film and television scripts. Or not! I had hoped to devote this essay to cinematic renderings of science (and scientists) under pressure to serve non-scientific agendas. But to my surprise, the story is rarely being told — and I wonder why. Aside from *The Insider*, a true drama based on the unexpected heroism of a whistle-blowing scientist working for a tobacco company (and perhaps *The Constant Gardener*, in which a fictional scientist reluctantly faces up to the human rights abuses of a pharmaceutical company), it is difficult to find stories featuring a scientist-hero in a David and Goliath scenario. The hero is far more apt to be a lawyer or journalist who doggedly gets at the truth. In popular culture the only worthy version of the scientist seems to be the forensic researcher who fights crime in his groovy lab to the hyped-up beat of atonal titration music.

To remediate this gap in the popular imagination, let me tell you a true story, a tragic story — my story — about a scientist (my husband) and the high price of personal and scientific integrity.

Phil was a geophysicist — the son of Lithuanian Jewish immigrants who spoke eight languages and settled in New York's Bronx. When he started second grade, the school system transferred him to a special school for gifted children. For his mother Dora, he was always "my son, the genius."

Unlike the fictional stereotype of the socially awkward nerd, Phil was brash, funny, and popular. He became president of almost every group he was attached to — student body president at Reed College, the elite liberal arts institution where he took his undergraduate degree, and also the president of the West Coast Association of Student Body Presidents.

If he hadn't chosen science, he could have opted for satire. These were the war years (World War Two, that is) and, in homage to Winston Churchill, he wrote a hilarious "Blood, Sweat and Jeers" column for the college paper. We all agreed that his rude, subversive wit — and delivery — was as thoroughly original and devastating as that of Mort Sahl or Tom Lehrer or Lenny Bruce. Would the ending of this story have been happier had he chosen a life of political satire over physics?

Politically Phil was anti-military, but fortunately since he was automatically exempt from the draft as a science major, he was spared the need to make any kind of formal declaration. However, in his graduate studies — with the horror of Hiroshima and Nagasaki burned into our consciousness — he deliberately avoided studies in nuclear physics or any other branch laden with military applications. By focusing on the study of the atmosphere between and around the planets, he was choosing to work with 'pure' science. Or so he thought.

However, universities in those days paid poorly for a young instructor with a growing family and were anemically funded for research. So when the Boeing Airplane Company — which up to that time had focused on engineering and civil aviation — announced its intention to create a scientific research lab devoted to pure science, the temptation to choose industry over academia proved irresistible.

This was an exciting, almost euphoric, time — working with management to conceptualize the labs, select the fields of study, design the buildings, and hire top international scientists. All of this, however, came after he had helped the company with a single military project. Boeing was competing for the original Minuteman Missile contract, and all they were asking Phil to do was to put together the proposal in proper and persuasive form. Other people had done the research and designed the prototype, and others would carry out the program if the competition were successful. Only his expertise in writing such proposals and his signature with his credentials were needed. Phil complied, and Boeing landed the Minuteman contract. In the grand, archetypal scheme of things this simple digression proved to be the contemporary equivalent to Faust's pact with the devil. And the devil doesn't necessarily collect immediately.

Several years later, after Phil joined the RAND Corporation in

Santa Monica as a Senior Scientist, the bill fell due. RAND is one of the original, high-powered 'think tanks.' Some of their other employees during that era were Herman Kahn (conceptualizer of the 'Doomsday Machine' and — along with Edward Teller — the inspiration for Stanley Kubrick's *Dr Strangelove*), James Schlesinger (Secretary of Defense with Nixon and Ford), and Daniel Ellsberg (*Pentagon Papers* and winner of the Right Livelihood or Alternate Peace Prize Award). At that time, about 60% of RAND's work involved government contracts. However, the company in their obvious eagerness to hire Phil, promised he would be able to work on the pure science projects he had wanted to pursue for so long. For his PhD dissertation at the University of California in Los Angeles, he had investigated the source of extra-low frequencies vibrations beneath the earth's surface, and after four years of intensive research had discovered a correlation with sun flare activity. He hoped to pursue some related hypotheses but unfortunately was never able to. Several decades later other scientists did pick up the torch and establish the fact that Phil's research had been a significant building block for future work. By then it was too late for him.

Recapitulating the Boeing episode, RAND too had a small job they wanted Phil to attend to first — a simple desk study that he could polish off quickly before going on to what he assumed he had been contracted to do. Questions had arisen about the defensibility of those Minutemen missiles that Boeing had built and been sinking into silos from Montana to Missouri at the cost of billions. What was needed was an assurance for the critics that the weapons were not vulnerable to Soviet attack.

From here on increasing weirdness creeps into the story. At dinner one night Phil declined to answer questions about his day at the office. Putting his finger to his lips, he motioned for me to follow him to the peach trees at the bottom of the garden. The children, curious, tagged along. Convinced that we were being listened to electronically, he urged us to watch our words and avoid any discussion of his work. Later, foreshadowing Gene Hackman's unforgettable role in Coppola's *The Conversation*, he took the phone apart to hunt for a bug. But since his practical skills didn't necessarily match his theoretical ones, the phone developed such an annoying hum we had to call in the company's repairman who in turn was so baffled he replaced the device.

This was the early 1960s, and Phil grew increasingly anxious about our cold war credentials — especially mine. We had both attended a college with a radical reputation and had an incriminating collection of leftist books in our library. Even worse, in my competitive tennis days, my women's doubles partner was a former secretary of the Young Communist League at the University of California at Berkeley and a close friend of Robert Oppenheimer. We had met Oppenheimer on a number of occasions — a gaunt, broken man with a soft voice and cavernous eyes, stripped of his security clearance and much of his reputation, partly through the hostile testimony of Edward Teller. He was an object lesson to us all.

A distinct chill had affected our whole community. Most of our friends came either from the UCLA faculty or the local aerospace industries — Douglas, Lockheed, and TRW (Thompson Ramo Woolridge). If pressed, they would admit they disapproved of the nation's incipient involvement in Vietnam and would prefer not be working on defense contracts. But the pay was good. People unfortunately really do prefer not to know or think about things when their job depends on not knowing or thinking about those things.

Even a non-scientist could have predicted the outcome of Phil's Minuteman study for RAND. Ensconced in their silos — however well camouflaged — they were irredeemably vulnerable. The Pentagon summoned Phil to Washington immediately. He returned a few days later in a highly troubled state, charged with the task of creating another desk study, tackling the problem from other angles, and coming up with the right answer. The truth was obviously not an option. Essentially he had been ordered to fake a scientific study and sign his name to it. Since this was personally impossible, he tried in good faith to demonstrate in his subsequent paper that, however one approached the question of the Minuteman's vulnerability, no solution existed. It was a sitting duck.

The second summons to the Pentagon resulted in a third and considerably more hostile injunction to produce the required evidence. He never returned to his office again. In fact he never worked again. However, it was a long time before the company noticed since RAND had a liberal policy about employees working odd hours and at home.

Meanwhile Phil began to scout around for other employment, only to discover that the doors which had swung open eagerly for him scarcely a year earlier were now locked.

Without question he was blacklisted, and his paranoia grew. One afternoon I noticed a partially burned bundle in the fireplace, which turned out to be a volume by Bertolt Brecht wrapped in one of my favorite paintings by Kandinsky — a couple of unabashed Marxists. The political purge was in high gear. While those items were readily reproducible, what really hurt was the disappearance of my an old 78 album of Paul Robeson's *Songs of Freedom* — a treasure that has never again become available in any format. It had special significance because Robeson spent an inspiring week on the Reed campus during our student years, visiting classes and hanging out in the coffee shop talking, mingling, and singing — especially those songs of the labour movement and the Spanish Civil War.

At this time Phil started to investigate a variety of quasi-religious, quasi-Eastern cults (in which Southern California is awash), seeking some source of inner power to fend off the forces arrayed against him. With his normal critical faculties totally in abeyance, he sought out the Life After Death Society, the Rosecrucians, Eckankar, Transcendental Meditation, and Scientology. He even spent a month on Catalina Island at a seminar with the Maharishi Mahesh Yogi where he claimed to have mastered teleportation.

None of his close friends shared my concern about his curious behaviour. And he certainly would not seek help himself because (1) that was not what he thought he needed, and (2) he couldn't risk losing his security clearance. The only incident that sounded a public alarm occurred under bizarre circumstances at St John's Hospital in Santa Monica where our family doctor sent him for a week-long battery of tests in a futile effort to determine the cause of a persistent low-grade fever. My suggestion that the cause might be psychological barely merited a response.

On the same floor of the hospital, in a large private room, lay Hollywood's fabulously popular singing detective Dick Powell. And Phil — who had decided that perhaps he should switch careers to film directing — slipped into Powell's room in the hope of making a contact and getting advice. In fact, he slipped in so many times that Powell's family called the police to protect the dying man from harassment.

From here on, the story grows dark — institutions, half-way houses, long disappearances, shock therapy, primitive neuroleptic drugs that caused gross side effects. His Beverly Hills psychiatrist, whose practice was limited to high-achieving, Jewish schizophrenics, claimed it was difficult to help anyone with such a high IQ because he had learned from earliest childhood that when his assessment of reality differed from that of others, he was the one who was right.

Exactly a decade after Phil's psychiatric breakdown, the government admitted the vulnerability of the Minuteman system. Later still, during the Carter administration, people toyed with the hare-brained idea of putting the missiles on train boxcars and keeping them moving — often through populated areas. Better still, digging an underground subway system across the continent in order to keep their whereabouts out of sight. Today they are still slumbering in their silos, amidst the wheat fields.

When I saw the film *A Beautiful Mind* (2001), based on the book of the same title about John Nash, the brilliant mathematician who suffered an extended psychiatric breakdown but nevertheless recovered sufficiently to be honored in his later years with a Nobel Prize for work he had done much earlier. I was struck by the uncanny parallels to Phil's story — except for the ending. In fact, the few details in the film that didn't ring true proved to have been freely adapted and altered from the original. Both men had been brilliant theoreticians, both were sincerely anti-war, both went to work for the RAND Corporation in the 1960s where they were sucked into Cold War defense projects, and both suffered psychiatric breakdowns afterwards.

Weapons research involves more money and a greater temptation for fraud than any other area. Projects like Star Wars (Ballistic Missile Defense System) have a certain lethal glamour that can lull the public to sleep. Even Dwight D Eisenhower in his prescient farewell address warned his countrymen about the obscene waste of money and resources — the way in which these expensive weapons systems take food, shelter, health care, and education from those in need and saddle future generations with debt.

Obviously disregard for and corruption of science suggest a staggering social failure. Throughout our popular culture — from Faust to Caligari to Frankenstein to Strangelove — we find a preponderance of negative images. Even in science fiction the scientist is often depicted as the bad guy — or the ineffective guy as compared to the militaristic action hero. Meanwhile, the archetypal stories that deal in a meaningful way with the clash of knowledge and power in our era are not being told. ❧

Understanding Black Anger

by Shirley Goldberg

It takes time to traverse the politics of history, confront guilt and arrive at an adequate memorialization of national crimes that also offers a possible path to reconciliation...

— Roger Cohen, Op-Ed "Race & American Memory,"
New York Times, April 17, 2008

Contemplating the unexpected and phenomenal rise of Barack Obama in his drive to capture the most important political job in the world, columnist Roger Cohen — with the special sensitivity of a former South African — calls our attention to the unfinished business of history: the unhealed wounds, the unatoned-for original sin. He notes that the United States has a magnificent Holocaust Memorial Museum, but as yet no adequate memorial to the 'ravages of race' — including the holocaust of the slave trade, the institution of slavery, subsequent racial discrimination, betrayal and denial of hope. One can only trust that when the Smithsonian finally does open its National Museum of African American History and Culture in 2015, it won't have been bowdlerized and sanitized the way the installation to commemorate the bombing of Hiroshima and Nagasaki had been.

A variety of extraordinary social forces have intersected to make the election of Obama possible. But along with the euphoria have come some bleak reminders. They started with a few cobbled-together, incendiary snippets spoken by Obama's long-time pastor and friend, the Reverend Jeremiah Wright from Trinity United Church of Christ in Chicago. Proving that a sound wave once born never dies but just goes on echoing throughout the universe, this deceptive outburst has been looping tirelessly through our mediasphere ever since — ending again and again with the ferocious crescendo of "God Damn America!" — a message that does not go over well in post-9/11, traumatized, and mismanaged America.

Not only did this sound-bite raise divisive racial issues and distort the tradition of Black Liberation Theology, it disrupted Obama's inspirational, seemingly post-racial campaign aimed at bringing people of all races, religions, ethnicities, and classes together to work for a better future. We've heard the message before, but never quite like this. The cohesiveness of Obama's history, life choices, and remarkably candid writing gives the message a fresh credibility.

In a random flight of association, he reopens memory files to the page on Jawaharlal Nehru, who traversed the vast land of India using the electoral system not just to promote his own candidacy but to educate the population about the democratic process and its potential. Obama, with his use of 'movement' language, his stress upon 'we' and 'you,' has likewise been promoting grassroots, bottom-up power. Altogether, he uses words in a more thoughtful, less programmed way than we expect from politicians. Leaving the details a bit vague, he stresses the power of hope over the power of nightmare.

When the Wright bombshell exploded, Obama responded to the educational possibilities of the moment with an astonishing speech on race and politics (Philadelphia, March 18, 2008) — a speech that recognizes the full complexity of the issue including the failures and legitimate grievances on both sides, a speech that merits inclusion on all social studies reading lists. The novelty of such a sophisticated response to a crude political attack elicited praise across the political spectrum.

Roger Cohen reacted gratefully: "For seven years we have lived with the arid us-against-them formulas of Bush's menial mind, with the result that the nuanced exploration of America's hardest subject is almost giddying."

Unfortunately the educational moment passed, and traditional partisan politics resumed. The originally hopeful vision of a colour-blind, post-racial campaign was no doubt doomed from the outset. Identity can be a confounding issue. Obama's autobiographical *Dreams From My Father* provides a complex exploration of his own identity. From the beginning of the campaign, he was often perceived as either too black or not black enough. There were those — including progressive liberals — who argued that a black candidate, no matter how over-qualified, could not win in racist America. The 'one drop' rule still prevails. And there were those in the black community who argued that he wasn't black enough. The experience of slavery wasn't in his DNA. Nor had he coped with 'Jim Crow' in his formative years. The son of a black father from Kenya and a white mother from Kansas, he had been raised by his white mother and white grandparents, grew up and went to school in multicultural Hawaii and multicultural Indonesia. Only in high school, through friendship with the son of a black American serviceman stationed in Hawaii, did he come in actual contact with the black American experience.

One can't escape the irony of the 2008 struggle for the democratic presidential nomination, pitting the first viable black candidate against the first viable female candidate, Senator Hillary Rodham Clinton. After the Wright episode erupted, Obama, who had previously swept to victory in several predominantly white states, began to lose the white vote in key swing states like Pennsylvania and West Virginia. Sensing their advantage, Clinton and her supporters collected and reiterated an assortment of poll numbers designed to prove that she was more successful with 'hard-working,' white, blue collar, less well-educated voters. At that point the science of political demography erupted all over the TV screen with maps and pie charts splicing the voting constituencies into myriad sets and subsets according to race, gender, age, economic status, and education. What had started as an historic race for change and renewal slipped back into divisive identity politics at its worst, with underlying racist sentiments exacerbated and many of Obama's young volunteers suffering brutal verbal abuse.

A further irony is afforded by the full text of the mesmerizing Wright sermons which fall into the long history of Black Liberation Theology with its nationalist message and its echoes of Old Testament prophecy. Wright's words need to be understood in that context. From the early days of slavery, the black church has played an enormous role in healing, educating, and nurturing its community. Coming out of an ancient oral culture, the church developed a powerful tradition of oratory, the rhetoric and cadences of which reverberate through the pages of Ralph Ellison, James Baldwin, and most of the great African American writers. The same cadences echo too in the rousing speeches of Martin Luther King Jr, Malcolm X, and Eldridge Cleaver. And, yes, more subtly — by way of Columbia, Harvard and an alternate life experience — in the eloquence of Barack Obama.

In Wright's original sermon the ringing "God Damn America!" conclusion is preceded by a long litany of black oppression from the slave trade, to the unfulfilled '40 acres and a mule,' to the horrors of lynching, to segregation, to medical experiments on black prisoners, to inferior schools, inferior housing, inferior health care, to the criminal disregard for the black victims of Hurricane Katrina. In its complete format Wright's indictment is hard to disagree with. It even makes sense to take a further step — to realize that a community so systematically degraded might fail to make clear distinctions between factual oppressions and more conspiratorial ones — such as the theory that US scientists created the AIDS virus in order to decimate the black population of the world. It also makes sense that blacks would be among the first to see 9/11 as the result of 'blowback' from America's own acts of terrorism — chickens coming home to roost, the metaphor that got Ward Churchill into so much trouble, the metaphor first uttered by Malcolm X as a dire prediction of things to come.

A member of the congregation, when questioned by the press about Wright's 9/11 sermon, replied that he wouldn't call it radical — it's just about being black in America. However, the media quickly branded the Wright sound-bite as 'hate' speech and labeled Trinity United Church of Christ as a 'hate' church — completely denying the vast amount of positive community work this popular, progressive, radically empowering evangelical black church has accomplished in the depressed south side of Chicago. The media have also worked hard to create suspicion about anyone who would — like Obama — remain a member of such a church and listen to such infamy.

White America finds it difficult to fully understand the complexity of black anger. Yes, the past was bad, but things are better now, aren't they? A persistent theme in African American literature is the imbalance of understanding of the Other. For his own survival the black slave had to understand the psychology of the master, whereas the master perceived no need to expend mental energy understanding what's going on in the slave's mind. The most humorous, bittersweet examples of this can be found in the short stories of Charles W Chesnutt, a black Cleveland lawyer of the late 19th century. This imbalance of insight prevails in any relationship where there is a power differential. And it certainly exists in the failure to understand the rhetoric of Jeremiah Wright and black anger.

Are things really better for blacks? School districts have been increasingly re-segregated. Affirmative action has been overridden. In 1967 black Americans earned 54 cents for every dollar earned by white Americans; in 2005, 57 cents — a gain of 3 cents in four decades. Testing the upper limits of black progress, the renowned photographer Timothy Greenfield-Sanders has recently made the film *Black List, Volume One* (2008) in which Elvis Mitchell, the former film reviewer from the *New York Times*, interviews twenty highly successful black men and women from the fields of art, literature, sports and politics. (Presumably *Volume Two* will deal with scientists and academics.) Beginning with personal experience and moving out into the social realm, each interview deals with the situation of African Americans in America today. *The New York Sun* reviewer, at its Sundance premiere, called it: "An inspiring mosaic… a meditation on how far we have to go as a nation in correcting the inequities that persist to this day." Obama, with his dual heritage, has commented wryly that he really knows he's black when he tries to hail a taxi.

In the "Chicago" chapter of Obama's *Dreams From My Father*, his analysis of the hate issue is triggered by an encounter with Ruby, a middle-aged black woman he has worked with closely on community projects. Incongruously, she is wearing blue contact lenses. This leads him to speculate about the inevitable degree of self-hatred within the black community — self-hatred for not being able to conform to society's standards for appearance or success — self-hatred leading in turn to a protective counter-narrative in which that hatred is turned against the whites. He asks whether Ruby can ever love herself without hating blue eyes. This troubles Obama because his mother had trained him to make subtle moral distinctions between those who mean harm and those who cause it out of ignorance or indifference. In the following excerpt he nails the psychological need for this hate within the black community and the role black nationalism plays in voicing it:

For a people already stripped of their history, a people often ill-equipped to retrieve that history in any form other than what fluttered across the television screen, the testimony of what we saw every day seemed only to confirm our worst suspicions about ourselves.

Nationalism provided that history, an unambiguous morality tale that was easily communicated and easily grasped. A steady attack on the white race, the constant recitation of black people's brutal experience in this country, served as the ballast that could prevent the ideas of personal and communal responsibility from tipping into an ocean of despair. Yes, the nationalist would say, whites are responsible for your sorry state, not any inherent flaws in you.

The single, most inclusive work of black American literature is Ralph Ellison's classic 1947 novel *The Invisible Man*, which uses a fictional disguise to not only summarize the whole social, political, historical narrative of the black in America, but also to develop the useful metaphor of invisibility. His unnamed black protagonist is invisible because he is seen only as a stereotype — not a complex individual. And, of course, the same observation can apply to any minority. In conclusion, Ellison asks: "Who knows but that, on the lower frequencies, I speak for you?"

Obama's church problem provides a good example of this kind of stereotyping. Would any white politician have been as seriously damaged by his church affiliation or endorsement — no matter how troubling? In addition to the sizable percentage of voters who are convinced Obama is a Muslim because of his name, countless others believe he must "hate America" because of Reverend Wright's passionate soundbites, always offered outside of historical and cultural context.

When Obama was first hired as a community organizer on the south side of Chicago, he was advised to check out Trinity United as the most popular, most active church in the neighborhood. He was drawn to it as an agent of social change. When he decided to join, it was a calculated choice. As he makes a point of explaining in *Audacity of Hope*, it had nothing to do with an epiphany, and for that reason it would not require him to give up critical thinking. His own spiritual background had been non-doctrinaire and basically humanistic. When his grandfather, during his Kansas days, decided the family needed a church affiliation, he chose the Unitarian-Universalist denomination for its multicultural mix of religions. And Obama has summed up the religious impulses of his anthropologist mother as reverence for life, a sense of joy, and her kindness.

Fortunately, in spite of the inevitable and depressing flare-up of racism, the historic selection of Obama as the Democratic presidential candidate suggested a major change in national consciousness which appears to be generational in nature. Polling indicates that race is not a consequential issue for those under 45 but still is for those over 45.

Part of this evolution has undoubtedly been nurtured by the representation of blacks in both television and film. (When the Smithsonian completes its National Museum of African American History and Culture, one hopes it will include a major film collection with a screening room and regular programming.) Especially significant has been the work involving blacks both behind and in front of the camera telling their own stories from their own perspective. The prime example is Spike Lee who has been making prize-winning films ever since his student days — films full of humor and outrage, targeting both white and black audiences, experimenting with various styles, both non-fiction and feature, in order to document the African American experience. Best known is his expressionistic *Do the Right Thing* (1989), set in

Bedford Stuyvesant, a poor black district of Brooklyn during a record heat wave, when a minor annoyance and stupid responses ignite the underlying racial tensions and flame out of control into police involvement, a death in custody, and a destructive, pointless riot. It's a flashy, seductive film featuring a great sound track and a screen full of hip, colorful urban culture, but what really lingers in the mind is the way Lee balances our sympathies and forces us to wrestle with the question of what is the right thing to do.

Following in quick succession were three powerful, in-your-face films dealing with racial flashpoints: *Mo' Better Blues* (1990) about the exploitation of black musicians, *Jungle Fever* (1991) about miscegenation, and his extraordinary *Malcolm X* (1992) which Norman Jewison had originally been scheduled to direct. With his characteristic tenacity, Lee sought out Jewison and convinced him that Malcolm X's autobiography was a story that had to be interpreted by a black director.

Subsequently he made a series of quieter films dealing in greater depth with the lives of black people inside the black community and designed more specifically for a black audience — such as *Crooklyn* (1994) about a black schoolteacher raising a family of five in *Brooklyn of the 70s, Clockers* (1995) about drugs as a way of life within the ghetto, and *Get On the Bus* (1996) about an assortment of black men on a cross country bus headed for the Million Man March.

He has also made a number of documentaries, the most notable of which are *Four Little Girls* (1997) about the terrorist bombing that killed four Sunday School pupils in an African American church in Birmingham, Alabama, during the Civil Rights Movement and his recent masterpiece *When the Levees Broke: a Requiem in Four Acts* (2006).

The Katrina tragedy struck while Lee was at the Venice Film Festival. For several days he shut himself in his hotel room following the events compulsively on CNN appalled by the sight of all those black faces pleading for help that didn't come. The story, as it unfolded, was so horrendous and unbelievable that he knew he had to document it for history.

The original agreement for a two-hour program for HBO quickly doubled into four. He made nine trips into the area and interviewed at least one hundred people who in a mosaic of their own voices — angry, bitter, tearful, injured, profane, and thoughtful — tell the story. To show the early days, he uses all available sources, a devastating assortment of media footage along with both amateur and professional video. The first hour deals with the storm and its terrible aftermath. The second hour explored questions of blame — including the persistent suspicion that some sections of the levees were intentionally dynamited to flood the poorer black section and protect other areas. The third hour, with the random diaspora of evacuees scattered in all directions, herded indiscriminatingly onto buses by National Guardsmen armed with AK-47s — resulting in frantic people looking for lost mothers, fathers, children — awakening a deep, painful, historic memory of slave families deliberately torn apart. And the fourth hour concluded with the monumental challenge of rebuilding.

Throughout this angry indictment, Lee reminds us of the rich heritage of the black culture of New Orleans. The whole film has a haunting musical score by trumpeter Terence Blanchard who has collaborated with Lee on many films. Lee opens with a long, unforgettable montage of colorful Mardi Gras scenes inter-cut with flood images — bodies floating face down in the water, people pleading for help from roof tops, cars crushed, homes uprooted, children air-lifted — all set ironically to the jaunty music of Louis Armstrong's "Do You Know What It Means to Miss New Orleans."

The end is equally memorable as it depicts a mock New Orleans Jazz Funeral with the Hot 8 Brass Band marching before an empty casket down a desolate, devastated street. The refrain of the song is "When I die… hallelujah, by and by, I'll fly away." But on the final verse, the vocalist alters the words to "New Orleans will never go away."

The guilt of the government — its ineptitude, criminal indifference, shoddy improvisations, and blatant racism — is so obvious that Lee never needs to raise his voice, never needs to be heavy-handed. It's all there in the tightly edited, tightly woven account. *When the Levees Broke* is a stunning work of documentary art as well as an invaluable historical record. It should also be a reference point for those who don't understand black anger, those who are so gravely offended by the words of Reverend Wright.

Half a century has passed since Martin Luther King inspired us with his "I Have a Dream" speech. As implausible as this might have seemed even a few years ago, an African American became president of the United States. At certain historical moments progress is not made by slow, incremental inching but by leaps. Perhaps that is such a moment. ❧

SCIENCE & RACISM

by James Alcock

The ability to think critically is not hard wired into our brains, nor is it simply an accumulation of common sense that develops as we grow up. Critical thinking involves the deliberative application of concepts developed across centuries of intellectual history, such as deductive and inductive logic, avoidance of logical fallacies, and consideration of base rates and control groups. Critical thinking also requires a willingness both to favour reason over emotion and to suspend judgement and live with ambiguity when the evidence is weak, confusing or beyond our ken. In the absence of critical thinking, we leave ourselves reliant on the easy interpretations that grow out of direct experience and the anecdotal accounts of others, interpretations which are all too vulnerable to error and delusion.

No human being can be at all times a critical thinker, no matter how much one might take pride in being so. Unfortunately, while it is often easy to recognize the lack of critical acumen in others, it is usually exceedingly difficult to realize just when we ourselves have sacrificed reason at the altars of pride, venal reward, illusory correlation or emotional solace. Thus, the hard-nosed sceptic of alternative medicine may believe that her reliance on large doses of Vitamin C to ward off colds is based in good science; it is not. The proud critical thinker may look askance at others' embrace of pop psychological fads or religious miracles or paranormal wonders, while he nonetheless marries extremely unwisely, or invests foolishly in a penny stock whose sole claim to virtue is a recommendation from an acquaintance.

Science, of course, is a systematized expression of critical thinking. Because science has been so obviously successful in its quest to understand and control various aspects of nature, it has taken on a sheen of near-infallibility for many people. But how do we recognize good science from its impostors? While that great pretender, pseudoscience, may be easy for some to spot when it is in the service of belief in supernatural phenomena, it often goes unnoticed when it involves less exceptional phenomena, phenomena that fit well with contemporary beliefs. Scientists themselves are not immune to pseudoscientific thinking at times, and therefore the critical thinker has to remain vigilant even with regard to claims emanating from the heartland of science itself. That is often difficult, for most people lack the skill and knowledge to evaluate claims from physics or biology or medicine. Suspending judgement, especially when faced with 'breakthrough' claims, is often the only reasonable course available.

Thus, all that glitters in science is not gold, and not all those who wrap themselves in the cloak of science bother to or even know how to apply scientific methods to the study of their subject matter. First, there are the impostors, those pretending to use science but who only borrow its name. Advertisers hawking everything from food supplements and over-the-counter remedies to engine additives exploit the reputation of science when they employ actors in laboratory coats and proclaim that the benefits of their products are 'scientifically proven.' Alternative medicine often dresses itself up in the raiment of its greatest opponent, leading to such oxymoronic terms as 'Homeopathic Science' and 'Chiropractic Science.' Even some 'modern' religions — Christian Science, Scientology — have borrowed from the reputation of science. There is no Vatican of Science, no trademark office to supervise labelling, and so such usage goes unimpeded.

Then there are the rogues, those who are trained in science, but manipulate their findings to satisfy a personal craving for power or influence or wealth, or to further a particular philosophical or political agenda. In only one of many such dramatic frauds that have come to light, in 2005, star South Korean scientist Hwang Woo Suk, who had published breakthrough scientific research reporting the cloning of human embryos and the extraction of stem cells, was found to have faked all of his human stem cell research.

And finally, there are the self-deluded, the generally well-trained and accomplished researchers who become distracted and slip into error. Again, examples are unfortunately abundant, and the realm of parapsychology contains many such people. However, so too does mainstream science. For example, in 1989, Pons and Fleishmann, two very competent chemists, shocked the physics world when they became convinced that they had produced nuclear fusion in a table-top apparatus: they were mistaken.

Despite all this, science does not veer very far off course, and eventually the safeguards built into the scientific method — in particular the demand for independent replication of knowledge claims — separate fact from chicanery and error. The unscrupulous or self-deluded scientist sooner or later is caught out, and the erroneous claims discarded. However, the reputation of science is often tarnished in the public eye as a result, and worse, there are some claims made in the name of science that cause very significant long-term harm because they reflect and give respectability to underlying social biases that disadvantage some groups of people in favour of others. One outstanding example of this is the subversion of science to the promotion of racism.

Of course, the use of spurious scientific claims to bolster Nazi beliefs about the inferiority of Jews is well-known. However, the Nazis were late-comers in terms of dressing up racism as science, and their agenda was obvious. Much less obvious, (and much less consciously deliberate, one would hope), were the efforts of some leading psychologists, particularly in the United States, to persuade their governments and their public not only that there is a scientific basis for grouping people into races based on the colour of their skin and other superficial characteristics, but that there is also a scientific basis for judging some such racial groups to be genetically inferior in terms of intellect.

The simplistic notion that we can summarize 'intelligence' by a number derived from a standardized test still plagues our society. However, the concept had somewhat noble roots, in that it grew out of efforts to identify children who were having difficulty in school in order to find ways to help them circumvent such difficulties. In the late 19th century, pedagogical authorities in France commissioned a psychologist, Alfred Binet, to develop an assessment tool to help pedagogues discover early on just which children needed more assistance, and then provide them with that assistance. This subsequently led to the concept of Intelligence Quotient (IQ), a ratio of a child's demonstrated 'mental age' to his or her chronological age.

Thus, the original purpose behind the development of IQ measurement was benign. Administer standardized tests to find which children were lagging, and then provide extra assistance to help them catch up. Taken in this light, a 'low' IQ should be no more stigmatizing than a low biology test mark or a low motor mechanics mark. Such marks do not indicate low 'intelligence,' but merely low performance, possibly due to any number of factors, including poor motivation. However, not many years later, Binet's test was brought to the United States, *translated* into English, re-standardized, and presented to the American public as the Stanford-Binet intelligence test. However, a subtle change had occurred. The instrument was now presented, by some of the leading psychologists of the day, as a measure not just of performance but of basic intellectual ability. Because the test items were culture-dependent to some extent — that is, the questions dealt with ideas that people growing up in the American mainstream were likely to be familiar with — they put immigrants and members of marginalized ethnic groups at a disadvantage. Nonetheless, the Stanford-Binet was quickly employed in support of the argument that people in certain ethnic groups are intellectually inferior, and the argument was convincing, for it led to changes in United States immigration laws and provided fuel to the eugenics movement.

The eugenics movement, a quest to weed out undesirable genes, also drew whenever it could from scientific knowledge to make its case. Again, the misuse of science led to the misuse of law. One notable example in Canada: in 1928, Alberta enacted the Sexual Sterilization Act, the only jurisdiction in the then British Empire to do so. The act was intended to prevent 'deficient' individuals from passing on their 'deficient' genes to the next generation, and it was implemented vigorously. The rate of sterilization of the mentally challenged continued at a high level, and the practice ended only with the repeal of the act in 1972. In the meantime, close to 3000 sterilizations had been carried out, and included amongst them was a range of people deemed unfit to reproduce, including unrepresentatively large contingents of people suffering from epilepsy, alcoholics, the poor, unwed mothers, recent immigrants and aboriginal people. Even the Nazi government of Germany turned to Alberta for specific advice on eugenics practices. In Nazi Germany, 400,000 people who were considered unfit to reproduce were sterilized.

To give this tragedy a human face, Leilani Muir was, in her childhood, classified as a 'moron' and sent to Alberta's School for Mental Defectives. At age 14, while undergoing the removal of her appendix, she was sterilized without her knowledge or consent. More shockingly, the order for her sterilization was signed by John MacEachran, who had initially set up the Department of Philosophy and Psychology at the University of Alberta. He was also the chair of the Eugenics Board from 1929–1965. He believed that by sterilizing children with low IQ test scores, the 'purity of the race' could be safeguarded and even enhanced. In any event, subsequent IQ testing later on in her life showed that Ms Muir's IQ was in the normal range. As a result, Ms Muir sued the Alberta government in 1996, and was awarded substantial damages. In 1999 the Government of Alberta reached an $82 million settlement with 247 other victims.

In the meantime, while eugenicists were promoting their beliefs to the public, something else sinister was going on in the name of science. To buttress the argument that some groups are genetically inferior to others intellectually, it is necessary to demonstrate that 'intelligence' is to a significant degree genetically determined, that 'nature' trumps 'nurture.' While various researchers had attempted to do just that, none of their efforts were entirely persuasive until along came Sir Cyril Burt, a distinguished British psychologist who focussed his research on the intellectual abilities of identical twins. By comparing the similarity in measures of intelligence of sets of identical twins separated in infancy and reared apart (thus sharing common genes but not a common environment) with the similarity in intelligence of pairs of fraternal twins reared together (thus sharing a common environment, but having no more genetic similarity than any pair of siblings), Burt assessed the relative importance of genetic and environmental factors on intelligence, as measured by standardized IQ tests. This research was the most extensive research of its type ever carried out and, supposedly, carefully executed and involving relatively large numbers of twin pairs. It appeared to provide strong evidence that genes, and not environment, are the primary factor in intelligence. This research seemed to justify the notion of racial superiority, assuming of course that some 'races' have inferior intellectual genes.

While Burt's evidence for genetic intelligence appeared overwhelming, and his credentials were sterling, it turned out that all was not as it appeared. Indeed, I was fortunate to witness personally the beginning of Burt's undoing when I was a graduate student in psychology at McMaster University in the early 1970s. The Chair of the department was Leon Kamin, and although his research focussed on learning in animals, he became involved in supervising a student who studied intellectual development in children. As he learned more about contemporary research into intellectual development, he began to read Burt's reports. Kamin noted something rather odd: correlation coefficients (a statistical measure) were numerically the same to three decimal places in two different studies, something that would be extremely unlikely to occur by chance. He then discovered that the correlation coefficient remained the same in some others of Burt's studies as well, and it was by way of searching for an explanation for this that Kamin eventually uncovered a massive fraud. Burt had apparently invented much of his data, and even invented the name of a non-existent co-author!

Although Burt's work was discredited in mainstream psychological science, there were others as well — people such as William Shockley, co-inventor of the transistor, and educational psychologist Arthur Jensen — who continued to defend and promote the view that intelligence is largely genetically determined, and that there are racial differences in intelligence. This view was echoed some years later in the published research of psychologist Philippe Rushton at the University of Western Ontario, who stated in defense of Burt:

Ultimately we will be able to predict IQ scores by taking a single cell from an embryo. For some, work on the genetics of intelli-

gence, and racial differences therein, challenges the Enlightenment assumption that knowledge is always better than ignorance. But scholars have accepted that the earth is not the center of the universe, and that man's closest living relatives are the chimpanzees. We can yet affirm our common humanity by accepting our differences. The disparagement of Cyril Burt is the most extraordinary case of counterfeit charges in the history of academic psychology, if not all of science.

The views of Rushton and others have been strongly opposed by many in the mainstream of psychology and science. Yet, such claims ultimately end up feeding racism, regardless of subsequent challenges to their authenticity. Society is at great risk of being harmed by spurious science when it offers information congruent with societal biases, for it provides a putative scientific basis for prejudice and discrimination.

Ultimately, we must learn to distinguish science from non-science and nonsense. Failure to do so imperils us all. ❧

CONSCIENCE IN THE PRINCIPALITY OF PROGRESS

by Jonny Diamond

PART ONE: MORE BLOOD ON THE TRACKS

The train I am on has just hit a deer. I'm on the way back into New York City, after a weekend in the country. I know it is a deer because as the conductor passes by his walkie-talkie spits out, amid anachronistic, pre-digital sizzle and crack: "just hit a deer, approx 4.7 miles south of Croton-On-Hudson."

When a train hits a deer, the noise is bad: a sack of rusted cutlery masticated in the darkness by 19th-century automata; or a thousand storm-frantic branches clawing at a thousand lead-pane windows. The commuters stir only slightly from their larval half-sleeps (technocrats in the foetal position, taking up two seats). Most of them are coming down from Albany, on a train that leaves the station in total darkness. They stir, some even blink awake, but after no worthy disaster reveals itself, no terrorist malevolence or bland malfunction, when it can be subconsciously explained away as obscure terrestrial interruption — indeterminate, benign — all go back to their morning gestation.

But I cannot. I have been cursed with this overheard sentence fragment, this blunt truth. I am stuck with the cinematically clichéd image of the deer on the tracks: an inviolate moment of quiet and mist on the eastern shore of the Hudson River shattered by the arch-villainous train, sleek, silver and impossibly solid, a force as purely destructive as it is indifferent to that which it destroys. This death, the cold red obliteration of this deer, will not leave my thoughts — it is an image unwanted and enormous and I curse the timing of the goateed conductor with the sour hands and ash-grey walkie-talkie.

But I realize there is metaphorical substance here, obvious, suspicious, unavoidable and blessedly distracting. In my distraction, I seek to isolate the allegory.

Begin with Ovid:

Actaeon, metamorphosed into a deer for the lesser transgression of human wonderment, rent apart by his own beloved hunting dogs.

So.

Progress, incarnate in the convenience and power of indifferent technology, destroys the living beauty of the natural world.

And.

By its destruction — by the unmaking of all that articulate bone and sinew and blood — the deer, symbol of what we had, becomes a symbol of what we've lost.

Wait. No. That's not what Ovid meant at all with the story of Actaeon. My random experience of a deer's blood and bone on dew-wet iron tracks, though secret and hidden, is insignificant; it does not have the narrative substance of an Ovidian tale, the proscriptive potency; it's lost to nearly everyone on the train, lost to the very characters in the drama who would benefit from a little mythic awfulness in their lives. Those characters caught in half-sleep, who don't know. And so the train is just a long silver tunnel to the City, a juddering womb daily birthing 345 passengers out through Penn Station into the cruel hum of midtown Manhattan.

PART TWO: THE BALLAD OF JANE & ROBERT

But maybe the persistent allegorical substance of The Deer and The Train can be transferred to New York, to the City itself: a heedless thing progressing through time and space; an engine of destruction operating outside the consolations of tragedy, operating beyond the human capacities to reconcile, to justify. New York City: a creation of humanity which long ago outstripped its need of human beings.

The story of progress in the City is one of forgetting, or more specifically, forgetfulness: a story of low-frequency communal amnesia in which all and none are culpable. The New Yorker, turning away from the accretions of the past (lest she become buried), turns instead to look forward down grand avenues that carve straight and deep beneath buildings giant and golden.

Novelist and essayist Colson Whitehead, when asked what made a person a bona fide New Yorker, described that amnesiac moment, walking by any given street corner, when one realizes that something has changed, but is unable to pinpoint exactly what. This change — dizzying, oneiric, overnight — is the fundamental experience of life in New York; immigrant, exile, arriviste (for this is the population of the City); each one succumbs, all forget. Indeed, this is the life of all cities, but in New York, capital of pure capitalism and ongoing reverence of naked ambition, the change is faster, bigger and greedier; it is a heedless, wilful pissing contest in which banal monstrosity and staggering beauty are nothing more than by-products.

If New York is modernity's Principality of Progress, then Robert Moses is its Medici, Richelieu and Stalin rolled into one; a man of preternatural wilfulness matched only by a diabolical singularity of vision, who aspired to bring theories of British Colonial rule to bear on the complexities of administering a modern city. This is the municipal despot — at one point he controlled ten of twelve city departments — who not only demolished the grand old Penn Station, but gutted neighbourhoods in the Bronx and Brooklyn to make way for highways, displacing tens of thousands of New Yorkers, single-handedly laying the groundwork for forty years of urban decline. (Those 'Projects' that people talk about with dread on TV crime dramas? Those were Moses' projects). The only redeeming thing about Moses was the catalytic volatility of his excess, which galvanized a retiring young urban theorist in opposition to the razing of Penn Station. Though unsuccessful in this first battle, she later gave Moses his first defeat over the planned Lower Manhattan

Expressway (which would've cut through what is now billion dollar real estate in SoHo). This urban theorist is none other than that great, adopted Canadian, Jane Jacobs.

The conscience in opposition to Moses' bullying hubris could only have been the soft-spoken Jacobs. She was the perfect Ovidian foe in that purest agon of the post-atomic age: progress vs. conscience; the wilful, eccentric autocrat vs the thoughtful pragmatist with a talent for inclusion and consensus; The Train vs The Deer.

Progress in the context of capitalism is often characterized as a religion (of which Moses would certainly have been a high priest); if so, then Progress As Religion is a kind of polytheistic animism. Money, Technology, Innovation are as local deities, propitiated with a fervour commensurate to that which can be gained, each functioning in a malign complex of ritual and sacrifice. Jacobs defeated Moses over the Lower Manhattan Expressway not because she had a more powerful God, but because she revealed the programmatic simony of Progress As Religion, and nailed her theses to the church door with a diverse group of human beings at her back. What gave Jacobs power over Moses was consensus, gathered in a humanist context, beyond distinctions of race, class and creed, based in a commonality between human beings who did not want to see their lives destroyed by the forces of greed and progress.

PART THREE: HEAR THAT WHISTLE BLOWIN'

If only I could stop the speeding silver train, march everybody off, and make them look at the remains of the deer; make them examine the catastrophic results of indifference, of progress unheeded, and force them to understand that we cannot, no matter how fast we travel, escape the consequences of our (in)actions.

But the train speeds still toward Moses' cloacal version of Penn Station, toward the giant grey city at the end of history, the half-sleeping commuters rustling beneath their ink-heavy daily papers.

And no one even thinks about looking out the window. 🐾

PART 4

Humanism, Education, Liberty & Responsibility

Humanism insists that personal liberty must be combined with social responsibility. Humanism ventures to build a world on the idea of the free person responsible to society, and recognizes our dependence on and responsibility for the natural world. Humanism is undogmatic, imposing no creed upon its adherents. It is thus committed to education free from indoctrination.

OUR UNIVERSITIES: HOW WE GOT WHERE WE ARE

by Ian Johnston

On important occasions most colleges and universities, even very new ones, like to invoke ancient traditions by dressing the faculty in strange clothes with multicoloured capes, robes, and funny tasselled hats and having someone intone choice phrases in an ancient language hardly anyone understands any more. These ceremonies, one assumes, are meant to remind everyone that the university is the only institution we have, other than the Roman Catholic Church and some native organizations, with roots in ancient times. If that's the purpose, then of course it's something of a sham. For almost all our universities are thoroughly modern institutions formed by a deliberate and decisive break with ancient traditions.

To understand the nature of this transformation, one needs to grasp the significance of at least three decisions which changed the relatively small traditional collegiate structure of the university into the huge modern multiversity. These changes have made our universities enormously powerful institutions, essential components of our social and economic life. They have also significantly affected for the worse the way we educate many of our young citizens.

ISSUE ONE:
THE RESEARCH ETHIC

The first change is well known — the decision made about one hundred years ago to enshrine disciplinary research as the heart of the college enterprise, so that we might emulate the spectacular successes of the German universities in the nineteenth century. What mattered now, above all other considerations, was advancing the causes of truth and of profitable new discoveries by hiring well-trained research specialists, giving them lots of time and resources to pursue independent research projects, and letting them take care of the education of undergraduates, particularly with an eye to the production of future researchers.

Since that time, especially in the last fifty years, the highest research degree, the PhD, increasingly has become the *sine qua non* qualification for almost all university faculty, and productivity in research and publication is now essential for promotion within the ranks. Of course, universities have always paid lip service to their responsibilities for having good teachers, but in practice that alleged priority has almost always been more a rhetorical flourish than anything else. What matters is the research qualification and research output. With these in place, one doesn't really have to worry too much about basic teaching qualifications — for example, a sufficiently fluent command of English so that undergraduates can understand what the professor is saying.

ISSUE TWO:
THE DEPARTMENTAL STRUCTURE

The second decision, which arises naturally out of the first, was to reorganize the university so that its key structural feature was the department consisting of faculty belonging to a single discipline, often narrowly defined, rather than a college composed of and run by a small number of faculty teaching a range of different subjects. Departments make disciplinary specialization very easy to manage, because such units more or less administer themselves, making all the key decisions about hiring, promotion, curriculum, equipment, and so on, subject only to the budget allocations determined by non-departmental administrators. And once the elective system of courses was introduced, the curricular role of the departments was standardized in a model which required each department to develop a range of credit offerings, organize its courses in a sequence which would produce departmental specialists (majors, honours, and graduate programs), and then compete with other departments for students.

This trend has turned the university into what can best be described as a Lego structure, something put together by assembling small, independent bricks and linking them in a mechanical aggregate (an important break with the more organic structure of the older institutions). Since the departments are largely independent of each other, bricks can be quickly and easily added or removed as circumstance requires: new demands are met by creating a new brick, and redundant departments are removed without any significant effect on anyone else. In such a structure, successful professorial work does not require any familiarity with what goes on outside the department or any vision of or concern for the university as a whole or for the student's experience outside one's departmental courses. And the major task of middle and senior administrative life becomes adjudicating the competing demands of different departments for resources. Such a model is also capable of infinite rapid expansion. The huge modern multiversity would be inconceivable without it.

This structure, once in place, gradually eliminated the differences among colleges, and a standardized model emerged. No matter what university or college one visits in North America (with very rare exceptions), the structure remains the same: an institution organized on the principle of more or less autonomous departments in their own physical space, staffed with research experts who must regularly publish results of their work, and offering a curriculum consisting of a selection of departmental courses, each worth a certain number of credits. The standards may vary, and there may be some minor differences in prerequisites and course combinations, but the basic arrangement remains the same. So far as coping with the curricular organization is concerned, in North America few students or faculty have any difficulty in moving from one university or college to another.

The major effects of these decisions are well known. Our universities have become the centres for an enormous amount of specialized research, often with amazingly successful results. Important research discoveries have increasingly been made in university departments rather than in research and development centres elsewhere or by private citizens, and the major prizes for pioneering research (especially in medicine and science) are routinely awarded to university professors. We look to our universities to provide the innovations which will keep our economy dynamic and position papers which will keep our leaders informed.

The emphasis on research has led, in many quarters, to a very effective partnership of the universities (who provide the research teams), the business community (which provides massive amounts of money), and the government (which provides money and facilities and, where necessary, appropriate legislation). Whatever questions we used to raise forty years ago about the probity of these arrangements and their effects on what a university is or should be seem to have disappeared. There was a time when people worried about the close connections between, say, the drug companies, federal legislators, and university postgraduate courses or between the Pentagon and various academic departments doing research on how to conduct the war in Vietnam or develop Star Wars, but we seem to have grown accustomed to such arrangements now. After all, the learned pate has always ducked to the golden fool. Interestingly enough, the phrase Academic Freedom, which originally was supposed to mean protection for faculty to pursue independent research and to speak out openly on public issues, has in recent decades as often as not come to mean protection from having to answer potentially embarrassing questions about sources of funding. Hence, the once popular notion that the modern university will act as society's disinterested conscience has become something of a joke.

The transformation of the university into the research engine for modern society did not happen all at once. It met considerable resistance, particularly in parts of Europe and Canada, where a much older tradition continued to insist on different priorities, and research qualifications and productivity were often not as essential a part of a university professor's work. But in recent years European leaders have recognized the economic cost of this tradition and, as a central part of their so-called Lisbon strategy to make the European economy the most competitive in the world, are promoting the Bologna process, an effort to streamline and standardize European universities so as to maximize their research output and their economic effectiveness. Canada made that transition forty years ago.

For all the obvious benefits this transformation has brought, there are some equally obvious problems. First is the enormously disproportionate amount of meretricious research, studies which make no significant contribution to the discipline or to the 'search for truth,' whatever that means exactly, and which are read by hardly anyone, not even by those in the same discipline. Since every professor is required to produce a steady stream of articles for publication in peer-reviewed journals, there has been a staggering proliferation of what is little more than academic busy work, much of it incomprehensible to anyone outside the immediate and often very narrow academic speciality.

Equally staggering is the cost. If we remember that a university professor teaches for about six hours a week for six months of the year, with generous time off for research every few years, and that his position brings with it a healthy salary, research facilities, and enviable fringe benefits, then we can understand easily enough that we are, in effect, spending massive amounts of public money to subsidize intellectual mediocrity (to use the politest term available). What is the total cost, I wonder, of those thousands and thousands of articles written by professors in education, literature, social science, history, and even science which disappear without a ripple. What would happen if we directed that money elsewhere, for example, into undergraduate education?

The research imperative is responsible for some very odd results, too. Outsiders are frequently astonished at the sheer drivel produced by some university researchers, especially those under the influence of the latest intellectual fad (like deconstructionism or the most fashionable psychobabble). Such fads are most evident in certain disciplines where it is difficult to find something original to say. Unlike the sciences, where research tends to move in a much clearer direction and there is an important sense of immediate priorities, many literary scholars, for example, are always circling around the same texts, and how does one contribute something new about, say, Shakespeare or Dickens? Well, one answer is to find a new theoretical framework and language, so that one can present old ideas in a new vocabulary. As the fashions change, the language changes, and new possibilities for published articles arise. But this is not progress: it is merely variety, trivial and short-lived intellectual play, as often as not characterized by a jargon incomprehensible to general readers (including undergraduates). And the New History, which claims that all aspects of life are equally important historically, that, in effect, Mickey Mouse is just as vital a subject of study as World War Two, has opened up an infinite number of scholarly research possibilities from, say, courtship patterns among medieval Languedoc peasants to the invention of the cheeseburger in Louisville, Kentucky.

The issue here, let us be clear, is not whether or not such academic research is personally stimulating or intellectually demanding or a contribution to knowledge or whatever. The issue is whether we should be spending massive amounts of public money earmarked for undergraduate education to subsidize it. Is the result worth the cost? I won't explore an answer here, but whenever I have to listen to another lament from the universities about their lack of funding, I'm tempted to remind the complainer that the greatest financial problem in our universities is the sheer waste of money spent on insignificant research and publication. Why not try a 'No-more-dollars-for-dreck' policy which supports the relatively few demonstrably excellent researchers to the hilt and insists that the rest of the money be spent in the classroom?

THE CENTRAL PROFESSIONAL MYTH OF FACULTY CULTURE

University faculty themselves are aware that most of what they produce as a group is without merit (how could they not be?), and since the vast majority of them cannot defend what they do by an appeal to its quality, they have come up with a frequently reiterated and almost universally shared justification. Conventional research and publication, they assert, is essential to good teaching. Unless a university professor is actively engaged in such scholarly activity, no matter what its value, she cannot be an effective instructor of undergraduates: she won't be up-to-date, intellectually engaged in the discipline, mentally alive, or whatever. This claim is enshrined in faculty handbooks and solemnly recited every time there's a plea for more research time or money.

There's only one problem: no one has managed to demonstrate that this claim has any validity. All empirical studies into this issue over the last few decades (and there have been several) have come to the same conclusion: there is no demonstrable connection whatsoever between conventional research and publication and teaching quality. And so what holds faculty culture together in the modern university is a myth, a wish-fulfilling assertion needed to justify light teaching loads and generous research funds. Most faculty reject this unpleasant truth out of hand, and over the years I've been pointing it out, I have met with a good deal of abuse and outright denial, a reaction not unlike that of Caliban when he looked at his face in the mirror and was unhappy with what he saw. He smashed the mirror.

When you think about it, there's more than a little irony in all this. Research is apparently essential to good teaching, except research that indicates such a claim is unproven. And given that the most important task facing almost all teachers of undergraduates is helping students learn to construct good arguments and to recognize shoddy ones, it is interesting, to say the least, that faculty culture rests on an argument so shoddy that it invites comparison with claims that something is true if anyone believes it or that creationism is just as scientifically valid as Darwinism.

In fact, university teaching is the only profession I am aware of where the extensive training and professional evaluation and promotion have nothing to do with one of the major requirements of the job. It's as if we hired and promoted our hockey coaches on the basis of their knowledge of the crystalline properties of ice or tensile characteristics of rubber or paid trial lawyers on the basis of their demonstrated expertise in some specialized area, like the history of Carthaginian maritime law, without regard to their courtroom performance.

Not surprisingly, the most deleterious effects of this transformation of the university into a research factory are experienced by those under-graduates who have no intention of becoming academic researchers (and these people make up approximately 90% of the student popula-tion). In many cases, they have to cope with enormous class sizes (an important way of keeping faculty teaching loads low), a bewildering range of options, increasing pressure to specialize, a lack of coordina-tion between one course and another, and teachers who lack some of the most basic requirements for effective instruction. Given that the vast majority of them have come to the university in order to pre-pare for a profession or to explore different career possibilities or to learn more about life, it's not surprising that there is frequent tension between them and an environment defined by professors with very narrow research interests and a fragmented curriculum catering to fac-ulty research priorities.

What's been lost to a large extent in these developments is the sense of an undergraduate education as an important transition from youth to adulthood, a time to explore intellectual choices, to gather a more intelligent sense of one's history, to read widely, without the constant pressure of a training in a specialized discipline to the exclusion of almost everything else, and to develop the social and academic skills necessary in professional life — something that used to be called (in a phrase that now sounds distinctly outdated) a general education as a preparation for citizenship.

The benefits of such a non-specialist education are widely recog-nized, but here again the tributes are more often empty rhetoric than principles which professors are eager to put into action. Most degree programs have some breadth requirements, but these are minimal and dealt with early on (if they are adhered to at all). The important direc-tion is always increasing specialization, treating all students as if they are potential research colleagues. So we routinely produce scientists with no knowledge of philosophy or politics or, for that matter, the his-tory of science, business graduates lacking any intelligent sense of the importance of ethics, and Arts or Education graduates who squeal in fright at the very mention of science or mathematics. And in almost all cases, none of these graduates will have been encouraged in their classes to acquire the general skills referred to above (in spite of repeated demands from employers for attention to these areas).

Where there are genuinely successful programs of general education, these tend to be confined to the first year (as in Arts I at UBC or King's College Foundations program). Curiously enough, although faculty have long acknowledged that these programs are extremely useful educationally and universities feature them prominently in their advertising as a mark of their excellence, such programs have had little effect on transforming the curriculum in the later years of undergraduate study, mainly because faculty teaching higher-level courses insist upon the prevailing specialist ethic. Yes, there are some exceptions (like the Liberal Studies program at Vancouver Island University, an upper-division program of General Education based on the Great Books approach, a program I was fortunate enough to teach in for several years), but these are rare indeed. Our curriculums are far more decisively shaped by what research-oriented faculty want to teach than by what students need to learn.

For that reason, the best known and most successful alternatives to the modern public university, like St John's College or Evergreen State College, are offered in institutions which began by rejecting specialist research qualifications and productivity and the conventional departmental structure and which insist upon a much more integrated curriculum in which instructors and students work together through a number of different disciplinary materials — an approach that is not so much interdisciplinary as non-disciplinary. Such an alternative recognizes an important fact of university life: function (what happens in class) is a product of structure (how the place is organized). For obvious reasons, any institution based on a conventional university structure will have great difficulty in creating and sustaining any significant alternative to the standard curriculum organized by independent departments. Even if some faculty are keen to introduce such alternatives, the imperatives of their professional culture will quickly snuff out their attempts or render them ineffectual.

That, too, is the reason why so many attempts to reform the undergraduate curriculum, from the famous Harvard Red Book (1945) on, have been largely unsuccessful. Since they fail to address the conventional structure of the institution, they amount to little more than minor tinkering — a new list of books, a new combination of first-year electives, a new breadth requirement, and so on. As well-intentioned as these often are, they leave untouched the features of faculty culture which create the problems they are trying to address. Ringing endorsements of lofty principles are no match for the entrenched realities of life in a specialized research department.

THE SOCIAL DIMENSION

Of course, in assessing the value of an undergraduate education one needs to be careful not to overestimate the importance of what goes on in the classroom. For no matter what the quality of teaching or the structure of the curriculum, the most valuable educational experiences have always tended to take place in the surrounding campus culture — in the fraternities, sports teams, debating societies, drama clubs, study groups, and so on, those places where young students have opportunities to socialize with each other. There's abundant evidence that in the traditional nineteenth century colleges, the teaching was often (perhaps even generally) extremely bad. The value of the experience emerged from the way it gave students so much generous access to each other. That's just as true today. It's no accident that magazine polls which produce a ranking of the universities based on student responses routinely favour the smaller institutions. And the high reputation of the elite private educational institutions in the United States has nothing to do with better facilities or more intelligent teachers and everything to do with the ways in which these colleges encourage or require students to interact outside the classroom in all sorts of ways.

That point is worth emphasizing because in recent years the surrounding campus culture in the public colleges and universities has withered considerably. Various factors, including the need to work to meet the rising costs of postsecondary education, the increasing numbers of mature students with outside responsibilities, the rise in part-time students, the pressure to take extra courses or achieve higher grades, and so on, have significantly decreased the number of students who have the leisure time to sample the wider cultural possibilities of campus life. Thus, the social experience of going to university is being increasingly defined by what goes on in the classroom, a forum not usually set up to encourage any conversation which is not firmly controlled by the all-powerful professor at the front.

One sign of this trend is the increasing concern about various problems on campus — drugs, alcohol, suicide, sexual aggression, and so on. It's not hard to link these to some extent with the stress and bewilderment experienced in the setting of a modern university, especially a huge and complex campus, like the University of Toronto or the University of British Columbia, and with the absence of a socially supportive network of friends (this is especially true, of course, in programs where students are not part of a core group which takes all its classes together). Attempts to alleviate these problems typically fail to address the root cause (the nature of the university itself) and instead appoint a Dean of Substance Abuse or a bevy of new counsellors or organize a workshop or distribute posters all over campus proclaiming a slogan or two.

The often impoverished social quality of the modern campus has in some quarters led to demands for a change in the standard teaching style — the lecture with the professor fully in control and a large group of students passively and obediently listening. If the opportunities for students to socialize outside the classroom are rapidly declining, some have asserted, then it's time to give them that opportunity inside the classroom, by a adopting seminar-style instruction and letting student conversation carry the weight of the class (a much more active learning process). Such a style is basic to the education of those applauded programs of general education I referred to earlier. In spite of the demonstrated effectiveness and popularity of such a style, however, it is hardly likely to have much effect generally for any number of reasons (it requires the professor to share power with the class and to redefine his approach to teaching, it cannot process the huge numbers of students needed to boost departmental numbers, it requires special physical arrangements, and so on).

None of these problems would matter nearly so much, however, but for the third of the three factors I have referred to, the decision to give the universities a virtual monopoly on entry into the professions. Whereas not so long ago there used to be a number of professions one could select and train for without going to university, now, thanks to what Michael Katz has called the biggest and quietest takeover in the history of capitalism, the universities have a stranglehold on preparing for professional life, and a student aiming at a profession has little choice but to sign up for the expensive and long sequence of undergraduate and professional certification courses at a university.

Why this happened is something of a mystery. There seems to be no compelling reason why many professionals need to be educated at a university rather than at a professional school with no commitment to research (eg, nurses, engineers, lawyers, chartered accountants, therapists, librarians, teachers, and so on) or why such professions should not offer alternative routes, the way many of them used to do. Perhaps it has something to do with the curious notion that a university degree somehow enhances the credibility of the profession. Whatever the reason, one might well ask, as many university professors who objected to this trend did ask, what on earth a well-qualified researcher is doing teaching students aiming at a practical profession? How is training for the professions compatible with the university's role as a research centre and with the professor's qualifications as a research specialist?

Such objections were, of course, brushed aside in the interests of enormously augmenting the social power and size of the university and the social prestige of the professions, so that what we have created, sadly enough, is a direct contravention of John Stuart Mill's eloquently liberal recommendation that while the government or its designate had the right to set the examinations needed to certify someone for a profession, there should be no monopoly on how a student prepares herself to take that examination.

Why should this matter? Well, first of all, putting all professional training in the hands of people paid to do research is very expensive.

After all, if we make teacher certification, for example, a postgraduate university program, then every teacher in it has to have a professorial ·contract insisting on a minimum number of teaching hours and a host of research perquisites. Once we insist that all entry into the nursing profession must go through the university, we have guaranteed that the cost of training nurses will be significantly higher than it was before. One might make similar claims for, say, programs in business or computer science or engineering, among others.

In addition, given the enormous social power this monopoly conveys, the universities, in conjunction with the professional certifying boards, have not been slow to milk professional training as a cash cow by making such training excessively long. Does someone preparing to be an elementary school teacher really require five or six years of university training? What about the enormous length of time required to get qualified to become a teacher of undergraduates? Why thirty-five years ago were my professors adequately educated with three years of undergraduate work at Oxbridge, while now my children have to go through anywhere from five to ten years of postgraduate work to meet the minimum qualification for a similar job (in a very expensive program which roughly half of the students who start fail to complete)? Here one might note, in passing, that, given the extensive use many universities make of teaching assistants, faculty tacitly acknowledge that the lengthy research qualifications required of teachers of undergraduates are unnecessary. While insisting on the importance of such qualifications, departments routinely waive them in their own courses in order to make use of a pool of serf labour, grossly underpaid graduate students, who, in some places, carry up to a third of the undergraduate teaching load.

Since obtaining professional certification nowadays is not so much a matter of demonstrating one's competence (in the way Mill had in mind) as of accumulating the required number of credits (and these are clearly not the same thing), it's hard to resist the notion that many of these professional programs are set up to maximize the university's enrolment and the income from fees (along with a guaranteed supply of bodies for specialized upper-division and graduate courses, which professors much prefer to teach) rather than to meet commonsense demands for entry into a profession. Well, those with a monopoly can, I suppose, erect as many expensive barriers as they wish, without caring about the debt a student must assume or how many competent people they are excluding from the professions because of the excessively high cost of getting certified.

The arbitrariness of decisions about the length of professional training is evident enough in the way universities and professional associations, working together, are quick to waive what they previously had claimed was essential in order to meet a shortage in the supply. I was supremely lucky in being able to get my high school teaching certificate in fourteen weeks over two summers (at the Ontario College of Education in 1956–57) and an MA (from the University of Toronto) in six months (in 1968–69), because the demand for teachers and professors was high. Looming shortages in some of the professions nowadays have already led to suggestions for drastically shortened undergraduate and professional programs, or arrangements whereby young professionals can start work and complete their certification part time, once they have an income. Implementing such suggestions is long overdue.

The point here, however, is not the optimum length of time it takes for this or that professional certification. The issue is the monopoly itself. Given that faculty organizations are quick to discipline any institutions which depart from the conventional arrangements (for example, by withdrawing accreditation or refusing to accept their graduates or blacklisting them), what we have is a system which acts in its own interests to oppress students and stifle alternatives. We promote competition in many aspects of our lives, recognizing that competition promotes excellence and variety and lowers costs. And we are quick to attack monopolistic business practices. With the universities, however, we permit competition for students but tacitly prohibit significant competition between the standard model of the research university and other alternatives.

These issues are well known. Writers inside and outside the academy have been calling attention to them for decades. But the universities and colleges for the most part continue with business as usual — an increasing emphasis on specialization and research, more fragmentation, larger and larger undergraduate classes, higher fees, longer programs, and so on. Experiments in various alternatives, like the BC college system, which often begin by trumpeting their potential for significant change, end up being quietly assimilated into the conventional university culture.

WHERE DO WE GO FROM HERE?

According to James J Duderstadt's *A University for the 21st Century*, the conventional model ('a Balkanized tyranny') is very poorly equipped to deal with a wide range of modern developments, so that the pressure for significant adjustments is becoming irresistible. There is a growing disconnect between what universities actually do and many of the social, economic, and educational needs the institution is meant to address. And many people are grumbling more and more about the cost of maintaining the public university system in its present form and the crushing load of debt students are having to assume.

Of course, there is, as there always has been, plenty of brave talk about ways in which the universities can reform themselves. But no one, it seems, is offering a significant challenge to the way in which the modern university is organized, and so such reform sentiments will, no doubt, go the way of all previous attempts in the past fifty years (at least) to improve undergraduate education. For a large college or university structured in the conventional manner is incapable of the reform necessary to achieve significant changes, particularly in undergraduate education and professional training. Our best hope for improvements lies in the development of new institutions with very different organizations and purposes.

Under this hypothetical scenario, we should encourage the universities to continue to do what they do best — valuable cutting-edge research and graduate programs for would-be researchers — and offer new alternatives which are wholly committed to student learning in a congenial environment and which reject the research ethic and the various features which arise out it (eg, departmental structure, narrow specialization, fragmentation, overqualified faculty, excessive cost, and so on).

However, given the university's tyrannical power over postsecondary education and the ways in which various alternatives routinely get swallowed up or stifled by the conventional structure, I don't hold any sanguine hopes that such obviously beneficial changes will happen soon. 🔖

REFORMING UNDERGRADUATE EDUCATION

by Gary Bauslaugh

A thinking man should always attack the strongest thing in his own time. For the strongest thing is always too strong.

— G K Chesterton, *GK's Weekly*, June 1925

Over the years there have been many cries for reform of university education, both within the academy itself and in the larger community. But the cries are faint now, much too faint, in the face of the rolling juggernaut of the modern university system. There are just too many students to deal with, and too many other things to occupy the attention of faculty members and administrators who could effect some change — some improvement — in the actual education students receive. And there are many privileges that go with employment in universities — freedom, status, money. A system in which these privileges are so entrenched is not likely to be amenable to change. As a result of these things, education has taken a distant second place in the hierarchy of important things that are done by universities.

What is in first place? What really captures the attention and imagination of university faculty and administrators, if it is not student learning? In a word, it is research. This is the single dominating feature of modern university life. Conducting programs of original research, with graduate students and post-doctoral fellows (and to a very limited extent with undergraduates), and seeking grants to do so, is viewed as the real business of universities. Success in research is necessary to get faculty positions in the first place, and to keep them (at least until tenure is awarded). With token exceptions, all the rewards for university professors, and all real status in the university community, comes from accomplishments in research.

I should mention that I am not suggesting in any of my comments here that research in itself is a bad thing; scientific research is one of the great undertakings of humankind. The achievements of such work — and in particular the insights we have gained into the natural world — have provided the basis for a rational approach to our existence, as well as providing us with many discoveries that have the potential to vastly improve human life. And the tradition of independent research carried out in universities, at least the scientific part of that tradition, is a big part of the extraordinary contribution that research has made to our lives.

It seems reasonable to suggest, however, that the role of universities in educating young people in our society is equally important, for, as we know all too well now, scientific knowledge without wisdom and responsibility is much more of a menace than a benefit. As we learn more about the natural world, and how to control it, it becomes increasingly important that at the same time we educate, in the fullest sense of that term, our citizenry. This means learning about history, philosophy, literature, artistic achievements — all of the things that enrich our understanding of the human condition and help us to gain a wider sense of responsibility and concern for present and future life on earth.

That such broader education assumes a much lower place — far below research — in the academic hierarchy can hardly be in dispute. The argument put forward by apologists for the status quo is that reverence for research leads to the best education anyway. The fact that undergraduate curriculum is mostly designed to prepare students for a life in academic research is viewed as a very positive thing; indeed there is a virtually exclusive focus on majors and honours programs, all designed to provide 'mastery' of a particular discipline, to the exclusion of any wider purpose, except insofar as that is accidentally and inconsistently achieved in the course of studying a particular discipline (and the few electives that are allowed in the course of this study).

Moreover, research skills on the part of faculty are much more highly valued than are teaching skills, further illustrating the imbalance in priorities. This is usually excused by lame comments that teaching cannot be evaluated anyway, but that research can be evaluated objectively. Both of these are dubious claims, to say the least, as faculty members who have no interest in or ability to teach continue to waste the time and money of thousands of students, and research is evaluated by counting pages in peer-reviewed publications, pages that often will never be read by any other person.

Students decide to come to university for a variety of reasons. Many are drawn by the realization that university graduation is the ticket for the best jobs in our society. Many just don't know what else to do. But it is safe to say that there is an abiding belief, even among those who have other motivations to attend, that they will actually receive a good general education, a belief that persists extensively in the population as a whole. It is not widely understood that most universities put almost no time or effort into providing such an education.

Once in a while some academic body, sometimes a university senate or perhaps a particular faculty or department, will try to address this problem in a serious way. There have been some remarkable efforts, such as "Discipline and Discovery: A Proposal to the Faculty of Arts of the University of British Columbia," written in 1965. This bold and eloquent plea for reconstruction of the undergraduate curriculum currently moulders away in obscurity, but rereading it inspires one with the realization that for many years others have been aware and have clearly articulated the real needs of undergraduate students:

Mental and emotional resilience is one of the irreducible elements of intellectual mastery and the BA program must be planned with this in mind. We believe that our proposals for general education work towards this end, because they constitute in outline a statement of the common centre from which the offerings of the faculty come and to which, sometimes deliberately, sometimes inadvertently, they bring back new ideas. This centre is a necessity for both student and scholar. For each of them it transforms the notion of a community of scholars from a rhetorical expression into a deliberate possibility; and this integrating process encourages continued vitality of intellectual effort. All too easily the life of the mind goes dead, and we share with the rest of this Faculty the determination to keep that life strong.

This heart-felt expression of the need to present a different curriculum, with the goal of giving students the general education — the overall intellectual development — that it is commonly believed universities provide, almost brings tears to the eyes of one who fought for years to bring such programs into colleges and universities. The tears don't quite materialize, however. There have been too many times when eloquent visions of a possible future in which undergraduate programs were actually designed to educate students in a way that helps them gain some sense of the ideas and events that have shaped human experience, and have them develop intellectual skills that would allow them to participate in an intelligent way in the continuing story of that experience. The tears, if they did come, would be from both the touching and eloquent expression of an important idea, and from the realization, once again, of the futility of this struggle.

Even small emerging degree-granting institutions, those with a real opportunity to provide leadership in developing improved programs of undergraduate education, and with little chance of contributing important new knowledge to the research world, become obsessed with the idea of research, believing that such is their only route to 'credibility.' But the opposite of that occurs. These places become fourth rate imitations of the large research institutions, instead of the first rate teaching institutions they could be.

There are many others who have noted this fundamental and intractable problem in undergraduate education. In 1991 the Report of the

Commission of Inquiry on Canadian University Education was published. The report was commissioned by the Association of Universities and Colleges of Canada (AUCC), and written by Stuart L Smith, a physician who was once the head of the Liberal Party of Ontario. I suppose the Association assumed that Smith was enough of an establishment person that he would do what consultants are normally expected to do, which is to give the answers the client wants. That answer (I am guessing) would be to the effect that education in Canadian universities is basically fine.

The Association, apparently, was less than pleased with the results: Smith took his mandate to provide an independent report seriously. George Pederson, a pillar of the Canadian university establishment and Chairman of AUCC, wrote an introduction to the Report. He damned it with faint praise, and concluded with the statement "The views contained in the report, however, do not necessarily represent the views of the Association or of its member institutions."

No wonder. After conducting extensive public hearings and doing much reading on the subject, Smith wrote the following words which must have curdled the blood of his sponsors:

> *Teaching is seriously undervalued at Canadian Universities and nothing less than a total recommitment to it is required.*

He went on to describe the difficulties of actually doing anything about it:

> *The Commission is convinced, however, that simply calling for this will accomplish very little. The experience in the United States is that repeated requests to 'do the right thing' have led nowhere. The forces at play, as described earlier, are simply too powerful and even the best efforts of well meaning administrators are unlikely to make much difference.*

The Smith Report caused some consternation in the university community, and it was widely denounced. Smith spent some time afterwards touring the country and giving talks, one of which I attended. He and I had actually been at McGill at the same time, though we did not know each other then. When we did finally meet after one of his post-Report presentations, I told him how much I respected his honesty and courage in standing up to the powerful 'forces at play.' I suspect that by telling the truth he forfeited many lucrative consulting jobs he could have had. And, sadly, Smith's Report too moulders in obscurity.

I don't mean to suggest that undergraduate education is all that is wrong with universities. But as humanists most of us believe that good general education is a prerequisite for a civilized society — our system of public education must produce citizens who have learned to think critically and have learned enough about society to apply their thinking skills in a sensible way. That ought to be the first goal of a university education. It is doubtful, though, that in most universities it is a real goal at all. ❧

THE COMPETENT LAYPERSON

by Mark Battersby

The doctor tells you that you have lung cancer and, because you have a number of different sites in your lung, the cancer has clearly metastasized. An operation would be useless, chemotherapy a painful and futile palliative. You probably have only a few months to live.

Do you accept the doctor's opinion and go home and die? Or do you take an intelligent interest in your problem? Did your education give you the confidence and skills to take such an interest? This is a very real question. Such a diagnosis was given to my sister-in-law several years ago. Fortunately Gail did not just go home and give up. A team of medical amateurs — my sister-in-law, a good friend of hers, my wife and I — set about learning about lung cancer and about the problems of diagnosis. I immediately gave her a copy of Stephen Jay Gould's wonderful *Discover* article on medical prognosis (The Median Isn't the Message, *www.cancerguide.org*) which I have long used in my critical thinking classes. Gould makes the point that whatever the 'average' life expectancy in a given diagnosis there are always outliers — individuals who dramatically exceed the average. Youth, general health, availability of excellent care, a positive attitude and even misdiagnosis, all contribute to the possibility that one is among the 'outliers.' Reasonable skepticism can be a source of hope.

My sister-in-law quickly transferred to a cancer clinic where doctors work together in teams and encourage patient involvement. The clinic's team of doctors raised some questions about the initial pathologists' report. What type of cancer cell was involved? Were the sites independent or linked to one another? After further testing it remained the opinion of the team, and particularly the clinic's pathologist, that the cancer sites involved identical (metastasized) cells — multiple site lung cancer was very unusual. Meanwhile we were in the clinic's library, assisted by a helpful librarian, studying cancer textbooks, *Medline* and *Scientific American*. We learned that the judgment of whether the cancer had metastasized was based on visual similarity. There appeared to be no clear means to check the reliability of the pathologist's judgments.

Our team of laypersons concluded that the experts' diagnosis was not well validated. Even though the pathologists disagreed about the cell type, the clinic's pathologist was "90% certain" that the cells were identical and hence had the same source. But, from our own research, we knew this 90% figure was just a subjective assessment of confidence and not a real measure of reliability. My wife, a lifelong reader of *Scientific American*, had read a study about DNA testing on colon and brain cancer. We asked why DNA testing wasn't being done in this case. The doctors at the cancer agency had not used such procedures in lung cancer cases (they now do). When they used DNA testing on my sister-in-law's lungs, it became clear — to the amazement of the pathologist — that the separate sites were independent. The cancer had not metastasized and the risk of an operation to remove the cancer was justified. It is over ten years since her operation and my sister-in-law remains cancer free.

Gail's life was saved by liberal education. Our team's actions and reflections embodied the ideal of a liberal education: intellectual autonomy. By dealing thoughtfully and carefully with expert advice, by bringing to bear disparate sources of knowledge, by understanding the structure of evidence and claims, and by having the confidence to raise questions, we were able to intervene in empowered, freeing and life preserving ways. None of our team had expert training in biology, medicine or any science, though all of us had considerable formal education and confidence in our ability to research and think about any issue. My own knowledge of critical thinking and general issues around statistical reasoning was certainly valuable. But the most crucial knowledge — my wife's awareness of DNA testing to diagnose cancer — resulted from her interest and pleasure in reading about science.

The confidence and intellectual abilities we used are ones that any college graduate should possess. Thanks to the internet everyone can have access to an incredible amount of information. But making good use of this access requires its own expertise. Because we are dependent on experts for most of what we know, intellectual liberation comes from the thoughtful and critical use of expert knowledge — call it the expert amateur or 'competent layperson.' Whether they're watching a movie or evaluating a medical diagnosis, competent laypeople are people who:

► have a broad understanding of the intellectual landscape;

► have strong generic intellectual abilities;

► know how to evaluate information and claims outside their area of expertise;

► can delve more deeply into an area of specialization with efficiency and appropriate confidence;

► are an informed and appreciative audience for works of arts and science; and

► have an informed appreciation and understanding of nature and society.

Competent laypeople know their intellectual limits, but also have the confidence and competence to expand them. Most of our lives are spent working and dealing with issues that are outside of our specific training. The sheer breadth of issues can seem daunting. In developing a liberal undergraduate program, we need to consider how we can best prepare students for such a full life.

The concept of a competent layperson is well suited to give practical meaning to another key goal: citizenship. In principle, the citizen is called on to make decisions about a wide range of matters, such as public health, allocation of resources, environmental issues, criminal justice, social housing, town planning, economic strategies, community morality, and international relations. Citizens must provide a critical audience for the debates, and more and more citizens are involved in direct action through advocacy groups. In either role, the citizen is called on to make judgments, express opinions and to vote on issues involving complex considerations and the input of a wide variety of experts.

The traditional enlightenment ideal of liberal arts as education for liberation — for freedom from the thrall of tradition and ignorance — continues to be a worthy one. Enlightenment philosophers were concerned to liberate people from accepting hand-me-down claims that were untested and unquestioned by the recipient. Intellectual liberation meant the rejection of such claims and the move to establish independently and personally the truth of claims.

While such advice was especially salutary at the beginning of modern science, the situation today is much more complex. None of us is equipped to establish, independently, most of the claims that we depend on. This is not a bad thing: it means that we can know many more things than we could if left to our own devices. The danger is that erroneous and misleading information can be passed on in the same way. Knowing how to evaluate and utilize sources is the key to sorting between knowledge and falsehood.

In my sister-in-law's case, we challenged our local medical authorities based on research reported by other authorities, not by doing our own pathology assessments. Nowadays it is remarkably easy to find not only popular sources of reliable information, but in many cases one can go to the actual fundamental research. Competent laypeople know how to find, evaluate and utilize this abundance of available research.

The current emphasis on 'practical' value of specific preparation for work misses the broader practicality of liberal education. While vocationally specific competencies and knowledge are often relevant to initial employment success, the abilities and knowledge necessary for our competency as laypeople enrich, in the longer term, all aspects of our vocational, intellectual, personal and social lives. Focusing explicitly on the development of the knowledge and abilities required for the competent layperson is the key to providing a more genuinely liberating education. It might even save our lives. ❧

THE GREAT
EDUCATION DIVIDE

by Jonny Diamond

I n-laws of mine recently received the unfortunate news that their daughter, Grace, hadn't been accepted to the school they'd been hoping for. She'd done well on all the tests, from math and logic to verbal acuity; and the tuition, though an exorbitant $16,000 a year, seemed manageable, as both parents are successful Manhattan professionals who run in the right circles (he's a real estate lawyer and she owns her business). But despite all the positives, competition was just too fierce for Grace to get a spot. The alarming thing, to me at least, is the fact that Grace was only three at the time.

Though the frenzy among well-to-do New York parents to get their children into the 'right' schools at the age of three is a fairly rarefied example, it speaks to a larger problem: Americans no longer have faith in their public schools. The idea of public education has been stigmatized by years of underpaid teachers trying to teach overflowing classes in poorly funded schools with few or no supplies. The focus for these put-upon teachers becomes less about well-rounded education and more about hitting targets for state and federal testing. As public schools are seen to decline, those with enough money move their children into private schools and, as the well off tend to clump together geographically, tax bases dwindle in depressed areas and public school budgets are slashed, which leads to a decline in quality, which leads parents with enough money to move their children to better schools... and so on. This unalloyed capitalistic approach to education, in which cost is the primary measure of quality, perpetuates a great and growing divide between the public and the private.

While it is difficult to censure parents for seeking the best for their kids, the degree to which children are pushed at a very early age is a reductive and distorting force. It's a force that favours the testable over the adaptive, the linear over the lateral; at every juncture, institutions seek to measure the aptitude of prospective clients (the language of the corporation has seemingly infiltrated every aspect of American society). Education then, especially on the assembly line of the public system, becomes more about scores and standardization; students become a series of numbers and ratings. If those numbers are low, a student is treated accordingly and placed in an educational stream that is increasingly difficult to escape from — the bifurcation is perpetuated, and democracy, which is sustained by an educated populace, declines.

But while I lament the state of American education, it must be said that my two favourite professors in university were Americans, both of whom came from working-class backgrounds, and grew up during the Depression. One, a gruff but mercurial lapsed-Marxist Pragmatist from the Midwest (note the capital P, as in the philosophical school of Pragmatism), the other, a grandiloquent lapsed-Catholic Irishman-turned-professor of aesthetics from New York City. Possessed of a celebratory skepticism about the world, these two men evinced an intellectual playfulness that was infectious. Most significantly for me, though, was the discovery that septuagenarians could be as full of dissent and anger as teenagers, belying with every breath the invidious and lazy notion that ideas — and more importantly, *ideals* — calcify with age.

The philosophy of aesthetics professor Edmund Egan was the son of a lay steward of the archdiocese of Manhattan. One is wary these days in America of religious dispositions, but recall for a moment the progressive-left Catholicism of the Depression, particularly in the urban northeast, along with the rabble-rousing of Dorothy Day and the egalitarian stridency of the trade unionist publication *The Catholic Worker*, and assumptions must be reconfigured. The New York described by

Professor Egan was inspiring, as he evoked the ecumenical tumult of a Manhattan childhood and the secular corrective of a street life that — despite its overt neighbourhood tribalism — offered all manner of creed and caste in any given five-block radius. He described a city that, after surviving a Depression and a war, found itself bursting with intellectual and artistic life in the late 1940s and 50s. Professor Egan told stories of Russian dancers performing with Balanchine's New York City Ballet, hanging in the air for an "honest-to-goodness five count;" nights singing and orating at the White Horse Tavern (including a tale he told with relish of being upstaged one evening at the legendary bar by a bleary Welsh poet named Dylan Thomas); watching Pollock argue with Rothko at the Cedar Tavern, only to be interrupted by Kerouac's bibulous attempts at impromptu poetry... The New York of the 1950s and its climate of intellectual possibility is the New York I am in perpetual search of, if not in place then in sensibility. Professor Egan is in many ways responsible for my move to the city.

The second of these two professors is a man named Kai Nielsen, a Midwesterner who experienced firsthand the rural deprivations of the Depression. If Professor Egan provided me with the inspiration for coming to New York, Professor Nielsen provided me with a way to think about America. I ended up accidentally in his class, Neo-American Pragmatism, after the far more exotically titled Continental Existentialism filled up before I had a chance to register. I went into the course with trepidation, as it was a 15-person seminar in what struck me as a thoroughly dull backwater of philosophical thought. How wrong I was. At the centre of this class was the writing of Richard Rorty, an American Pragmatist whose philosophical program I came to adopt as my own (insofar as a non-practicing, dissenting Unitarian secular humanist can comfortably 'adopt a program'). Rorty didn't seem to be making grand claims about the Universe or Man or the salvific powers of philosophical purity, rather he was talking thoughtfully about kindness and love, economics and literature, film, art, physics, politics... in short, he was writing about all the stuff I wanted to read about — and this, apparently, was philosophy! Here was a thinker who abhorred the hermetic, often absolutist divisions of the academy, someone keen on de-emphasizing the importance of his own academic discipline, or at the very least, removing the stuffing from the shirts of those analytic philosophers perpetually at the ready to label most of the liberal arts with the deadly-scornful epithet 'fuzzy thinking.'

Happily, I believe that my fuzzy, catholic liberal arts education has prepared me to be an engaged citizen of a democracy. Though its success is perhaps difficult to quantify, and almost impossible to reduce to a statistic, my Canadian public school education has given me the vocabulary to fight against those who would treat art and literature as educational after-thoughts. Rorty's optimistic insistence that philosophy can actually concern itself with the problems of the world has become my own.

These three men — the two professors, Rorty — and their ideas have been fundamental to my intellectual life as an adult, and I picked them up for a steal: the total cost of my four-year Canadian university education was less than one year of Grace's preschool tuition. Sadder still though than that stark fact, is the unlikelihood now of working-class American children, be they rural or urban, ending up as philosophy professors. So long as education is seen as just another stall in the market place, the public/private divide in America will widen, and only the children of privilege will receive the kind of education we all deserve. And no democracy can survive that. 🌿

REED REMEMBERED

by Shirley Goldberg

What has gone wrong with the University? Or, more properly — what has gone wrong with the Zeitgeist? Postsecondary institutions are microcosms of their time and place. At their best they are microcosms of what their society believes an ideal world should look like. I was lucky enough to attend such an institution.

Today the financial pressures on students, in addition to an overall sense of hopelessness about the future of the world, combine to discourage the kind of rampant curiosity about abstract ideas and alternative realities that is vital to the process. Unpopular concepts are avoided. Almost no one is echoing the rallying cries of the students of the 1960s: "All power to the imagination! Be realistic — demand the impossible." We've forgotten George Leonard's wonderful title: *Education as Ecstasy*.

We used to debate the desirability of the university as an 'ivory tower' completely removed from the grime of the marketplace and the political arena, an idea that doesn't make much sense today — perhaps it never did. The friction between the theoretical and the real creates electricity. At the most extreme, this friction can cause a state of intellectual and ethical euphoria — the kind that has been stirringly recreated in a couple of documentaries, *The Mao Years* and *Have You Heard From Johannesburg?*, which I shall talk about later. Both deal with optimistic and disruptive student movements that actually accomplished large social benefits.

In my student years at Reed College in Portland, Oregon, during World War Two, we endlessly speculated about such issues. And many went on to make major contributions to society. For a long time this small, liberal arts college in the rain-swept Pacific Northwest produced a higher percentage of graduates who followed through to complete their PhD and MD degrees than any other college or university in the United States.

No matter what our major field of study, we were all required to take a massive two-year humanities program. Like the Great Books programs at the University of Chicago and St John's College, it operated on the theory that a functioning democratic society needed a shared cultural base. St John's went so far as to call it a "survival program." The great texts of the past would serve, as Matthew Arnold noted, as "touchstones" against which to measure the new.

Such a humanities program can be spun in many different ways. At Reed, which had been founded by a Unitarian, the spin was humanist all the way. We began with the Greeks — man is the measure of all things. And Barry Cerf's unforgettable lecture comparing the world view of the *Oedipus Cycle* to that of the *Book of Job* would have converted almost anyone. The Judeo-Christian *Bible*, as well as the *Bhagavadgita*, Lao Tsu's *Tao Te Ching* and the *Koran* were studied for their literary value as much as their philosophy. The inclusion of a few key documents from diverse cultures sharing the planet was invaluable in pushing back boundaries, and mitigating apprehension about the 'Other.' In contrast to the stories I hear about students today who have difficulty relating Plato to their own lives, we automatically used everything we studied to question our own realities.

The instructors were exceptional. Despite extremely low salaries even for that time, they had chosen Reed because of its rewarding teaching environment with 98th percentile students at an eight to one ratio. Of course, as our psychology professor frequently reminded us, "If you are the cream of the crop, God help the skimmed milk!"

One of the most radical experiments at Reed was the absence of grades. Throughout four years of study we forgot that grades existed, that they were covertly being recorded for the purpose of graduate records. For high-achieving students this had a truly miraculous effect in removing anxiety and refocusing attention purely on the content and on the thrill of the thought process — ideas that defied gravity and flew. Serious discussion could erupt wherever students met.

Contributing to the creative experience of our education was the degree to which the planning of the program facilitated individual interests. If we were intrigued by the work of Euripides or John Stuart Mill or Kafka, we were encouraged to read further even at the expense of other texts on our extensive reading list. The essay tests were sufficiently broad to accommodate various coherent combinations of information. As far as the humanities program was concerned, Reedies didn't traipse through four years in lockstep.

Another radical aspect of our education was a complete adherence to the honour system. In the current situation, with papers and exam questions marketed on the internet, such a policy may seem preposterous. But the invisibility of grades made us worry less about what the professor wanted and take more pride in our own concepts. Tests were distributed in the classroom, but we could go anywhere — the library, the dorm, the coffee shop, the sunny steps — to write them. We were treated like responsible adults who recognized that cheating primarily harms the perpetrator. Since it also harms the community, students who were aware of cheating had the option of taking the case to the Student Council who in turn, with impeccable secrecy, would investigate and pass judgment. In four years I knew only of one such case.

This honour code extended to every aspect of campus business. Years later after experiencing some thefts, the bookstore put up shelving at the entrance for the storage of books and bags. In protest, four students — two men and two women — stashed their books and backpacks and then, slowly and deliberately, took off every item of clothing, folding them neatly on the shelves before entering the store.

At Reed in the early 1940s no idea was too dangerous to be examined. The era was post-Great Depression and post-Spanish Civil War, both of which had radicalized many of the best minds of the time. It was also pre-Cold War and pre-Corporate Dominance. The big ongoing campus debate was Stalinism vs. Trotskyism. However, in a straw vote for the 1944 presidential election, republican Thomas Dewey (with his funny little Charlie Chaplin moustache) won out decisively over democrat Franklin D Roosevelt. So much for the danger of letting kids play around with risky dissent! To this day, the traditional red Reed t-shirt features the Reed seal, the Griffin, surrounded by the words "Atheism, Communism, Free Love" — not as a profession of belief, but as a thumbing of the nose at a society that is shocked by those concepts.

Many, however, had deep commitments. One friend, whose parents both taught in the California University system and whose only brother died in the Spanish Civil War, spent his summers organizing the dock workers of Long Beach for the Trotskyite cause. One of our favorite professors, Lloyd Reynolds, was later investigated by HUAC (House Un-American Activities Committee) and consequently suffered a period of suspension. Fortunately his story ends on a grace note. After he was able to return to the classroom, which he did with a new specialty in calligraphy, he won a well-deserved national award as "The College Teacher of the Year."

Our faculty was in every way an interesting lot — for instance, our enormously popular, charismatic sociology professor who years later moved on to the University of California where he gained notoriety as "Professor by Day, Second Story Man by Night." It seems that he furnished a 'love nest' entirely with items stolen from the homes of famous movie stars — a lamp from Gary Cooper, a chair from Norma Shearer, etc. All this hit the headlines shortly after he had been quoted in a major newspaper while attending a national conference as saying: "Most people don't know what us sociologists are up to." I am certain that at some level his escapade was a calculated experiment.

Many of our guests at the college were larger-than-life participants in 20th century history. They would come for a week, speaking in classes and mingling informally with students about campus. I particularly remember Alexander Kerensky, who had been the leader of the provisional government in Russia from the overthrow of the Tsarist government in July of 1917 until the Bolsheviks stormed the Winter Palace in November. By the time he came to Reed, he was working at the Hoover Institute in California writing his memoirs about the Russian Revolution as a turning point of history. In connection with his visit we were introduced to the cinema of Sergei Eisenstein — *The Battleship*

Potemkin and *October* (which was anything but flattering to Kerensky).

Another visitor was Paul Robeson, the great black singer who had visited the Soviet Union and roamed Leningrad with Eisenstein in the late 1930s and who spoke passionately about music, politics and race relations. Only a few years later he would be stripped of his passport and blacklisted, falling into a long, sad decline.

Contemporary turning points were not neglected either. At a time when the United States government was totally in support of Chiang Kai Chek, and almost nothing was known about what was really going on in China, two articulate young student followers of Mao Zedong gave us their own vivid version of the Peasant Revolution. We had a front row seat on history — in dramatic contrast to the present climate of fear, in which an institution has to think twice before inviting a Palestinian scholar to speak.

At times like this when movements for peace and social justice seem stymied and most students are keeping their heads down, it is valuable to be reminded of these moments of solidarity and the thrill of burning with a hard, gemlike flame. We have become much too afraid of dissent and chaos. And much too focused on personal and short-term goals.

After twenty-five years of teaching in the post-secondary system, I look back on my Reed experience as an almost imaginary landscape. However, no matter how hostile the era, the potential of "education as ecstasy" never dies. The study of the humanities can be as filled with epiphanies as ever. And it certainly is more necessary than ever for the perpetuation of our democratic values and our ability to deal with the many problems that obviously lie ahead. The times are against us, but if we don't like the Zeitgeist, it's our obligation to reconstruct it. ❧

PART 5

HUMANISM & RELIGION

Humanism is a response to the widespread demand for an alternative to dogmatic religion. The world's major religions claim to be based on revelations fixed for all time, and many seek to impose their world-views on all of humanity. Humanism recognizes that reliable knowledge of the world and ourselves arises through a continuing process of observation, evaluation and revision.

FAITH & THINKING

by Trudy Govier

I recently spent eight months teaching in a small Mennonite college where a pervasive and all-consuming issue was the legitimacy of faith-based hiring criteria. The issue was whether permanent jobs should ever be awarded to persons who were non-Christians. (As a visitor avowing agnosticism, I could be tolerated on the assumption that my temporary presence would not lastingly affect curriculum and planning.) How was religious faith to be reconciled with academic research, learning and teaching? For my colleagues, this question implied a profound dilemma. If hiring was restricted to Christians, then how could the college claim to be inclusive, academically responsible, and seeking the best candidates? But if hiring was not restricted to Christians, then how could it preserve its Mennonite character and role?

When my appointment began, the discussion was more than five years old and still all-consuming. Many aspects of the issue troubled me. I couldn't assent to faith framework, was hurt by the nearly ubiquitous presumption that people 'without faith' had no moral values, and was frustrated by the time and energy this issue drained from my colleagues.

From my perspective, the most troubling aspect of faith-based teaching and research has to do with resistance to evidence and argument. I found it impossible to accept that one should be proud of one's narrative as to how faith had structured one's academic career; such narratives provided the basis of weekly seminars, in which I did not participate. I could not support the presumption that such narratives were appropriate at all, much less suitable for consideration at tenure and promotion committees.

How could a person of 'no faith' write successfully about topics like forgiveness and reconciliation? My apparent success at doing just that was the basis of my appointment. Even so, it posed a threatening challenge to some. I was angry when an administrator interpreted the success of my entirely secular lecture on political problems and strategies as demonstrating just how vital it was to have a 'faith' perspective on the dilemmas of reconciliation. If a fact supports your faith, well and good. If that fact seems not to support your faith, then reinterpret it so that it will. Your reasoning can protect your faith. Does this kind of thing have to happen? Is it necessarily involved in 'faith'?

As a philosopher and author of a widely used text on critical thinking, I believe that fundamental assumptions should be examined and counter-arguments dealt with in a more honest and straightforward manner. Thinking with integrity requires taking objections seriously — and that's incompatible with constructing self-serving and *ad hoc* hypotheses to get rid of them. How, I wondered, could it be intellectually responsible to maintain one's faith by reinterpreting any counter-evidence?

What is faith? From a logical perspective, there are two fundamental aspects. First, a belief that is held as a matter of faith is not fully supported by cogent arguments. Second, such a belief is resistant to counter-evidence. We tend to interpret what we experience so as to maintain those beliefs we hold as faith.

In the context of the Mennonite college, the term 'faith' was used to refer to religious faith, primarily Christian religious faith — a faith committed to belief in the existence of all-powerful, all-knowing personal Deity who created the world and sent Jesus Christ to be its saviour. In this picture, God can maintain relationships with His creatures. He may chose to intervene in terrestrial events and may even be expected to do so in response to the fervent prayers of sincere believers.

Christianity is one of several major religious faiths. But not all faith is religious in nature. If we understand faith in terms of its basic functional and logical qualities — its organizing character and its relation to argument and evidence — it is clear that there are also forms of secular faith. People may, for example, have faith in science, money, the market economy or technological progress. Or even each other.

A person such as myself, who thinks that resisting counter-evidence is generally objectionable, has to acknowledge that persons of religious faith are not the only ones who engage in this style of thinking. Many secular people do that too. Religious faith and secular faith are similar in the way they handle evidence and argument.

To the outsider, religious faith may seem like dogmatism and closed-mindedness, imprudent, conflict-producing and even dangerous, given its departures from responsible reason and reasoning. Religious faith has inspired great deeds and great horrors. Similar things can be said about secular faith. If you don't think secular faith can be harmful, pause a moment and think about faith in Marxism. Or the market economy. Or technological progress.

To the objection that faith, as requiring evidence-resistance, is not appropriate in education and research, there was in the Mennonite college a standard answer. I will call this response the Theologian's Reply. To produce it, you cite cases of secular faith, claim that there is a lot of it around, even in schools and universities, and maintain that from the point of view of logical credentials, religious faith is no worse. You then infer that religious faith is respectable, even commendable, from a logical point of view. Many secular people hold central tenets as matters of faith and are unwilling to revise such tenets in the face of objections, counter-evidence and glaring failures of fit. (Consider, for example, market economics. Some people cling dogmatically to a fundamentalism of the market, despite consistent evidence that markets do not provide certain necessities of life such as clean air and decent housing affordable by the poor.)

In his influential book *The Structure of Scientific Revolutions*, Thomas Kuhn deemed such inflexibility to be an essential feature of 'normal science.' He described cases in which scientists ignored or reinterpreted counter-examples that could have upset their favourite theories. In one especially iconoclastic passage, Kuhn even claimed that scientific theories are relinquished not because people have been convinced by rational arguments for and against them, but because old scientists eventually die. Then new ones, favouring new ideas, take over. Without going all the way with Kuhn, we cannot rightly ignore the fact that evidence-resistance characterizes much secular thought, including some scientific thought.

Still, I never found the Theologians' Reply convincing. I couldn't help thinking it was based on a well-known logical error — the fallacy of 'two wrongs make a right.' Assume that evidence-resistant thinking is not, in itself, desirable. If so, then the fact that secular people engage in it won't render it correct for religious people to do so. Evidence-resistance supports irrationality, dogmatism, and imprudence. It rationalizes self-indulgent thinking. It seeks to justify our clinging to beliefs in the face of counter-evidence; it provides excuses for self-serving reinterpretations of arguments and evidence.

There are logical, prudential and ethical reasons against the dismissal of counter-evidence. Using *ad hoc* hypotheses to protect our favourite claims is not compatible with intellectual honesty and integrity. Evidence-resistant thinking is a problem whoever is doing it, and the fact that there are many secular examples does not render religious examples unproblematic.

Whether secular or religious, faith is resistant to change. Yes, secular faith and religious faith are analogous in this important respect. But there are aspects of religious faith that make the problems particularly deep and disturbing, opening doors to deep bias and abuses of power and authority. Christian faith typically presumes a link between religious faith and moral virtue, so that adherents regard a loss of faith as undermining norms of action and even the meaning of life itself. Eternal salvation depends on one's faith and that, to say the least, provides a deep motivation to sustain faith commitments. Other factors are the weight of tradition, community, and authority, which can make 'losing one's faith' seem a social tragedy. By hypothesis, God is a supernatural Being. His non-empirical status means that experiences and observations can readily be reinterpreted so as to support favoured views about His nature and activities.

As human beings, we often cling to the fundamental beliefs that shape our sense of the world. We have a pronounced tendency to cling to our beliefs and to indulge ourselves by failing to re-examine them when it would be appropriate to do so. Still, we can think through counter-evidence — and we should try to do it honestly and flexibly. Changing our minds can be a good thing, even on matters of faith. ❧

THE NATURE OF BELIEF

by James Alcock

Our reason is quite satisfied, in nine hundred and ninety-nine cases of every thousand of us, if it can find a few arguments that will do to recite in case our credulity is criticized by someone else. Our faith is faith in someone else's faith, and in the greatest matters this is most the case.

—William James

Our heads are chock-full of beliefs, beliefs about the physical world, philosophy, religion, politics, health, families, friends, ourselves. Many of these beliefs are widely shared: For example, countless people around the world believe that American astronauts have walked on the moon. Hundreds of millions, if not billions, believe that their minds and personalities will continue to live on in paradise long after their bodies have stopped functioning and all their cells have died. Countless others believe that after death, they will be reborn many, many times in a long cycle of reincarnation, before finally being absorbed into a Godhead. Most Canadians believe that smoking causes lung cancer, while a majority believes that some people have psychic powers that allow them to move objects by the power of the mind alone, or to peer into the future, or to communicate directly with other minds without the use of any physical channel. And millions of children are led to believe, by the elders whom they have learned to trust, that an ageless old man at the North Pole spends his time making toys, and then one night a year, delivers them in his reindeer-drawn sleigh to children all over the world.

Which of these beliefs do you share, and which do you reject as preposterous? And what are your reasons? Of course, you long ago gave up any belief in Santa Claus, but that disbelief was widely shared in the adult world, and so the renunciation is not surprising. However, you no doubt believe along with the rest of us that American astronauts have walked on the moon. If so, on what basis? "Everybody knows that!"? Sorry, not good enough. "I watched it happen, on television." Yes, but we have also watched people disappear in the transporter room on Star Trek only to reappear somewhere else; as realistic as that may appear, we recognize it to be fiction. "It is written up in an encyclopaedia." Yes, but does that necessarily make it true? One's belief in the moon landings is not nearly as easy to defend personally as we might like to think, for we do not have any direct evidence. Ultimately, the belief relies on our trust that reporters, newspapers, television stations and governments have told us the truth, and on our confidence that in a free society, it would be nearly impossible to perpetrate such a lie.

However, while we may it find silly and paranoid that a small but vocal group of people believe that the moon landings never occurred, and that the television broadcasts were faked as part of a propaganda campaign, what evidence do you or I really have to persuade them that they err and we do not? And what should we say to the hundreds of millions of Chinese citizens who continue to believe that Mao was a great and kindly man? How do we persuade them that their government has deceived them and hidden from them Mao's murderous history, while assuring ourselves that we have not been similarly deceived, and that the moon landings were real? And how do we disabuse the majority of Americans who wrongly believe that the terrorists who destroyed the World Trade Centre in New York came into the USA through Canada, and were sponsored by Iraq?

So, no matter how rational we like to think that we are, and no matter how much we pride ourselves on being able to think critically, ultimately many of even our most deeply held beliefs are not verifiable in any practical sense, but are necessarily rooted in our trust in others, and in our confidence in their intelligence and wisdom. Our faith in the accuracy of our beliefs is often, as William James put it, faith in someone else's faith. Such trust and faith is important, of course. Civilization would never have progressed if each individual and each generation was unwilling to accept the beliefs of the preceding generation and insisted on learning everything from scratch. We are unlikely to develop Mendeleyev's Periodic Table of the Elements on our own, or to appreciate the nuances of Shakespearean drama without some instruction.

SOURCES OF BELIEF

Beginning in childhood, we depend first on our parents and later on teachers, and even later on peers, to provide the information upon which we base our beliefs. Young children are uncritical consumers of information fed to them by adults, and at a young age, children can readily be led to believe in almost anything — that there is an ageless toymaker at the North Pole, that Zeus and other rollicking Gods inhabit Mount Olympus, that Christianity, Islam, or Hinduism represents ultimate truth, that the earth is a globe, (and not flat, as our senses suggest), and that Americans once walked on the moon. As they grow, and pass through years of formal instruction at school, they are expected to come to believe an astonishing array of other 'facts' as well, facts about geography, chemistry, biology, who started the First World War, what really happened on the Plains of Abraham, and who assassinated John Kennedy. This is for the most part a good thing. However, unless children are also taught to question, to challenge and not merely to accept something as true because a teacher or textbook deems it so, then the pattern of blind acceptance of what authorities pronounce may continue throughout their lives.

In addition to formal and informal inculcation of beliefs, we also learn directly from our own experiences. This learning can occur on an intellectual level, as when we cut a tree down and it falls the wrong way, and through reason and logic, we determine how to control the fall the next time we tackle a tree. In this case, a number of factors, including our intelligence, our reasoning skill, and our ability to interpret the situation correctly will influence our ultimate belief about the best way to cut down a tree. This learning can also occur automatically, 'experientially,' as a result of the way our nervous system is built. The experiential route to belief begins with the automatic discovery of patterns in the vast amount of sensory input that we receive from the world around us, (or sometimes even from within our own brains). We are born with this capacity to find patterns, both in terms of sensory stimuli and the timing of events. With regard to the latter, even young children learn associations amongst objects and events based on temporal pairings of what they perceive around them. An infant who makes contact with a hot stove while creeping around the floor feels pain, and will avoid such contact in future. This happens automatically, without necessity of any cognitive intervention, for any subsequent imminent contact with the stove will (as a result of what is called classical conditioning) automatically produce autonomic nervous system arousal, which in turn creates both a negative emotional response and a motivation to avoid the stove. As the child's intellectual abilities grow, the hot stove will later be understood in terms of cause and effect; it will be seen to have caused the pain.

Such temporal contiguity is the basis for much of our learning, and while this learning process is vital in allowing us to survive and function in the world, it is not tied to truth, in that it does not depend on there really being a causal relationship between the two events. If you become very ill after having eaten Roquefort dressing, you may automatically become anxious the next time that someone offers you a salad with that dressing, but it may be that the dressing had nothing to do with your illness; it just happened to have been ingested shortly before your sickness. The learned association is the same whether the Roquefort had anything to do with the illness or not. This process, where we see a causal relationship in the absence of evidence about the actual causal chain, is referred to as 'magical' thinking. Thus, people may come to believe that they have been cured of an ailment after taking homeopathic treatment because the symptoms went away after taking the nostrum. This is the error of post hoc ergo proctor hoc — after the fact, therefore because of the fact. Take the remedy, feel better, and give credit to the remedy. This leaves us very vulnerable to becoming hooked not only on quack therapies, but on many other things as well, such as gambling, horoscopes and belief in the supernatural and paranormal.

Humans also learn by observation of course. If someone drinks poison and dies, we do not have to try it for ourselves. Again, however, we are vulnerable to the error of *post hoc ergo proctor hoc*. Seeing should not always lead to believing.

There is a further complication insofar as our appreciation of the world around us is concerned. Our brains are very powerful pattern detectors, and because of this, often go far beyond the information that is available. You never see half a person sitting behind a desk. Your brain fills in the rest, for you know that this is a whole person, and the desk is obscuring the lower half. On the basis of a little information, we fill in the rest, using the categories of objects and events that we have learned about in the past. As powerful as this is, it does leave us vulnerable to error. If you see a faint object in the sky and hear an engine, you may actually perceive, and later remember, something that was much more airplane-like than the image formed on your retina. We construct our perceptions, and our memories, matching sometimes fragmentary incoming information to objects and events with which we are familiar. Once we have made that match, both perception and memory now are based on the result. If you see a strange, fleeting light and identify it as a ghost, your memory of that event will be much more ghost-like, and your belief that you actually saw a ghost is likely to go far beyond what might be justified on the basis of the fleeting image that you saw. We are all prone to perceiving what we expect to perceive, as we project our beliefs onto new information. To the extent that our perceptions and interpretations are distorted, so too will be the beliefs that grow out of them.

The experiential and intellectual routes to knowledge described above sometimes lead to competing views of the world around us. You may truly believe, based on your intellectual consideration of the facts before you, that your nephew's pet garter snake will not hurt you, and yet, you may find it impossible to force your hand to pick it up because of autonomic arousal and a fear response. You *believe* that the snake is not dangerous, but your autonomic nervous system has learned a different lesson. Similarly, you may be strongly intellectually opposed to racism, and yet in certain circumstances find yourself feeling uncomfortable in the presence of people of a particular racial group, without really knowing why. Based on your beliefs, your intellect insists that you are not prejudiced; your autonomic nervous system reacts differently. The pity is that it is usually easier to bring belief into line with emotion than vice versa, and unfortunately this is what most often happens.

In sum, then, our beliefs are based both on information received from authorities and upon our own direct experience or, more precisely, on our interpretation of that experience. This leads to error in the first instance when our authorities are mistaken, and in the second, when the well-documented biases and vulnerabilities of experiential learning produce a distorted appreciation of reality.

FUNCTIONS OF BELIEF

Beliefs reflect our understanding of how the world works, based on our past experience and what has been communicated to us formally and informally by others. If you did not believe that the highway continues on the other side of the hill, if you did not believe that it is safe to eat the food in your favourite restaurant, if you did not believe that headache medicine sold in pharmacies is not laced with cyanide, if you did not believe that you can predict the behaviour of people around you based on your knowledge of people in general and your past experience with specific individuals, then the world would be a very difficult place in which to live, and your ability to deal with it would be severely compromised. Every situation would have to be evaluated anew, and our cognitive resources would be quickly overwhelmed.

Beliefs are motivating. They can produce powerful effects and even lead to dangerous behaviours. If you were truly to believe that you can jump unharmed to the ground from your balcony on the 40th floor, then the next time that you are in a rush to get downstairs, you may take a shortcut, in all likelihood your last. The rest of us, not sharing your belief, would label you, and your belief, as having been psychotic. If you truly believe that your God wants you to wreak havoc on unbelievers, and that you will gain honour and eternal happiness in an afterlife if you kill unbelievers by blowing yourself up, then we should expect fireworks. If your airplane goes down in an arctic winter, and you believe that it is possible to survive in these circumstances, you are much more likely to be able to do so than if you accept that death is imminent and that there is nothing you can do to help yourself. The former conviction elicits problem-solving, the latter, passive acceptance of one's apparent helplessness.

Some beliefs, because of the destructive effects they produce on behaviour, justify the adjective 'toxic' or 'pathological.' When we read of mothers who pray that their sons and husbands will become suicide bombers, because they believe that this will make them martyrs and give them glorious afterlives, or when we read about people who are solidly mired in their belief that certain groups of people, categorized perhaps in terms of race or skin colour or sexual orientation, are 'scum' or 'subhuman,' therefore justifying ethnic cleansing, or gay-bashing, we see the awesome and destructive power of belief.

Beliefs are important in helping define who we are, and our beliefs about ourselves determine our self-esteem. If you do not believe that you are intelligent, worthy, attractive, or likeable, your life will suffer greatly compared to the individual who has more positive beliefs about him or herself. Indeed, erroneous beliefs can set in motion self-fulfilling prophecies: the individual with low self-esteem, who believes that he or she is unlikable and uninteresting, is not likely to behave in a manner that will bring others to find him or her interesting, thereby providing ultimate reinforcement and justification for the initially faulty belief.

Beliefs serve an important group function, for shared beliefs contribute strongly to social cohesiveness and facilitate the coordination of efforts in the pursuit of mutual goals. In the long run, this benefits most individuals in the group. In addition, positive beliefs about the group nurture individual self-esteem. Why is identifying oneself as an American, or a Canadian or a humanist, or a Christian or Muslim, so important to people in particular circumstances? A good part of the answer is that it adds to self-esteem. Most Canadians probably recall that at the moment that he won his Olympic Gold Medal, Ben Johnson was one of them, a *Canadian*, and *Canadians* had won gold. Yet, as soon as they were faced with the shocking news that he had lost his medal because of a positive urine test, he suddenly became identified as a *Jamaican-Canadian,* and even a *Jamaican immigrant.* Canadians did not want their group image, and therefore to some degree their own self-image, tarnished by his actions, and we tried to preserve the belief that Canadian athletes are not cheaters.

STABILITY OF BELIEFS

People vary in their willingness or capacity to consider opposing views and to change their beliefs as a result of logical analysis or new information. The spectrum runs from the credulous individual, easily and uncritically swayed by any new information, to the open-minded critical thinker who examines all new relevant information and who relies on methods to test the validity of the beliefs, to the dogmatist who clings tenaciously to his or her beliefs and who rejects conflicting information out of hand. While there are personality differences amongst people, with some being generally more dogmatic or open-minded or credulous than others, very few would fit any one of those three descriptions all the time. Most of us present a mixture of all three types, sometimes open-minded, at other times, credulous, and at yet other times dogmatic, although we are unlikely to recognize these chameleon-like shifts in ourselves.

Although beliefs do change based on new information and experience, many beliefs are extremely stable over time. This is usually a good thing, for it would be maladaptive if all our beliefs changed readily with every bit of influence, but it can also lead to stubbornly-held erroneous beliefs. Belief stability is promoted by a number of factors:

FACTOR 1: WIDELY HELD BELIEFS

When a belief is held almost universally, then there is little reason to question it, and it is unlikely to change. Centuries ago, few people questioned the belief that the earth is flat, and that one would fall over the edge if one got too close. Even though no one had ever seen anyone fall over the edge (or so we *believe*), they did not question the assumption because it was common knowledge, and 'made sense.' Today, almost no one questions the belief that the earth is a globe, for it is also common knowledge and 'makes sense,' even though we do not have direct personal evidence to support the belief. We have not sat on a dock watching a tall-masted ship as it disappears over the horizon, with the top of the mast being the last to go. And flying to Europe or Australia provides a personal experience no different from that one would have on a flat, saucer-shaped earth. As for pictures from space, recall once again *Star Trek*.

FACTOR 2: BELIEFS WITH EMOTIONAL INVESTMENT

The more important a belief is to us, the more likely it is to resist change. If, for example, you believe that modern Italy is an older nation than Canada, then you are wrong, at least according to my trusted authorities. Once you consult a reference source that you trust, you will no doubt immediately correct your belief. It is not an important belief, there is no emotion involved, and emending it has no negative consequences for you. On the other hand, if you believe that eating a healthy diet and getting regular exercise is important for good health, and you are devoted to exercise and good nutrition, then this belief is likely to be more resistant to contradictory arguments. A newspaper article suggesting that exercise is bad and that we should all consume more fat is not likely to lead to a change in your belief.

We try to avoid having to change important beliefs, and often resist through rationalization or other intellectual manoeuvres. For example, racists hold very negative stereotypes of minority groups, and yet may in some circumstances have to admit that the members of a disliked minority group with whom they work are 'nice enough;' however, this usually does not weaken the prejudiced belief at all, for these 'nice enough' people are seen as the 'exceptions.' Indeed, these 'exceptions' can then serve to defend against the charge of being a bigot: *"Some of my best friends are…"*

FACTOR 3: BELIEFS THAT BOLSTER SELF-ESTEEM

As indicated earlier, some beliefs serve to bolster our self-esteem and for that very reason, they resist change. The belief that Canadians are the peace-keepers of the world may no longer actually be true, but many Canadians resist giving up that belief because it contributes to their national pride and indirectly to their self-esteem. Similarly, Americans believe that they stand for human rights around this world, and are resistant to examples that suggest otherwise.

FACTOR 4: PRESSURE TO CONFORM

Since a large proportion of our beliefs is shared with the people in the society in which we live, the larger society rightly or wrongly often takes a keen interest in them. Some beliefs therefore resist change because they are seen as being very important for group success. On the other hand, beliefs which seem to threaten the structure of a society or the perquisites of the powerful are often suppressed by the group leadership. While democracies attempt to protect the right to individual belief, as long as one is not harming others, rejecting important group-held beliefs can lead to pressure to conform to the majority belief, and if one does not, to ostracism, incarceration, or even violence. One might truly believe in the communist vision of a better world for all, but expression of such belief may be dangerous to one's well-being in as it was in the United States on the 1950s. People in the Middle Ages who pointed out the irrationality of the Inquisition and the witch burnings were usually themselves condemned as witches.

FACTOR 5: PRIMITIVE BELIEFS

Belief stability is also assured in part because new information is less likely to be accepted as true if it is at odds with our existing beliefs. In particular, some beliefs are so deeply held that they are accepted axiomatically. These have been labelled *primitive beliefs*. Belief that objects left unsuspended fall to the ground, or that people cannot become invisible, or that God exists, or socialism is good, or socialism is terrible are all examples. New information that is contrary to these primitive beliefs is likely to be rejected as not worthy of consideration. A committed capitalist is unlikely to pay attention to information suggesting that the government should give more money to the homeless. A person who is very skeptical about the paranormal is unlikely to give much consideration to someone's account of having seen a ghost or having watched a psychic bend a spoon.

Differing primitive beliefs create a gap between believers and sceptics, whether in regard to religion, the paranormal, political philosophy or whatever. If we know 'deep down' that communism does not work, or that God exists, or that there are no ghosts, or that when your body dies, there is no spirit to live on, then it is difficult to have a meaningful dialogue with those whose primitive beliefs incorporate a belief in communist philosophy, God, ghosts or survival. Sometimes, however, a dramatic experience — whether interpreted correctly or not — may change our primitive beliefs in what is referred to as a *conversion experience*. Saul on the road to Damascus, the doubter of the paranormal who succumbs emotionally to a powerful 'paranormal' experience, the very ill person who has long ridiculed homeopathy but seems to recover suddenly after being persuaded to try a homeopathic remedy, all of these are likely to promote passionately their new belief. Unfortunately, conversion to scientific rationality never seems to occur in such a dramatic moment.

FACTOR 6: TRANSCENDENTAL BELIEFS

Religious beliefs are in general very resistant to contradictory information or experience. First of all, they are typically acquired at a young age, before critical thinking skills have had a chance to take root, and many of the basic concepts become primitive beliefs. Secondly, people typically evaluate religious beliefs in a different manner than they do other beliefs. As psychologist Jerome Frank pointed out, religious and other supernatural beliefs are typically held within a different framework than are more mundane beliefs. While beliefs about the everyday world form part of what he labelled the Scientific-Humanist Belief System, and are subject to the rules of logic, religious and other supernatural beliefs are not. They belong to a second belief system, the 'Transcendental Belief System,' which does not involve logic at all. It is based on 'faith.' Indeed, faith is often trumpeted by religious leaders as a badge of honour, making one worthy if one ignores reason and accepts extraordinary claims on the basis of faith alone. Thus, most people would reject as extremely unlikely a claim that a particular model of automobile will go 200 kilometres per litre of gasoline (Scientific-Humanist Belief System). However, when another 1000 children starve to death after the devout have prayed for the end of a famine, this is not considered as possible evidence that there is no God or that prayer does not work. Rather, the central, primitive belief is maintained, and rationalization is found: *"God works his wonders in mysterious ways;" "the good die young;" "every prayer is answered, and even no answer is an answer."* Such a belief system is all but impervious to disconfirming evidence because nothing ever is seen to be disconfirmation. In addition, when such challenges are deemed to be sinful in themselves, as is the case in some religions, then any such questioning elicits guilt, which is assuaged only when the questioning ceases and the beliefs are reaffirmed.

FACTOR 7: RELATED BELIEFS

Beliefs also resist change if they are interrelated with a number of other beliefs that would also have to change along with them. For example, if a devout Roman Catholic moves toward the belief that women have as much right as men to be ordained as priests, then that modification of belief would doubtless affect other important beliefs, such as the belief that priests should not marry, or the belief in the infallibility of the Pope. The need to examine and possibly change a whole number of related beliefs often leads to no change at all.

FACTOR 8: DEEPLY HELD VALUES

Beliefs are difficult to change when they relate to values. Values are deeply held ideas about right and wrong, good and bad. These are often, but not necessarily, tied to religion. They typically are instilled in childhood and reflect the prevailing morality of our group or society at the time. Because they are shared, there is rarely a need to defend them, at least not within the group, although it is not uncommon for the youth of one generation to challenge the deeply-held values of the preceding one, something that was massively demonstrated in the 1960s.

Values are often so fundamental that behaviour not in keeping with them elicits great emotion. In summer 2006, for example, a hue and cry was heard across the country because three young men had relieved themselves against the War Memorial in Ottawa. And no doubt most of us view incest and slavery as totally reprehensible and indefensible (these are values again), and we would likely experience strong negative emotion were we to listen to someone seriously try to defend either. Yet, we often fail to recognize that other people with differing values react in the same way that we do when our values are offended. While readers of this anthology are likely to support the legalization of gay marriage and view it positively, for some people opposed to this new reality, gay marriage strongly offends their value relating to the 'sanctity of marriage.' Just as we would react viscerally to the idea that incest or slavery should be legalized, so might they react to legalized gay marriage, something that for some is even theologically forbidden. Dialogue is difficult with regard to value differences, and if we only reject the views of such people as being ignorant or bigoted, or if we try to persuade dissenters through logical analysis, then we are usually doomed to failure, for we have ignored the important role that values play in determining and defending such beliefs.

CRITICAL THINKING

This discussion so far has focused on content, on *what* we come to believe. And, in the right circumstances, people can come to believe virtually anything — AIDS is being deliberately spread in Africa by the CAI; fluorinated water is good for you; fluorinated water is bad for you; after you die, you are judged for your sins and then spend an eternity in Heaven or Hell; if you die a martyr's death by blowing up yourself and others in service of some cause, you will live in splendour for eternity; consuming too much fat will clog up your arteries; chiropractic neck manipulations will cure just about anything.

What is more important than the content is the *process* by which we come to believe. Do we simply accept as fact whatever anyone tells us is fact, so long as it is consistent with our primitive beliefs? Virtually no one is that naïve. At the very least, we choose our sources. We are aware that we need to consider the possible motivation of the source — is someone trying to sell us something or manipulate us, or is the source unintelligent or unreliable? Even for the most careful of thinkers, the source is important. A real example: about twenty years ago, there was a report stating that any normal male can produce breast milk; all he has to do is allow a baby to suck on his nipple regularly for about three weeks. Do you believe it? You probably would dismiss it out of hand were you told that this had been written up in one of the sensational-ist tabloids such as the *National Enquirer*. In fact, however, this article appeared in the *Globe & Mail*, and was attributed to a Harvard Univer-sity endocrinologist. That changes things, doesn't it? Suddenly, it is not so easy to treat the claim as foolish. So, do we continue to reject the claim because it is opposed by common sense? Do we accept it because it came from a Harvard endocrinologist?

What we should do in this case, and in every case where we are con-fronted by new information from what seems to be a reliable source but that does not fit with what we already believe, is to suspend judge-ment. We do not have a good enough basis to accept the claim, nor a good enough one to reject it. If the claim is important to us, we should pursue more information, and finding out how other endocrinologists view the claim might be a good first step.

Suspending judgement is just as important when dealing with unusual information fed to us by our own senses. While one may be told, "I saw a ghost, and now I believe in ghosts, and so would you if you had seen what I saw," that individual would have been wiser not to jump to that conclusion, but rather, once again, to suspend judgement pending the collection of more data. if available. If we do not rush to judgement, then we have time to deliberate, and employ whatever logic and critical thinking skills at our disposal, and gather more information.

Critical thinking does not come automatically to us. We have to work at it; we have to acquire it. Science, a formalized version of critical thinking, began to emerge when scholars such as Copernicus decided that beliefs about the world need to be vetted by empirical testing. It did not matter to Copernicus, when the data indicated otherwise, that Ptolemy had dictated that the sun moves around the earth, or that

Christian dogma placed the earth at the centre of the universe. We need to remember this as individuals. How might we actually put our beliefs to the test? Often we have neither the expertise nor the means to do so, but if we were to realize even just that, then we would be less likely to view our beliefs as unadulterated truth.

In closing, it is important to realize that our brains are essentially belief-generating machines, or 'belief engines.' Our beliefs will always map imperfectly onto the domain of reality. While we can often see the error in other people's ways, and even roll our eyes at their credulity, we usually take for granted that our own strongly-held beliefs are well-founded. Where belief is concerned, we all live in glass houses, and we need to be careful when throwing stones. However, by promoting critical thinking, encouraging logic and discouraging dogma, there is a good chance we can improve the ratio of sense to nonsense amongst our beliefs and those of our fellow human beings. If we are to survive as a species, faced as we are with weapons of mass destruction, pandemics, and environmental degradation, we will need every bit of good sense that we can muster. ❧

ON THE ORIGINS
OF MY HUMANISM

by Jonny Diamond

My father has always been a little too fond of Groucho Marx'
great line, "I refuse to join any club that would have me
as a member." For the last forty years, the club in question has been the Unitarian Universalist Church, where,
every Sunday, he has shown up as an official "non-member observer."
My father is proud of his status as a sanctioned outsider and guards
it rigorously, rebuffing any attempts at what he perceives as "mission-
ary acquisitiveness" by incoming chaplains — as he sees it, "an outfit
devoted to secular inquisition and freethinking debate needs its apos-
tates, too."

My parents met at Unitarian fellowship in the early 1970s. My father,
an altar boy turned atheist, son of socialists and publicans, "popped by"
after a morning on the slopes to see what it was all about; my mother,
a second-generation Unitarian, daughter of gardeners and cartograph-
ers, was immediately taken with him. From the very start, the heart
of their relationship was intellectualized argument, a loving refusal to
cede any point until its inverse has been adequately demonstrated. As it
turns out, there is no better place for this kind of thing than a Unitarian
fellowship, something I would come to understand at a very early age.

The fellowship in question (I've never been able to use the term "congregation") must have had an average age of sixty, and was comprised of a diverse group that convened each Sunday, an amateur parliament of progressive agitators delighted at the prospect of weekly debate on topics ranging from the opening of the Chinese economy to the redemptive power of modern art. For a young boy in suburban Toronto, the life, history and experience brought to bear on these discussions was as compelling as it was intimidating. No subject was taboo. Everything was questioned. Scepticism was encouraged, but cynicism was frowned upon. Non-dogmatic atheism, rational enquiry, a deep secular reverence for art and nature — and all of it topped off with better coffee than the Methodists down the street.

One of the central figures in my memory is an elderly woman named Trudy Weiss, perhaps because she was the first adult I can remember seeing eye to eye with (literally). With her wiry black hair and thick-rimmed glasses above a ready smile, Trudy was a fixture at the Unitarians for most of my young life. She was an Austrian Jew who'd survived a year at Dachau, the significance of which I only came to grasp after she was gone. Though never shy about sharing her opinions at the Fellowship (she and my father once argued about the moral dimension of suffering all the way out the door and into the parking lot), Trudy was at her best hosting people after meetings. Her crowded, informal salons, which consisted of a series of heated conversations across a single long table laid out with cold cuts, pickles, cheese, bread, coffee and wine, were a marvel to behold. Around this table could be found the usual suspects: Jim MacDougal, a quiet, lapsed Anglican beloved of the younger set for his annual dramatic Christmas readings of Dickens, O'Henry, and Stephen Leacock, for which he'd don a holly-leaf bowtie pinned with a red berry; Dagmar Kominova, a morose, black-clad Czech who always sat at the rear of any gathering, perpetually on the verge of escape; the Gerard family from Manchester, a pale collection of Edward Gorey characters, marshalled furtively in and out of fellowship by a paterfamilias who was always introducing the Russian anarchists into any discussion; Larry the Tool and Die Maker who would go on to write the incisively titled *Philosophy For the Tool & Die Maker*, which my father spent years attempting to edit into coherence. Finally, there was Laura, a single mother, who, as far as I can tell, never missed a

Sunday, despite the fact she had two elementary school-age daughters. Laura, as she was not hesitant in letting us know, had grown up in thoroughly unromantic working-class Windsor, and though she'd always understood the importance of a college education, hadn't yet managed to acquire one. The enthusiasm and hunger she brought to each discussion, and the curiosity she displayed regarding books she hadn't read or movies she hadn't seen (and the discipline she displayed in consuming them) impressed on me early the value of such things.

Laura was one of the "converted" as my father described them, the closest thing Unitarians have to zealots; people who've discovered the possibilities of free rational enquiry later in life, and realized how much fun it can be to really talk about things that matter. (In my family, one is expected to discuss religion and politics at the dinner table — those who avoid these subjects, or any subjects, are deemed suspect.)

Looking back at the make-up of the fellowship, I realize that most of its members were "converts." And though of diverse backgrounds, they were united in a search for a way to escape the orthodoxies of their former lives. Perhaps "search" isn't the right word, evoking as it does the possibility of a project completed. What was really going on was a discovery of the inherent value of "searching," the present continuous human need to explore doubt to its fullest, discovering more through sustained uncertainty than could ever be gained by the finality of religious certitude.

As a twelve year old, all of this marvellous ecumenical haggling and freewheeling intellectualism seemed a matter of course, a natural state of affairs obtaining throughout the grown-up world. And even though I soon realized the secular humanism of my Unitarian youth wasn't actually present in *all* aspects of Canadian society, I came to understand and appreciate Canada as a place relatively free of ideological fundamentalism, founded on the virtues of compromise and consensus. Never would I appreciate those virtues more than upon my move to America.

In a land where more people believe in the existence of angels than they do in universal healthcare, where declarations of atheism amount to political suicide, and the commander of the military consults with a higher power, the primacy of religion in American life is undeniable.

Here, unlike most of the Western world, it takes no small amount of moral courage to espouse Enlightenment ideals, a position fewer and fewer seem willing to take. As the world moves closer to a clash of fundamentalisms, it has never been so important to defend secular humanist values, to preserve forums for the kind of freethinking scepticism that captivated my parents, my young self, and all those refugees from orthodoxy. Without the instinct to question, and the informed doubt that is its by-product, "democracy" is just another war cry.

Since the initial publication of this essay, my father died a peaceful death in his mid eighties. Below is a portion of the eulogy I delivered at his memorial, which serves as further explication of the origins of my humanism and its evolution.

I was very lucky to have had the chance to talk with my father in the month before his death, when he first fell ill. We spoke of many things, my father and I, but mainly we spoke of death, and the imminence of his own. He told me he was saddened by the prospect of the end, that he loved this fleeting world and all its complexities and contradictions. He told me that he wanted more: more sunshine, more laughter — simply, more. But much like Socrates, who I only invoke by comparison because my father once played him on stage, he refused the consolations of eternity, didn't, as they say "find God in the fox hole." He recognized that his life was coming to end and had no need for the mysteries of any particular beyond, the mysteries of existence having proved more than enough. And so, at the very end he remained true to those beliefs he'd held for 50 years, holding to an intellectual commitment with his younger self.

This, perhaps, above all the other lessons he left me, is the most valuable: that we need not outgrow our beliefs, that idealism is not a rash phase, not merely the province of youthful passion; that intellectual honesty is far more powerful and necessary in bad times then in good... There is an oft-used aphorism trotted out by those old men in power to justify the gradual impoverishment of their ideals: "A man at twenty who is not a liberal has no heart. A man at forty who is not a conservative has no brain."

The life of my father who, to the age of 84, maintained his passionate commitment to social justice, civic generosity and the welfare of all people, is stark rebuttal to that bleak dictum. To his dying day, in what must be a lesson to us all, he refused to let the world harden his heart.

And this, surely, is one of the signal things we must do when we come to praise the dead: share with each other the lessons they have given us; be generous and expansive with the good they have bequeathed the world, in both word and deed, honoring their lives not with mere adjectives but with action. Above all else, we must forever strive to redistribute the wealth of their good works and wisdom.

As Wittengstein remarked on the death of his father, "He lived a life worth dying for." Today, as we celebrate the life of my own father, Jack Diamond, I can with certainty say the same thing. ❧

ONCE BORN, TWICE SHY

by James Alcock

Jesus answered and said unto him,
Verily, verily, I say unto thee,
Except a man be born again,
He cannot see the kingdom of God.

—John, 3.3

Heaven is restricted.

Being kind, decent, law-abiding, caring and helpful is not enough to gain admission. Seek no entry here, all ye Hindus, Buddhists, pagans, atheists and other non-Christians, no matter how upstanding you may be as citizens, parents, friends and neighbours. Even belief in Christian doctrine and adherence to Christian morality is not enough. To get into Heaven, you must be Born Again.

To Roman Catholics, one is 'born again' through baptism, in which the stain of Original Sin is cleansed away as one repents for personal sin and is transformed through God's grace. Unless one is baptized, then, one cannot go to Heaven. Consequently, infants who die without having been baptized, even though free from personal sin, have no hope of ever entering Heaven. Instead, their souls are assigned permanently to Children's Limbo (*limbus puerorum*), a state of happy oblivion somewhere between Heaven and Hell.

To fundamentalist Christians, however, Heaven has tougher entry requirements, and baptism is not enough. They interpret being Born Again as the active acceptance of Jesus Christ as Lord and Saviour, although this concept is not without ambiguity. And there are even more rigid limitations for some Christian sects. Jehovah's Witnesses, for example, believe that only a total of 144,000 souls will be 'born again' in the Resurrection and admitted into Heaven. Given the six and one-half billion people alive today, not to mention all those who have gone before, this means that the vast majority of people will never get to Heaven if the Jehovah's Witnesses are correct.

Born Again Christians constitute a large and growing segment of the population of the United States, a group with considerable collective political clout that can count amongst its members some of highest political powers in the land, including the former American President, Vice-President, Secretary of State and Attorney-General. A 2004 Gallup Poll reported that 45% of Americans are Born Again Christians, while fewer than 10% of Canadians describe themselves in this manner. This reflects a substantial difference in general religious belief between the two countries: according to another recent poll, while 59% of Americans consider religion to be important to them, only 30% of Canadians feel the same way.

Born Again Christians in the United States are leading an attack on reason and science. For example, more and more states are imposing limits on the teaching of evolution in science classes, as creationism and its dressed-up cousin 'intelligent design' make their way into science classes.

What is it like to be Born Again, to believe fervently that the Holy Scriptures are infallible and literally true, to believe that God and Jesus are constantly watching over you, to believe that you will one day go to Heaven and be reunited with your (Born Again) loved ones, to believe that there is Satanic evil always present in the world that must be opposed, to believe that we are soon coming to the end of worldly existence as predicted in the Book of Revelation? I can tell you what it is like from first-hand observation, although for the record, I have only been born once, as was documented in the family Bible of one of my uncles. Inscribed in that Bible was a list extended family members and two columns of dates labelled 'Born' and 'Born Again.' I noted that dates were inscribed in both columns for most family members, even for grandchildren as young as two or three years, but for my siblings and myself, dates appeared only in the 'Born' column. My aunt saw me looking at the list and expressed the hope that she could soon add a date for me under the second column as well. (That never happened).

I was reared in a very tolerant and loving home. I was encouraged to think, but I was also taught to believe in Christianity, and was an active Christian until my late teens, at which time, over a period of two or three years, I wrestled with my faith, struggled with the resulting guilt elicited by questioning it, and eventually became a non-theist (a term I prefer to 'atheist' because of all the negative connotations that term can elicit). My father had been reared as a Baptist in England, but never showed any indication of having any religious faith whatsoever. He never spoke of religion, never attended church and never even closed his eyes when my mother said Grace at each meal! However, neither did he attack religion. Live and let live.

My mother was a member of the United Church of Canada, and this is the church in which I was reared. As most Canadians recognize, this is a generally tolerant, socially-progressive church which has often been on the forefront in promoting social justice. It was comfortable with intellectual inquiry and, at least in retrospect, seemed to be generally low in dogmatism, and rather practical in many ways. I vividly recall that when I was about 14, my Sunday School teacher, who also happened to be the school principal in my little town, told my friends and me that we were now old enough to take Communion. However, he cautioned that we should only do so if we were prepared to make every effort to stop sinning, and he went on to tell us that he was not yet ready to make such a promise, and therefore would not be taking communion himself! Shades of St Augustine in his *Confessions*: "Oh Lord, make me pure. But not yet!"

My mother's family of origin was very religious; all but one of her siblings had been Born Again. Moreover, one of her brothers was an ordained evangelical minister, as was his wife. I had regular contact with my aunts and uncles, and one of my aunts lived just doors away. Thus, my everyday exposure to the spectrum of religious belief went from no religion (my father), to tolerant religion that encouraged intellectual inquiry (my mother and the United Church), to fundamentalist religion that rejected any questioning of a literal interpretation of the Scriptures.

To my fundamentalist relatives, as for other fundamentalists that I have met later in life, religion was the central core of daily existence. Virtually every picture on the walls of my relatives' homes involved a religious theme. No decoration of the human body was allowed: no lipstick, no jewellery. Christmas trees were of course pagan and to be eschewed. Movies were considered sinful. (My uncle counselled my older brother that he could not attend church and go to movies as well. My brother elected to stop going to church!) Every decision my relatives made involved God in some manner. Should I change jobs? Pray, and let God guide the decision. Should I buy this house? Put in an offer, and if God wants you to have the house, it will be accepted. Why did the airplane crash? God in His wisdom ordained it, for some reason beyond our comprehension. Further exposure to Born Again religion came several years after my father's death, when my then septuagenarian mother remarried, to a very strict Born Again Christian. He practised his faith to a fault, even saying grace over doughnuts at the doughnut shop. He fervently believed that the United Church was satanic and made my mother feel guilty for having brought us up in that church.

What has always struck me about my religious relatives, and other Born Again Christians whom I have encountered since, is the righteous certainty they have about their beliefs. Their absolute certainty that the Bible is literally true, their absolute certainty about what is right and wrong, produces intellectual rigidity, if not intellectual rigor mortis, for no reflection or discussion is necessary when one knows the truth. This intellectual rigidity in turn leads to intolerance of those who do not share the fundamentals of their belief system, an intolerance that contrasts sharply with the message of Christian love and acceptance of all that was taught to me in the United Church. Such intolerance leads sometimes to emotional abusiveness, as when, the day my father died, another aunt told my mother with some apparent sadness that since my father was not Born Again, his soul would already be in Hell. Even other Christian denominations are rejected as false religions. One of my aunts described to me how she was working to bring a number of unfortunate sinners to the Lord — a pregnant unmarried teenager, a young drug addict and a Roman Catholic. I asked her if I had correctly heard 'Roman Catholic' in the same list as drug addict and pregnant teenager. She replied that I had heard correctly, for all are outside God's Grace.

Religion in general to some extent, and all-encompassing fire-and-brimstone fundamentalist religion in particular, constitutes a belief system from which it is difficult to extricate oneself, even when motivated by reason to do so. Being reared from infancy in a religion generally makes it all the more difficult, for one has come to accept the basic tenets of the faith before intellect has fully developed. The intrinsic control mechanisms in religion are barriers to reason, and the more fundamentalist and dogmatic the religion, the more powerful are these mechanisms.

BARRIER TO REASON #1:

Faith must not be questioned. If religious teachings do not make sense, or even if they seem absurd, they are nonetheless true and are to be accepted on faith. A simple example: When quite young, I was puzzled about the Bible. How could it be, I asked my Born Again aunt, that with only four human beings extant in all of creation — Adam, Eve, Cain, and Abel — and leaving only three after Cain killed Abel, Cain left his parents and went away and got married. "Whom did he marry?" I wondered. It is wrong to question, I was admonished. You must accept it on faith. (I was subsequently interested to learn that in the famous Scopes trial in Tennessee in 1925, prosecutor William Jennings Bryan, who was defending Christian faith against Godless evolution, was unable to answer the same question about Cain's wife put to him by defence lawyer Clarence Darrow).

BARRIER TO REASON #2:

Guilt. If questioning one's religion is wrong, then to ask such questions means that one is even more of a sinner, and this leads to guilt, which severely dampens one's enthusiasm for further inquiry. Personally, I continued vainly to search for evidence to support my childhood faith. Once, I even devised a way to show God's existence. My father arose early every morning and set out cereals for breakfast, and he always put the cereal boxes at the same end of the table, day after day. I prayed to God that, as a sign, could he please have my father put them at the other end of the table the next morning? I did not want to ask for anything that would interfere significantly with the laws of nature, but this seemed eminently doable without any untoward effects on the way the world works. No such sign was forthcoming, however. My father did not vary from his routine, or perhaps I would now be writing for a religious organ rather than this sort of book. Did I lose my faith? One cannot escape that easily and absence of evidence is not evidence of absence. However, my guilt level increased, for I had been taught by my aunt that God does not like to be tested or trifled with. I was guilty of wanting proof for that which should be accepted on faith.

BARRIER TO REASON #3:

God is watching, and sees into our hearts. While those who are not religious may enjoy their 'guilty pleasures' from time to time, it is not so easy for the deeply religious, for God is always watching. Even examining religious precepts in a critical manner will not escape divine attention, and one will have to account for these unfaithful thoughts on Judgment Day. There is no escape.

BARRIER TO REASON #4:

Ignore contrary evidence. There is little discussion or true debate within a dogmatic religious group. Views contrary to the orthodox position are easily dismissed either because they are misguided or because they are inspired by Satan, who always lurks, waiting to tempt people to stray from the path of righteousness. And of course the views of any people who have left the faith are discounted: either they have answered Satan's call, or they 'obviously' never had the true faith to begin with. While I respect people's rights to their religious views, I regularly find that many Christians, and fundamentalists in particular, reject the value of anything I have to say as an ex-Christian, telling me that obviously I have never experienced the true faith. Inded, Born Again Christians go even further, rejecting the notion that I was ever a Christian to begin with. First of all, I was never Born Again. And secondly, "The United Church, you say..."

BARRIER TO REASON #5:

Social pressure. Threat of social rejection by people you care about is a powerful deterrent in religious and secular settings alike, but all the more so, I believe, in dogmatic religious settings. Straying from the path will bring considerable pressure from those around you to return to the flock.

BARRIER TO REASON #6:

Much to lose. Religion involves carrots as well as sticks. In accepting the doctrinal beliefs and not questioning them, and in living one's life according to the dictates of the faith, there are undoubtedly many rewards. For Born Again fundamentalists, these rewards include being one of God's chosen, knowing that you are in God's hands and being watched over, knowing that you will go to Heaven when you die, and having certainty about what is right and wrong in life. Leaving the faith means giving up these comforts.

These barriers to reason make it very difficult to leave a religious belief system, especially one that is as all-consuming as Born Again Christianity. This is not to say that Born Again Christians are not good and decent people, but it does mean that they are very restricted in their willingness and ability to give fair consideration to points of view that conflict with their doctrinal beliefs. Moreover, because of the conviction that they are living in the manner intended by God, they need not draw a distinction between secular and sacred. They believe that their faith should rule, even with regard to the secular concerns of daily life.

Of course, not all Born Again Christians are cut from the same cloth, and my relatives were undoubtedly amongst the most conservative and doctrinaire. My aim is not to stereotype those who claim to be Born Again, but to point out just how hard it is because of these barriers to reason to leave a religious belief system, especially one that is as all-consuming as Born Again Christianity. I am not threatened by religious faith in general, and I certainly respect and admire the devotion of many religious people to great humanitarian causes. Moreover, there are many people who are both religious and intellectual. However, there is danger when religious fundamentalists — of any religion — try to shape the world to suit their literal interpretation of ancient texts. This ultimately leads to a division between believers and non-believers, not just on a religious level, but also on a political and emotional level. Such a schism has been at the root of much human carnage across the ages. Unfortunately, the earth is rumbling and the cracks are becoming wider. ❧

The Darwinian Mind

by Robert Weyant

I n his notebooks, where he recorded ideas he was not yet ready
to publish, it is clear that Charles Darwin (1809–1882) had come
to think of the human mind as being the activity of the human
brain. This view of the human mind was a necessary component of his overall view of human beings that allowed him to discuss the
evolution of human mental characteristics. Clearly, the human brain
was a material organ that could be changed through the processes of
evolution. If the human mind was simply the activity of this evolved
human brain, then the mind might also be thought of as having evolved
and both its evolution and its functioning could be studied scientifically. In his view, the whole argument for evolution — his whole life's
work — made no sense if humans were excluded. This was true despite
the fact that in his initial work on evolution, *On the Origin of Species*
(1859), he made almost no mention of the human species. But, in fact, it
would have been difficult for anyone to read and understand *The Origin*
and miss the implication that we too are a product of the evolutionary
process.

And what of the human mind? What Darwin said, close to the end
of his great exposition, was:

> *In the distant future I see open fields for far more important
> researches. Psychology will be based on a new foundation, that of*

the necessary acquirement of each mental power and capacity by gradation. Light will be thrown on the origin of man and his history... And as natural selection works solely by and for the good of each being, all corporeal and mental endowments will tend to progress towards perfection.

Look at the words used here: 'psychology,' 'each mental power,' and 'mental endowments.' There is really no question that mind was a part of his grand scheme right from the beginning. However, it is interesting that Darwin appears to maintain the traditional distinction between 'corporeal' (ie, physical) and 'mental' endowments. I think he was just being careful, attempting to ruffle as few feathers as possible until his ideas relating to evolution were accepted. Nowhere in his writing is there any indication that he viewed 'mind' as having an incorporeal basis.

What Darwin had suggested in *the Origin* he later made explicit in *The Descent of Man, and Selection in Relation to Sex* (1871) and *The Expression of the Emotions in Man & Animals* (1872) where he discussed a number of human psychological activities from speech to ethical behaviour, cooperation to emotional expression, sexual attraction to belief in a deity as having their roots in the behaviour and psychology of other species. That is, he argued for a continuity of psychological processes from other species to human beings. Early in the second chapter of his work on *The Descent of Man* Darwin wrote, "My object in this chapter is solely to shew that there is no fundamental difference between man and the higher mammals in their mental faculties." Human beings are different in the sense that the behaviour of any species differs from that of other species — but these are differences in degree, not differences in kind. What is crucial is the continuity; he saw us as existing on a mental continuum with other species — a natural continuum. This was a major change in Western thought because it moved human nature from the non-material world into the natural world. That change, in turn, created an intellectual environment that opened up new possibilities in everything from literature to the law, social practices to science, ethics to economics and served as a basis for new theories of how the human mind works, just as Darwin had predicted.

What had led Darwin to this revolutionary view? He had been studying medicine at Edinburgh University for two years when, in 1828 at the
age of 19, it was decided that he was not really cut out to be a doctor.
By his own admission, young Charles preferred roaming the woods,
hunting, gambling and drinking to studying, but the deciding incident
seems to have been two operations he witnessed, one on a child, where
the sight of the pre-anesthetic patients, strapped down and screaming
in pain, led him to run from the operating room before the surgery was
complete. "The two cases," he later wrote, "fairly haunted me for many
a long year." His father, Doctor Robert Darwin, decided that Charles
would go off to Cambridge and study to become a clergyman. This
may seem to have been a somewhat odd choice for a family that leaned
more towards freethinking than orthodox Anglicanism, but we have to
view the situation as a well-to-do 19th century father would think of it.
Such a career was often less a 'calling' and more a 'living.' Adrian Desmond and James Moore, in their admirable biography of Darwin, have
described things this way:

> Dr Darwin, a confirmed freethinker, was sensible and shrewd.
> Was the Church not a haven for dullards and dawdlers, the last
> resort of spendthrifts? What calling but the highest for those
> whose sense of calling was nil? And in what other profession were
> the risks of failure so low and the rewards so high? The Anglican
> Church, fat, complacent, and corrupt, lived luxuriously on its
> tithes and endowments, as it had for a century. Desirable parishes
> were routinely auctioned to the highest bidder. A fine rural 'living'
> with a commodious rectory, a few acres to rent or farm, and per-
> haps a tithe barn to hold the local levy worth hundreds of pounds
> a year, could easily be bought as an investment by a gentleman of
> Dr Darwin's means and held for his son. It was an inducement for
> a young man to subscribe to almost any creed.

Charles rather liked the idea of being a country parson with time to
roam the woods and hills in search of new plants and animals. He had
some uneasiness concerning just how much of the dogma of the Church
of England he really believed but, he later wrote in his autobiography:

"... as I did not then in the least doubt the strict and literal truth of every word in the Bible, I soon persuaded myself that our Creed must be fully accepted. It never struck me how illogical it was to say that I believed in what I could not understand and what is in fact unintelligible." Looking back on his plans from his old age, Charles felt that, considering how much he was later to be attacked by various religious groups: "... it seems ludicrous that I once intended to be a clergyman." His future in the ministry was never, Charles recalled, formally given up. Rather, it "died a natural death when on leaving Cambridge I joined the Beagle as Naturalist."

HMS Beagle, a ship of the Royal Navy, was supposed to spend one or two years mapping the coasts of South America. Instead, when the Beagle sailed on 27 December 1831, it was destined to spend five years sailing around the world and it brought Charles Darwin to a new understanding of the world of living creatures, including human beings. On board the Beagle were three young inhabitants of Tierra del Fuego who had been brought to England on a previous voyage to be 'civilized.' Having learned some English as well as English manners and customs and having even been presented to King William IV and Queen Adelaide, they were now being returned to their homeland in the hope that they would be a positive influence on their less civilized families and neighbours. Darwin's first encounter with those less polished natives came on 18 December 1832 when the Beagle reached Tierra del Fuego. He wrote in his diary:

It was without exception the most curious and interesting spectacle I ever beheld. — I would not have believed how entire the difference between savage and civilized man is. — It is greater than between a wild and domesticated animal, in as much as in man there is greater power of improvement.

This experience and others that shortly followed may well have given Darwin his first inkling that the psychological difference between humans and other species was not absolute but could be greater or lesser depending upon the conditions of life. Here were human beings whose only clothing was an animal skin thrown over their shoulders, who spent much of their time naked in wet and freezing conditions, who had no permanent shelter, whose guttural language he felt, "does not deserve to be called articulate," whose diet seemed to consist of whatever shellfish and birds they could find along the shore and about whom he remarked, "If their dress and appearance is miserable, their manner of living is still more so."

On 16 January 1833 a group from the ship were on shore and came across traces of a fire that was still warm that the Fuegans advised them had probably belonged to an individual who was a 'bad man,' an outcast who was living alone. Charles recorded, "How very little are the habits of such a being superior to those of an animal. — By day prowling along the coast & catching without art his prey, and by night sleeping on the bare ground." These experiences continued with Darwin drawing comparisons between human and animal behaviour. On 25 February he wrote:

Whilst going on shore, we pulled alongside a canoe with six Fuegians. I never saw more miserable creatures; stunted in their growth, their hideous faces bedaubed with white paint and quite naked. — One full aged woman absolutely so, the rain and spray were dripping from her body; their red skins filthy and greasy, their hair entangled, their voices discordant, their gesticulation violent and without any dignity. Viewing such men, one can hardly make oneself believe that they are fellow creatures placed in the same world… How little can the higher powers of the mind come into play: what is there for imagination to paint, for reason to compare, for judgment to decide upon. — to knock a limpet from the rock does not even require cunning, that lowest power of the mind. Their skill, like the instinct of animals is not improved by experience; the canoe, their most ingenious work, poor as it may be, we know has remained the same for the last 300 years. Although essentially the same creature, how little must the mind of one of these beings resemble that of an educated man… Whence have these people come? Have they remained in the same state since the creation of the world?

The point here is not whether Darwin's assessment of the Fuegians was fair, nor whether it was simply an expression of the racial prejudice of a Victorian Englishman against anyone who was not a Victorian Englishman. Rather, the point is that already, in 1834, he was beginning to think in terms of a psychological continuum. Not simply a continuum of human abilities as between what he would term 'savage' and 'educated' men, but also a continuum between the mental abilities of human beings and those of other species. Young Charles Darwin had no answers for his own questions, but clearly the wheels were turning. Speculations and queries in his diary were to become research interests and chapter headings in his later writings.

Later, as he began to put his ideas together, Charles opened a number of notebooks. These contained ideas he was uneasy discussing publicly and they help us see how his thoughts developed over time. For example, by 1838 he not only believed that species had evolved, but he also clearly had the idea of natural selection which he would not make public until the Origin appeared in 1859. In addition, his notebooks also tell us that he was, by then, a convinced materialist in the sense that he thought of the human mind as being a material, evolved set of processes located in the human brain. In his notebooks for 1838 he tended to use the words 'mind' and 'brain' interchangeably and specifically asked, "Can we deny relation of mind and brain... What other explanation — can we suppose some essence." He had come to believe that the study of animal behaviour, rather than metaphysics, was what would provide an understanding of the human mind.

Thus, in the 'M' notebook be wrote, "Origin of man now proved... He who understands baboon would do more toward metaphysics than [John] Locke" and "Plato says in Phaedo that our 'necessary ideas' arise from the preexistence of the soul, are not derivable from experience. — read monkeys for preexistence." In the 'C' notebook on the transmutation of species, Darwin mused, "Thought (or desires more properly) being hereditary it is difficult to imagine it anything but structure of brain hereditary" and he followed this idea with the exclamation, "Oh you materialist!" His materialism appeared on a number of occasions such as the comment in the 'N' notebook:

To study metaphysics, as they have always been studied appears to me to be like puzzling at astronomy without mechanics. — Experience shows the problem of mind cannot be solved by attacking the citadel itself. — the mind is function of the body, — we must bring some stable foundation to argue from.

An understanding of how the physical body works might have to come first, but the ultimate goal was to storm "the citadel itself" — the human mind. Furthermore, he saw a mind evolved through the laws of nature to be a mind that obeyed the laws of nature. In the 'M' notebook Darwin wrote, "one doubts existence of free will every action determined by hereditary constitution, example of others or teaching of others" and "I verily believe free will and chance are synonymous. Shake ten thousand grains of sand together and one will be uppermost, — so in thoughts, one will rise according to law." This simple mechanistic view of how the brain works would have to change with increased knowledge in both biology and physics, but the materialism holds good.

Ideas on the emotional continuum between animals and humans, which were to reappear thirty-four years later in *The Expression of the Emotions*, first appear in the 1838 notebooks. For example, in the 'M' notebook Darwin wrote:

Seeing a baby ... smile and frown, who can doubt these are instinctive — child does not sneer, because no young animal has canine teeth. — A dog when he barks puts his lips in peculiar position, and he holds them this way when opening mouth between interval of barking, now this is smile... The distinction as often said of language in man is very great from all animals — but do not overrate — animals communicate to each other... some say dogs understand expression of man's face. — How far they communicate not easy to know, — but this capability of understanding language is considerable.

The idea for the 1872 book on *The Expression of the Emotions* may be found in the 1838 comment that, "The whole argument of expression more than any other point of structure takes its value from its connexion with mind, (to show hiatus in mind not saltus between man and Brutes) no one can doubt this connexion." Looking backward rather than forward, Darwin's experience with the inhabitants of Tierra del Fuego appeared in his notebooks in the form of the comment, "Compare the Fuegian and Ourang-Outang, and dare to say differences are great."

In *The Descent of Man* Darwin argued that virtually all human emotions and many human intellectual functions, including reason and morality, exist in simpler forms in non-human species. Of course he realized that there were observable differences in the mental powers of animals and human beings but these differences were, he argued, of degree, not of kind. They were, as he put it, "connected by the finest gradations." The 'mental faculties' of human beings exist in other species, but to lesser degrees. Thus, human beings mentally, as well as physically, are continuous with other species. And how might this continuity of behaviour and abilities have come about? Darwin wrote:

> ... in each member of the vertebrate series the nerve-cells of the brain are the direct offshoots of those possessed by the common progenitor of the whole group. It thus becomes intelligible that the brain and mental faculties should be capable under similar conditions of nearly the same course of development, and consequently of performing nearly the same functions.

The equation seems clear — similar evolved brain structures equals similar evolved mental faculties and psychological functions. Nowhere in Darwin's thought is there any suggestion that the existence of mental powers and behaviours are not the result of causal factors either in evolution or in processes such as learning and adaptation. On the basis of anecdotal evidence and extrapolations from observed behaviour he credited non-human species with such emotions as pleasure, pain, happiness, misery, terror, suspicion, courage, timidity, love, maternal affection, grief, indignation, jealousy, emulation, shame, magnanimity, excitement, wonder and curiosity. He concluded that, "Most of the more complex emotions are common to the higher animals and ourselves." He also attributed to non-human species such abilities as imitation, attention, memory, imagination and reason. On the last of these attributes he remarked, "some animals extremely low in the scale apparently display a certain amount of reason. No doubt it is often difficult to distinguish between the power of reason and that of instinct."

'Reason' was bound to be contentious as it was the ability that traditionally marked off human beings from other species since only humans were thought to have a non-material rational soul. Darwin presented examples of animal behaviour chosen to support the assertion that in many instances it is reason, rather than instinct, that lies behind the animal's actions. Having presented a mass of evidence concerning the similarities in human and animal behaviour, he then observed:

> It has, I think, now been shewn that man and the higher animals, especially the Primates, have some few instincts in common. All have the same senses, intuitions and sensations — similar passions, affections, and emotions, even the more complex ones; they feel wonder and curiosity; they possess the same faculties of imitation, attention, memory, imagination, and reason, though in very different degrees. Nevertheless many authors have insisted that man is separated through his mental faculties by an impassable barrier from all the lower animals... It has been asserted that man alone is capable of progressive improvement; that he alone makes use of tools or fire, domesticates other animals, possesses property, or employs language; that no other animal is self-conscious, comprehends itself, has the power of abstraction, or possesses general ideas; that man alone has a sense of beauty, is liable to caprice, has the feeling of gratitude, mystery, &c.; believes in God, or is endowed with a conscience.

He proceeded to argue that many of these abilities are displayed by non-human species and, in the case of such behaviours as articulate language and a belief in God, in which he agreed that non-human species did not engage, he argued that it would be a relatively small step from what they already do to the activity presently peculiar to humans. Since Darwin's time, of course, the study of the comparative behaviour of humans and animals has uncovered far more similarities between the species than even he had realized.

In general, the existence of such 'higher order' abilities peculiar to human beings as self-consciousness, individuality, abstraction, the possession of general ideas and a belief in God (some of which have been demonstrated in animals since he wrote) depended, for Darwin, on the existence of adequate reasoning powers and an articulate language. But because both reason and language were, in his view, the products of an evolutionary process, the general point was maintained that while these may be important observable differences between humans and other species, they are differences of degree and not of kind. He even described the process by which human morality (he termed it the *moral sense*) could have evolved out of social instincts which any species living in social groupings would have had to develop. When his first child, William, was born in December of 1839, Darwin kept a detailed record of his development from "the first dawn of the various expressions which he exhibited," to show how animal-like actions appear in the developing human being.

In *The Descent of Man* he described a second evolutionary mechanism, sexual selection, which, in addition to natural selection, provided explanations of various human and animal behaviours, particularly mating behaviours and displays. The whole point of the evolutionary exercise was, after all, not simply survival but reproduction — getting your genes into the human gene pool. Darwin couldn't have expressed it that way since he didn't have the concept of genes, but that was what he was arguing.

Perhaps this is enough to give a general overview of Darwin's ideas, his evidence and his theorizing about the psychological continuum between animals and humans. The 'Darwinian Mind,' then, was the natural product of the processes of evolution on such physical structures as the brain, along with learned behaviours appropriate for the circumstances in which the particular species lived. There was no unbridgeable psychological gap between human beings and other species, even in relation to complex behaviour. ➦

PART 6

HUMANISM & IMAGINATION

Humanism values artistic creativity and imagination and recognizes the transforming power of art. Humanism affirms the importance of literature, music, and the visual and performing arts for personal development and fulfillment.

Myth & Fantasy: A Humanist Perspective

by Shawn Dawson

yths," Joseph Campbell once succinctly said, "are stories about the Gods." More elaborate and accurate definitions are certainly available, but this gets at the essence and helps explain much of what I suspect is the typical attitude of humanists toward myth. Humanists are secular, and so we reject Gods. Myths also represent or are associated with much of what we are trying to get away from; they are linked to religion, superstition, a pre-scientific way of looking at the world, a lack of concern for the truth, and our dark and primitive past.

Such at least is what a no-nonsense (William James might have called it 'tough-minded') humanist might say about myths. There is much about such a position that I think is absolutely correct, perhaps above all its firm commitment to the truth. Believing in the literal truth of myths does require something more than merely the suspension of disbelief. It seems to require either a willingness to sacrifice the truth in favour of something else (psychological certainty, for example) or a tendency for compartmentalization, that is, dividing your beliefs into a region reason can touch, and another reason cannot. But is there not, or can there not at least sometimes be, more to myths than that?

I think the answer is yes. There are many theories about myths and

I will not go into them here. However, Joseph Campbell's understanding of them seems to me insightful. Campbell's basic thesis is that there are shared motifs running through all myths and that these express universal commonalities in the human psyche. His position has been criticized for having an undue psychological emphasis and in particular for relying too heavily on Carl Jung's psychology. Be that as it may, that there are shared motifs or themes in mythology seems undeniable, and it seems plausible that this is the locus of their significance. If so, then myths are important at least because they express universal human concerns, or what we might call universal truths about the human condition.

What are some of these themes or concerns? Running throughout mythology we find concerns about death, the longing for immortality, food, sex, marriage, love, pregnancy and birth, childhood, the transition to adulthood, violence, conflict, and war, to name a few. For example, a Greek myth about romantic love imagined that humans were once combinations of male and female, until Zeus split them apart. For ever after, the halves sought each other out, in order that they might be reunited and once again complete. This myth strikes me as beautiful and expresses an important truth about romantic love — we feel as if the other person completes us (and I would not restrict this to only heterosexual love). The whole panorama of life and experience common to all human beings is arguably represented in myth, and so myths are important. At their best, myths can remind us of what is important in life; they can inspire us, cheer us, comfort us, embolden us, entertain us, in short, help us in many situations and along many stages on life's way.

On the other hand, myths also represent negative experience, and the stories may have negative consequences. There is a subtle yet disturbing effect of such a myth as the Old Testament story about Adam and Eve being expelled from the Garden of Eden for eating from the tree of the knowledge of good and evil, which in my view then sets the tone of the whole Bible as being against knowledge.

When we think of myth as mainly having to do with the supernatural, in the long view, our society appears to be relatively *demythologized*. Although religious fundamentalism may be on the rise in the past few years or decades, over the span of the past two or three hundred years there has been a definite progression to a more secular society. Still, the old myths linger on. In many ways, humanists stick out precisely because we are dissenters from the dominant mythology, namely a kind of amorphous theism. But it may be comforting to think of the long view, and to have hope, and to work, for a time when society as a whole has outgrown the supernatural.

There is another sense in which the word 'myth' is often used — that is, 'myth' as a misconception. Merriam-Webster's Online Dictionary provides this definition of myth: *2a: a popular belief or tradition that has grown up around something or someone; especially: one embodying the ideals and institutions of a society or segment of society.* In this sense, society is as satiated and intoxicated with myths as ever — the myth that success can be measured in terms of money and possessions; the myth that beauty is on the outside, that is, in physical attractiveness; the myth that education is only of value insofar as it contributes to a person's ability to earn money; the myth that religion has some special authority over or insight into morality or ethics. Myths, in this sense of the word, pervade our society.

It is also difficult to draw a sharp line between myth, in the broader sense of stories about the Gods and the supernatural, and fantasy, which the Oxford English Dictionary defines as *a product of imagination, fiction, figment.* Fantasy is, however, particularly associated with the arts and literature. Myth and fantasy share many of the same themes or motifs. However, perhaps the crucial difference is that whereas fantasy is willing to acknowledge that it is a product of the imagination, myth often pretends that it has loftier (and typically divine) origins. For example, there is an understanding, however implicit, between authors of novels and their readers that the novels themselves are fictional. On the other hand, many Muslims believe that the Koran is the literal word of God (Allah) and that it is absolutely true and inerrant. Fundamentalist Christians have similar beliefs about the Bible. To humanists, the Koran and the Bible are documents with very human origins and thus we regard them as at least partially mythological.

I have two recommendations, one unsurprising and one perhaps somewhat surprising and controversial. First, we should not reject all myths and fantasy outright (were it possible to do so), but neither should we accept them uncritically. What we must do is be judicious in our response to myths and fantasy. This sounds easy but requires more thought and vigilance than we might realize. What kinds of myth and fantasy are we getting from the popular media? To what are our children being exposed? What kinds of habits of thought and values are we learning from myths and fantasy prevalent in our society, and are these what we really want? I am certainly not suggesting censorship, but rather that we ought to be thoughtful and aware of what myths and fantasy we (and our children) are consuming.

My second recommendation is that humanists consider doing more to create, encourage, and promote broadly secular, and, in particular, humanist fantasy and myth. There are two main reasons for doing so. The first is to meet our own emotional, aesthetic, and moral needs. The second is to reach out to non-humanists. I cannot help but think it would be better if there were more humanists in society, but I have no desire to go door to door. What I am suggesting is that we try to find ways to reach people who are open to humanism, but who don't know much about it. Some of these people may be more likely to be attracted to humanism by a beautiful poem, an engaging novel, or a poignant piece of theatre, than by a tightly constructed argument, although we should continue to produce those too. [Editor's note: see 'Science, God & Philip Pullman,' Part 6)

The noted skeptic Michael Shermer has often said that human beings are pattern-seeking, story-telling animals (see *Why People Believe Weird Things* and *How We Believe: The Search for God in an Age of Science*). Myths and fantasy are simply some kinds of stories that we tell each other and have been telling each other for a very long time. These stories can be true or untrue, and good or bad, among other distinctions we can make between them. I do not think our fondness for stories is going to go away, nor do I want it to, but I do hope that humanism can find more stories of its own that are worth telling and retelling for many years to come. 🌿

Beyond Literalism

by Gary Bauslaugh & Gwyneth Evans

God said it, I believe it, and that settles it.

— posting on the front of a fundamentalist tour bus

The issue is obvious where religious fundamentalists are concerned. Their reading of ancient manuscripts as the true, unambiguous word of God leads them to believe that the direct or literal meaning of the words leaves no room for interpretation. What it says is what it means, and without question it speaks the absolute truth.

Rationalists, of course, have many problems with this analysis. For a start, how can anyone be so certain of the sacred origins of these texts, when facts about their authorship are murky and obscured by the passage of millennia? What about differences in translations, which often change the meaning of key passages?

And then how can a single interpretation of these texts be extracted with absolute certainty, particularly when contradictions abound, both within particular interpretations and between different ones, all held with equal fervor? Is it not important to try to set the words in their cultural and historical context — very different from life in the contemporary world, very much more limited in understanding of science and the natural world? And how can the idea of metaphorical rather than literal meaning be so roundly dismissed? How indeed? These familiar objections would seem sufficient to challenge literalism in the interpretation of so-called Holy scriptures, but, as we all know, such literalism — such reductionism — is rampant throughout the world, and threatens civilized world order.

The threat comes from hugely unwarranted certainty. If one is somehow convinced of the absolute and unambiguous truth of particular scriptures, then there is no room for the tolerance that is necessary for peace in a world of many cultures and beliefs. Most philosophers accept the idea that pluralism is a necessary component of a peaceful human society — that different beliefs, practices and principles must be accepted (within reason) for people to live together in any sort of harmony. Human society, taken as a whole, is not monolithic, and is not likely to ever be, nor would we want it to be. Instead it reflects the complexities of the human mind, and the infinite richness of human thought.

This does not mean that we must accept the idea of cultural relativism, where all beliefs have equal validity; it does mean that we must be very circumspect and tolerant in attempting to circumscribe acceptable thoughts and practices. This is, sometimes, a perilous balancing act, for a humane society cannot tolerate, for example, genocidal aggression or any form of extreme human cruelty, wherever it exists. But we must ensure that interventions of any sort are based upon secular principles of human compassion, and not arbitrary rules of religious origin. Religious literalists are the enemies of the search for reason and moderation in the understanding of and acceptance of human differences.

There are more things in heaven and earth, Horatio,
than are dreamt of in your philosophy.

—Hamlet

This famous quote from Shakespeare is often used to validate the idea of openness to the possibility of the supernatural, and a literal reading would certainly support such an interpretation. But Shakespeare was no literalist. His writing is rich in multiple meanings, and nearly four hundred years of scholarship and performance have increased, rather than simplified, the possible ways for us to understand and interpret them. Hamlet's friend Horatio was a rationalist, studying philosophy at the University of Wittenberg, where his course of study would have been heavily grounded in logic. Horatio can make no sense of the appearance of the ghost of Hamlet's father, and Hamlet chides him for his narrowness. There is something in human experience that is unattainable through logic, Hamlet is saying. Though a simplistic interpretation of this passage would be that ghosts are real, a deeper assessment of Hamlet's words instead reveals a recognition of the complexity of the human mind and feelings, and the possibilities of human imagination: according to Hamlet, logic is not all.

The essential problem with literalism is semantic reductionism. Words are taken at face value, with their modern connotations and context, and no understanding of a possible subtext. The meaning of language is reduced, sometimes to the point of trivialization. Certainly that is true of the religious fundamentalists, referred to above. They trivialize the meaning of ancient scriptures, which are critical components of human culture. But they are not the only ones doing this.

When you have a strong negative reaction to someone, you can be certain that they're reflecting traits that you also possess.

— or similar words by Carl Jung, Deepak Chopra and many others

The problem of literalism is not, unfortunately, limited to religious fundamentalists, though they are likely the most egregious and pernicious practitioners. Literalism pervades and influences human thought, wherever humans are, in many complex and sometimes unfortunate ways. And sometimes those most aggressive in condemning the literalism of religious fundamentalists are guilty themselves of a different kind of literalism.

If we can separate thought processes into two broad categories, let us think of them as being linear and imaginative. One is not superior to the other — both have been crucial to the emergence of modern human society. But they are clearly different. Linear thinking is the basis of logic and science; it leads to the establishment of fact, to the extent that fact can be established. Imaginative thinking is different from logical, sequential thought, though of course it can be richly informed by it. Imaginative thinking is also informed by human experience, by feelings and visions of existence that may well have nothing to do with logical thought. It is, therefore dangerous (as Plato said) in that it can lead us away from realism, but it is of immense value in the enrichment of human life, and to gaining insights into the human condition. Love, to use an obvious example, is influenced by reason, but flourishes in the imagination. The intense attraction one human can feel for another is not, generally, a logical calculus of merits and demerits, but is a flight of glorious imagination. There are of course risks in this, but who would have it any other way?

Well, it must be admitted that some people would. Dr Laura, the socially conservative radio talk show host, often has berated those who claim that love was the basis for their marrying someone. "You wouldn't buy a car that way — you would examine all the advantages and disadvantages," she would exclaim (in this or some similar fashion.) "How can you choose a husband based on feelings?" She does have a point. But were the world populated exclusively by people of such determined and often banal rationality we can imagine a sterile place indeed. Do we want a world in which emotion is displaced by calculation? *Star Trek's* half-human, half-Vulcan Spock has a certain charm, to be sure, but his most endearing moments are when he shows his less logical human side. And without emotion what sort of art would the Vulcans have, what sort of music, what literature?

It is artistic genius, in its many different expressions, that shows us the full richness of imaginative thinking, and illustrates the sometimes reductionist limitations of linear analysis and the literalism that it can lead to. Literalism seeks one meaning where there may be many, and loses meaning where such meaning is other than the end result of a calculation. Linear analysis, by itself, excludes metaphorical meaning — the human insights and understandings that are gained, and human feelings that are evoked by great works of art, music and literature.

The scientist shows us the vital importance of rigidly logical thinking in pursuit of knowledge of the physical realities of the world — there is no other reliable way of establishing facts. But if facts were all there were to understanding and experiencing life then our greatest works of literature would be encyclopedias. Science is necessary to the gaining of factual understanding of the physical realities around us, and taking us beyond superstition, but most scientists understand that science itself can say little about the vast richness of human imagination.

But clearly there is a problem in the desire of some people of a scientific bent to want to extend the literalism — the rigid linear thinking — that is so crucial to scientific success to realms where it is not so serendipitous. Unfortunately this is seen at times on the part of humanists, who seem oblivious to the irony of their disdain for religious fundamentalists. They, like fundamentalists, describe religion in a singular (though different) way. Such humanists describe religion as simply irrational and therefore to be dismissed, choosing to ignore the good deeds that are performed by many religious organizations (how many soup kitchens do humanists operate?) and the many great works of art, literature, music and architecture that have been inspired by religion, and the community life that provides support and comfort for its members. Those who like to think that religion is merely a worthless delusion are engaging in another form of reductive literalism.

An artist is a magician put among men to gratify — capriciously — their urge for immortality. The temples are built and brought down around him, continuously and contiguously, from Troy to the fields of Flanders. If there is any meaning in any of it, it is what survives as art, yes even in the celebration of tyrants, yes even in the celebration of non-entities. What now of the Trojan War if it had been passed over by the artist's touch? Dust. A forgotten expedition prompted by Greek merchants looking for new mar-

kets. A minor redistribution of broken pots. But it is we who stand
enriched, by a tale of heroes, of a golden apple, a wooden horse, a
face that launched a thousand ships...

—James Joyce in Tom Stoppard's play *Travesties*

The problem of literalism is clearly evident in the world of artistic expression. Consider, for example, state-sanctioned Soviet art, controlled by thought police who insisted on purging it of any potentially complex metaphorical meaning and instead ordered rationally obvious depictions of what were thought to be worthy communitarian activities — a typical product is gigantic statuary of stylized tractor farmers raising well-muscled arms in gestures of victory. The literal message of a glorification of labour in the service of the state, and rigid controls placed by the state on the formal presentation of that message, preclude the possibility of subtlety, complexity, or alternative meanings. Those Soviet works have interest now as curious historical artifacts, but few people find in them the richness of insight and human feeling captured by less constrained artists, for example in the sculpture of Donatello, Michelangelo and other artists of the Italian Renaissance. Such artists may have often focused on religious themes, but this in no way diminished their metaphorical vision, as did Soviet censorship. State censorship condemned many of the imaginative works of the composer Shostakovich, while heralding the banal as appropriate expressions of the values of the state and people.

Literalists want art to convey a direct meaning or moral: art as an extension of rational thought. It is to be a logical exposition or demonstration of some specific element of the human condition, not an imaginative exploration of themes and the rich complexities inherent in it. But the latter, not the former, comes much closer to describing the true nature of art. This concept largely eludes the literalist, for art is not analysis or straightforward exposition; it is imaginative exploration. A poem is not an argument.

Shakespeare's plays have enriched human life as much as the work of any artist. His words, few of which are concerned with the hard facts that literalists seek, have immeasurably added to our language with their poetic expression and vivid illustration of the depth and complexity of human thought and feelings.

The moving words of Portia's speech to Shylock in *The Merchant of Venice*, to take just one example, illustrate the nature of mercy more eloquently and compellingly than any philosopher or psychologist has:

> *The quality of mercy is not strain'd.*
> *It droppeth as the gentle rain from heaven*
> *Upon the place beneath: it is twice blest;*
> *It blesseth him that gives and him that takes:*
> *'Tis mightiest in the mightiest: it becomes*
> *The throned monarch better than his crown;*
> *His sceptre shows the force of temporal power,*
> *The attribute to awe and majesty,*
> *Wherein doth sit the dread and fear of kings;*
> *But mercy is above this sceptr'd sway;*
> *It is enthroned in the hearts of kings,*
> *It is an attribute to God himself;*

Even the literal mind which objects to Portia's reference to God in the final line will surely be able to resonate with the humanity and compassion of the ideas in the figurative and beautiful language of this speech.

It is rare to see a production of one of Shakespeare's plays, particularly of the great tragedies *Macbeth, King Lear, Hamlet* and *Othello,* that does full justice to the words contained therein. Often directors will attempt to impose a single meaning on these complex texts — a particular 'interpretation' of the play — building on a logical analysis, drawing out a particular idea that can be elicited from the script. But such directors inevitably lose much in doing so. The tragedies are intricate works which, when done successfully, bring out the strongest feelings of recognition of our common humanity, with far more emotional complexity than could any essay on the topic. These plays, like great music or great art, inform us in a way that no logical exposition, or less accomplished work of imagination, could ever do. That most of the contemporary productions of the great tragedies are less than fully successful ought not to stop one from going to see them, for even in diminished form these productions convey some of the richness of the text. There are almost always moments of pleasure in hearing the words expressed in different ways, and almost always new feelings and insights aroused by even less than expert portrayal of the great artist's words. And when a production does more fully succeed it provides a deeply engaging and rare emotional human experience.

As a form involving almost all the arts — literature, theatre, music and the visual elements of stage and costume design, opera is a valuable illustration of the potential depth of a work whose literal significance — the text or libretto — may not be at all satisfying. Opera, an art form which has inspired passionate admiration since the 16th century, is on the surface often illogical, even silly: in a story being enacted on stage, the dramatic action generally halts while the actors (who often look nothing like the characters they represent) sing about their feelings and dilemmas, often in phrases repeated over and over. It is easy to make fun of opera, but to dismiss it because of its literal improbabilities is to miss out on a life-enhancing experience, a great human creation. Even accepting the basic premises of opera, however — that the drama will be conveyed through the music, both orchestral and sung by characters whose nature is conveyed by their voices rather than physique or physical acting ability, an overly literal response will limit our reaction to certain major operas in the standard repertoire.

Operas of the verissimo tradition like *La Boheme* and *La Traviata* have an immediate appeal: the stories are realistic, and the social and psychological context of the passions and problems undergone by the characters readily arouse a humanist's understanding and empathy. In operas based on a fairy-tale or fable tradition, however, like *Turandot* or *The Magic Flute*, viewers may have a hard time making literal sense of the hero's choices and actions, and thus finding meaning in the opera.

Why Calif should persist in courting the murderous Turandot, with her irrational aversion to men, while ignoring the generous, good-hearted Liu (who, given the relative demands of the singing parts, is usually much younger and slimmer than Turandot) makes almost no literal sense at all; only if the opera is seen as a fable, about the power of love, can its resolution have meaning.

Both of these operas are set in fantastic realms (any viewer of *Tur-andot* expecting it to be an historically-accurate depiction of life in ancient China will hastily be disabused), while *La Boheme* and *La Traviata* have specific social and historical settings, which prepare us to expect motivation and action of a realistic rather than primarily symbolic nature. Only by distinguishing between these different types of opera, and looking for a different kind of meaning, can we go beyond frustration at the literal inconsequence of works that deal with human emotion and human experience in a metaphorical, non-realistic way.

Shakespeare's plays and the great operas are all examples of the power of imaginative human expression, which asks of us, in response, to draw on all our resources of imagination, flexibility and openness, for a rich reward. We will now turn to some contemporary examples, two films, that relate to the issue we are targeting in this essay — the relationship of humanism to imaginative thinking and metaphorical expression, and the problem of literalism in the humanist movement.

❧

Is not the truth the truth?

— Falstaff in *Henry IV, Part 1*

In 2003 a documentary film, *Capturing the Friedmans* by director Andrew Jarecki, examined the puzzling case of the well-to-do Friedman family living in upper state New York in the 1980s. The father, Arnold, was a university professor who also taught computer classes for children at his home. Following the discovery of some child pornography in the home Arnold and one of his sons, Jesse, were arrested and convicted on charges of child abuse. The film, looking at the story from different perspectives, won the Grand Jury Prize at the Sundance Film Festival in 2003, and that same year was nominated for an Academy Award. The film was widely praised by critics, though not everyone was enthralled by it.

The film is remarkable for its illustration of the elusiveness of truth. Reminiscent of the Japanese fable that was made into the memorable

1950 film *Rashomon* by the great Japanese director Akiro Kurosawa, it shows how, even with plenty of witnesses, it is very difficult to ascertain exactly what has happened in certain complex human situations. It is about the hazards of certainty, and about how preconceptions can mislead us.

Chris Mooney is a leading skeptic in the United States, having written many articles for magazines such as the *Skeptical Inquirer* as well as books such as his powerful and effective attack on the Bush regime in *The Republican War on Science*. Mooney was one of those not so enthralled by this film. In a review of *Capturing the Friedmans* (CSICOP Online, *Doubt & About*, July 7, 2003) Mooney writes, "the director ignored his duty as a responsible documentarian to actually seek the truth." Mooney believes that this is an 'ethical' responsibility of documentarians. But is a documentary necessarily different from, say, a poem, in which the search for truth is undertaken in a figurative or metaphorical sense? Suppose a person making a documentary is seeking truth through lyrical and poetic images, as in the classic *Man of Arran*, rather than detailing a succession of facts? Is such a film-maker unethical? And is it not the case that such film artists, if they are good at what they do, can convey a greater sense of the complexities of reality than might a strictly explicit description and analysis?

A documentary can simply be a literal exposition, as close to the facts as possible, or it can be something more expansive or speculative. But it reaches its highest levels as art not, as Mooney wants to think, when it is simply explicit. Rather, documentary is at its best when it causes us to think more broadly about general implications, and to ponder more deeply about the complexity of life, and to feel more sympathetic to those who are different from us, and to gain insights and feelings about the shared human experience. To achieve this, a documentary maker cannot simply 'tell' people what to think, anymore than a teacher can really help students by telling them what to think. Both, at their best, work in subtler ways.

Mooney misunderstands the purpose of *Capturing the Friedmans*, which is metaphorical rather than explicit. Seeking actual truth (or someone's stab at such truth) certainly can be a worthy goal, and a film about the Friedmans could have simply made a case for their innocence, or for that matter of their guilt. Mooney is convinced of their innocence, but the case is not so clear as he would have it. He dismisses Jarecki's balanced presentation of the evidence as "postmodern ambiguity," based on the probability that much of the evidence against the Friedmans was the result of hysteria that was rampant in the 80s about organized groups of pedophiles. There were indeed many victims then of such hysteria. Were the Friedmans such victims? Mooney is sure of this, though the Friedmans did admit guilt and Arnold was a previously-convicted pedophile.

"Is not the truth the truth?" Falstaff, when he said this, was not so naïve as the literal meaning of this phrase would suggest. He was mocking the supposed truthfulness and false honour of those of higher station who cloaked their bad actions in noble words. Mooney in effect says that the truth is the truth and ought to expressed — but without Falstaff's sense of irony. It is as if naked truth is obvious and is all that matters.

But Jarecki was after bigger things than a simple attempt at exposing the truth. Instead he chose to demonstrate something of the capricious nature of human life, and of the difficulties we all have in deciding what to believe, and about the elusiveness of final truth. While Mooney dismisses a comparison, drawn by the *New Yorker*'s David Denby, with *Rashomon*, the comparison is apt. One may be based upon a fable, the other on a real event, but they both explore the same troubling, intriguing, important subject: how different people have different recollections and understandings of things that have happened to them.

Mooney excoriates Jarecki for not having the courage to state where he stands, and accuses him of using the uncertainty for promotional purposes. Jarecki's defense is elegantly stated in a quote of his in the last paragraph of Mooney's review:

What I would like is that people leave and say, 'you know, I've seen a lot of films where at the end, I'm supposed to think something. And here, I'm not supposed to think something. I'm just supposed to think.' That is my hope.

Mooney says this is the easy way out. But as any good teacher knows, leading people to think is really the hard way out. Teaching is not telling.

As Mooney admits, many people did come away from the film with a strong suspicion that the Friedmans were innocent. If they did so they likely had a much more considered and thoughtful assessment of this than if the documentary had simply made a case for their innocence.

Telling students what to know and what to think, instead of leading them to think, is an all-too-common predilection of teachers. It is too common as well in the humanist movement. Mooney, though he is a very bright and accomplished man, limits the value of some of his work by aggressive certainty regarding truth. Ambiguity is more than a post-modern fetish; its recognition is the first step beyond literalism.

Many films, and virtually all the best films, have a metaphorical aspect to them. The 2013 film *All is Lost* lends itself to both a literal and a metaphorical response. On the screen we see Robert Redford, sailing alone in the Indian Ocean, awakened by his yacht striking the corner of a huge steel container adrift at sea. As he tries to repair the gash in his yacht, he is overturned in a tropical storm, and eventually has to hurry onto his life raft and leave his provisions and technological aids behind. The elderly sailor (the only character in the film) becomes dependent on ancient aids — a sextant and charts, and finally the most primitive tools — a fishing line and hook, a message sealed in a bottle.

The film is interesting enough on a literal level as we admire the sailor's resourcefulness and courage, and wonder at the final scene in which he swims up from the depths to clasp the outstretched hand of an apparent rescuer. But one might ask, as I heard one puzzled film-goer say as she left, "What was that all about?" As metaphors, the events and images of the film are much more intriguing. A solitary man in a boat is a resonant image in itself, suggesting the voyage of life that inevitably leads to death and absorption into the infinite. The absurdity of the presence of the container floating far out at sea recalls both the way our society is "fouling the nest" of our environment, and the bleak, inarguable facts of illness or accident which befall us unpredictably, without any evident reason or justice.

As the sailor is gradually stripped of all the equipment he has so carefully provided and skillfully uses, he embodies King Lear's desperate vision of man as a "bare, forked animal," helpless against the elements of nature. In the powerful images near the end of the film, the round raft bobbing in a vast featureless ocean is echoed by the shapes of a full moon, and a school of fish circling beneath. These round shapes emphasize the elemental process the sailor in experiencing, bereft of his technological aids and returning in death to nature. Is the final sight of a hand reaching out to grasp the drowning sailor's hand an actual rescue, or a wish-fulfilling hallucination accompanying his death, or an ironic recollection of the human contact he had avoided in choosing to make this solitary journey?

While the film may appeal on a literal level as an adventure/survival story, it is much more interesting and thought-provoking when some of its powerful visual images are explored for their philosophical resonance.

❧

Whenever religious beliefs conflict with scientific facts or violate principles of political liberty, we must respond with appropriate aplomb. Nevertheless, we should be cautious about irrational exuberance… If it is our goal to raise people's consciousness to the wonders of science and the power of reason, then we must apply science and reason to our own actions. It is irrational to take a hostile or condescending attitude toward religion because by doing so we virtually guarantee that religious people will respond in kind. As Carl Sagan cautioned in 'The Burden of Skepticism,' a 1987 lecture, "You can get into a habit of thought in which you enjoy making fun of all those other people who don't see things as clearly as you do. We have to guard carefully against it."

— Michael Shermer, *Scientific American*, September 2007

The themes of *Rashomon* and *Capturing the Friedmans* — unwarranted certainty and the elusiveness of truth — are of considerable relevance to the humanist movement in North America, and to the sometimes strident certainty with which humanists express their views. Unwarranted certainty is the bugbear of irrational belief. It is relatively harmless to hold irrational beliefs (as everyone does) so long as those beliefs are not held with unwavering and committed certainty. It is likely that beliefs are natural to humans and probably have survival value. But we know, now, or ought to know, that absolute certainty is an intellectual error. That is one of the central lessons of science, but art too helps us understand this crucial point.

Films such as those discussed above remind us of this point. Seeing the difficulty of knowing what actually happened in a relatively straightforward set of circumstances should give one pause when considering such questions as the meaning of life and the existence of God. The presence of any supernatural being seems highly unlikely, to be sure, but aggressive expressions of atheistic certainty are not an effective way of persuading people to think more critically about such matters; expressing such certainty simply validates the acceptability of absolutist thinking. How do we, as humanists, make the point about rejecting absolute certainty, which of course leads to the justification of all sorts of abusive actions, if we ourselves reflect a similar attitude?

To be credible, and to be intellectually consistent, humanists must not exhibit the same sort of implacable certainty that many belief systems encourage.

Humanists are not always at ease in imagined worlds — worlds of metaphorical language. Humanists tend to prefer logical thinking; they like to find the right answer. They like to present sound, logical arguments that, alone, should be sufficient to persuade others to our way of thinking. Humanists, like Plato, are often leery of the dangers and imprecision of imagined worlds. And, because of this, they sometimes pursue our comfortable certainties with, as Michael Shermer puts it, an "irrational exuberance."

But human imagination, and its expressions in art, explores the ambiguity that is central to metaphorical thinking and which conveys, as much as it is possible to do so, the full depth of human experience. Art enriches our own lives and engenders empathy for the human condition. It is neither didactic nor necessarily explicit; rather it is indirect, working through images and allusions. It is by nature metaphorical, not literal.

If metaphors are dangerous things, so are most things of human value — honesty, food, love and sex come to mind. Humanists, too, can have their lives enriched by metaphorical thinking. The imagined world belongs to all of us.

❧

I'm not making fun of your friend, Madame, I assure you. I know how intelligent and learned he is. It's a question of 'doctrine.' This man who is so skeptical has grammatical certainties. Alas, Madame Straus, there are no certainties, even grammatical ones… Only that which bears the imprint of our choice, our taste, our uncertainty, our desire and our weakness can be beautiful.

—Marcel Proust, Letter to Mme Straus

The pure rationalist will likely have his or her facts straight, but may lose the deeper meaning those facts might otherwise illuminate: a sort of truth may emerge but it is likely to be a superficial, and not a 'beautiful' one. On the other hand, of course, the person who solely lives in the imagination will have no way of assessing a relationship to reality. The rationalist can count word frequencies in Shakespeare, but may have trouble seeing beyond the surface meaning of those words. The non-rationalist will see lots of meanings but may be unable to relate those meanings to any of the actualities of life.

Humanists — especially humanists, for they want to make the one life they will have, and the one world they will live in, as rich as possible — ought to embrace not only reason but the metaphorical meaning of Hamlet's words to Horatio — that logic is not all. There is more to life than is dreamt of by reason alone. ❧

HARRY POTTER
& THE HUMANISTS

by Gwyneth Evans

L ike JRR Tolkien's Middle Earth, the imagined world of JK
Rowling has become enormously important to the North
American public. The release of each new book in Rowling's
series was anticipated by both children and adults with a
fervour that marketing strategies alone cannot account for. Unlike
Middle Earth, which is a self-contained world separate from the real
world we know, the magical dimension inhabited by Harry Potter and
his fellow wizards coincides with and interpenetrates our everyday
world, and has been imagined so consistently and vividly that huge
numbers of readers, including many generally uninterested in literary
fantasy, are caught up in the stories, rereading them many times and
making their characters, events and places part of their own mental land-
scapes. Should humanists worry about this? Should we be troubled that
young people (let alone the adults) are absorbed in stories about problems and adventures in imaginary worlds, rather than soberly confronting the innumerable problems and tasks of our own, real, world? I think
not, for a number of reasons. For one thing, we can rejoice that books
of such appeal are not mere 'swords and sorcery' tales where the strongest and most cunning win out, but have as their deepest, and most
evident, values such essentially humanist qualities as integrity, loyalty,

compassion. Harry, like Tolkein's heroes, makes ethical choices which are neither popular nor easy.

A more fundamental concern, however, about the artist's creation of an imagined world, particularly in work aimed at young people, is whether or not such a creation deludes or deceives the reader. The literary genre of *fantasy* is sometimes confounded with the psychological, clinical idea of fantasy, involving self-deception or delusion. Nonetheless, it has often been observed that literary fantasy is less likely to deceive or mislead children about the nature of reality than overtly 'realistic' stories can do. The 'Once upon a time...' opening that leads the young child into a fairy tale signals that what follows bears a symbolic, rather than direct, relationship to the everyday world. The exaggerations, illogicalities and extravagances of fantasy announce that this is story — an invented world, not what one is to expect in everyday life. The realistic story, on the other hand, does lead readers to think that real life works in the same way, and so may more readily raise anxieties and false expectations. I doubt that any children have been injured by running at the rail station barrier trying to get to Platform 9 1/2 to catch the Hogwarts Express, or staked much on the hope that shouting one of magic words taught in the Hogwarts' Spells course would actually make anything disappear or mend itself.

In the first volume, Harry Potter discovers a world of magical beings and people with magical powers which exists alongside our ordinary world, but as such is clearly a world of make-believe and, especially in the earlier books, play. Beyond the excitement of the adventures, much of the delight of the books lies in their playful details such as the Weazleys' clock which has on its dial, in place of numbers, comments such as 'You're Late,' and the marvellous invented game of Quidditch with its object the capture of an erratic flying ball called the Golden Snitch. By clearly signaling that this is an imagined world, a world of play or make-believe, fantasies like the Harry Potter books do in fact help children distinguish between fiction and everyday reality. The psychological and thematic significance of the books is conveyed indirectly and symbolically, through adventures which involve exploration into unknown, sometimes forbidden, territories; discovery of secrets, especially those related to identity; combat in defense of one's friends and the vulnerable, and the recognition of who one's friends and enemies really are.

What the adventures and discoveries of Harry Potter do not involve is any revelation that the speculations and beliefs of psychics and religious people in the 'Muggle' (non-wizard) world in which we readers live, are actually true. Harry and his friends have no time at all for their vague and incompetent Divination teacher who deals in New-Age-style fortune-telling and prophecies. While styles and attitudes of the teachers, and pupils, at Hogwarts resemble those of any real-life school, with degrees of exaggeration appropriate to the preadolescent energy and humour of the story-telling, the fantastic elements of the school-building itself, with its disappearing stairways, magical banquets and talking portraits, and the curriculum of courses, in Potions, Charms, Transfiguration, and Herbology (taught by Professor Sprout), are sheer fun. Their relationship to our real, everyday world is that of invention, embroidery, play. Entering the world of the Harry Potter books invites suspension of disbelief, not belief — and that is an important distinction.

In *The Science of Harry Potter* (2002), Roger Highfield, Science Editor of *The Daily Telegraph* and popular explicator of scientific matters for the layperson, uses the Harry Potter books to look at 'how magic really works.' Covering a great range of topics, Highfield leaps lightly from one field of knowledge to another, as he relates recent discoveries in brain scanning to Hogwarts' Sorting Hat, in embryology to Hagrid's magical creatures (with a side trip into mythology), in nuclear fission to the Philosopher's Stone. As well as intriguing and amusing the adult reader, *The Science of Harry Potter* might prove a good way of drawing young readers of fantasy into an engagement with discoveries and competing theories in psychology, chemistry, zoology and physics in the real world. Rather than dismissing Rowling's fantasies as escapism, Highfield shows how their playful invention is not the foe of *real* knowledge and understanding of the world, but provides its own unique delight, related to though not the same as scientific understanding. ❧

THE RULE OF LAW

by Mike Matthews

Rules are rules, and rules are probably meant to be broken, but laws are things of iron. They feel good; it's great to know that horrible behaviour is against the law, and that the law can crack down on lawbreakers. Crack down! Get 'em Stevie! We can feel secure because there are laws in place. Providing they are in place, providing the final decree has been signed, and providing we wanted this deal in the first place.

Often we have little choice. First, last, and all our lifetime we encounter the Laws of Nature. This includes matters as immense as the movements and mutations of galaxies, and the physics, thermodynamics, and hydraulics of hurricanes. Such laws are often beyond our ken, and certainly beyond our defiance or dispute.

However, as important and as ever-present any Law of Nature is the Law of Nachos. You cannot put enough cheese on your nachos. No matter how much you put on. You grate what we call 'copious' amounts of cheddar cheese on your corn chips, and put them under the broiler for a few minutes. When the nachos come out of the oven, there is very little cheese on them. You put them back in the oven with more cheese grated on them. Guess what? They come out dry and bare again. The cheese slips away somehow, or it vaporizes, or cheese mites, thousands of those little invisible critters, get in there and make off with it.

A very bad law that we have here in BC is a regulation that comes into operation on the car decks of the BC Ferries. The regulation is generally stated as the Law of the BMW, and it requires that the car alarms of these up-market vehicles shall go whoop-whoop-whoop as soon as the ferry moves away from the dock and into deep water. This moronic noise pollution has been going on for years now, yet neither the ferry authority nor the federal government (via the Marine Act) have taken the appropriate action of simply banning these vehicles from the ferries in the first place, or arranging the appropriate resources — gangs of eight to ten husky sailors — to hoist the BMWs up off the deck and drop them overboard, whooping their wretched lungs out, into the waves.

Another vehicle law, simple but deadly, is one of the Rules of the Road. The law here mandates that the traffic light on the highway will change against you if you are trying to move along the highway briskly. As we all are, eh? So that traffic light, just by turning red whenever we approach it, will ensure that we can't build up any momentum, which in turn ensures that we cannot get anyplace anywhere near on time.

Once we do get there, wherever that may be, we encounter the Law of the Land. This law says that a piece of land, a property, real estate, is worth the price it can fetch, and not a penny-farthing more nor a pfennig less. Any time that a house price is quoted, it is simply and utterly a wild guess, nothing more. This law has lately had interesting applications, both in the lunatic south of our continent, and in our own country. Folks unable to manage their sub-prime mortgages have walked away from them, or slunk away, or melted away, thrown into vats at the glue factory perhaps. This was not the end of the business, for the lending companies, the banks, and the stock market have followed the folks into the tank. We don't know where this will end. We don't know if it will end. We are all giggling about this, but it is a nervous giggle.

Here, as so often, we are facing the Law of Unintended Consequences, which means that all sorts of miserable, horrible things that could not be expected, or even imagined, will happen. The usual way of expressing this idea is the succinct 'shit happens.' This does not mean that we live in an unpredictable universe. Rather, this law describes situations where a much closer look at what we are about might save us from grief, situations where intention and attention are at odds, where what we see, or do not see, is prompted by our heart instead of being governed by our head.

Above all, we must have room in our head for the Law of Large Numbers, sometimes called the Lore of Large Numbers. Understanding this law, these principles, means that we understand, accept and bow down before the brute fact of big things, big numbers and their crushing effect on littler things. It means recognizing that while it is true that the bigger they are the harder they fall, it is far more true that, as the coach told us, the smaller they are, the further they can be flung. The Law of Large Numbers means that you can't win.

Yes, laws sometimes go too far, far beyond natural sense. Among the commandments that Moses brought down from Mt Sinai were those forbidding us to steal or to kill. Yet those have turned out to be among our more favoured and frequent activities, killing especially.

We kill animals and eat them up, which perhaps is not unfair. Were the animals in command of the technology they might quite likely do the same to us, and as it is some of the larger animals, provoked or trapped or feeling out of sorts, will chase us and chew us. But we kill our own people, our own species, and we have done this, breaking the law of Jehovah or Yahweh, for some time. Yea, all the long time we have been here, according to the old books. Shakespeare's King Lear, speaking of his sons-in-law, had one wish: "Then kill, kill, kill, kill, kill, kill!"

And we do. We kill Scribes and Pharisees, Israelites and Muslims, Jews and Christians and Ammonites. We kill Africans and Asians and Europeans. We killed Saxons and Anglo-Saxons, Frenchmen and Scotsmen, Irish rebels, Wat Tyler's men. We killed Native people all over North America and South America. Americans, Canadians, and Mexicans, neighbours, killed one another in sallies back and forth across the borders of North America. We killed Germans and Italians in battles, and we dropped bombs on the civilians in their cities. We dropped nuclear bombs on Japan. Now we kill Afghans because they won't give up their traditional agricultural practices.

We kill individuals who displease or disobey us. We hung and gutted Ned Ludd and we swung Johnny Dillinger. We poisoned and gassed and electrocuted those deemed criminal. A young man, a religious leader who committed no more crime than riding a donkey without a licence was, according to the law of the time, whipped through the streets of his city with timbers loaded upon his back, then killed by hammering spikes through his hands and feet and thrusting a spear into him intercostally.

Nonetheless, our laws reiterate that old commandment, no killing. Dying, on the other hand, is readily available to us, providing we accomplish it in a manner that meets the approval of the father of the young man on the donkey. We must not seek to command or control the end of our lives. "The Almighty has fixed his cannon 'gainst self-slaughter," warned Hamlet. Professor Somerville assures us that with any release from existence that we consciously choose or arrange, "we lose the gravitas of death." Euthanasia, happy death — an offense against Nature.

We are to wait for disease, accident, misadventure, or the impersonal murders of war to carry us, gasping or screaming, out of this world. We are to go to our deaths without any preparation beyond prayer: "O Lord God Almighty, I pray to thee that the missile flying toward my dwelling, targeted at me and my family by modern weaponry, electronic guidance technology, shall change mid-flight to a bouquet, a posy, a fistful of forget-me-nots." We are, after all, skilled at prayer. "O Lord of Hosts, I beseech thee to make the pavement beneath, seventy stories below me, turn out to be, when I arrive at it, a cushioning billow of cloud in thine eternal heaven."

We are forbidden, by the law in some jurisdictions, to take our own deaths into our own hands, no matter how clearly and strongly we wish to die, no matter our bewilderment, desolation and pain. Nor may we, no matter the extremity of our agony, no matter how great the pity and the caring of those around us, be helped hence, be assisted on our way to the exit.

So says the law, a blind and cowardly law. Charles Dickens' Mr Bumble, in words about the law that are useful to remember, suggested that the law should have its eye opened. ❧

SCIENCE, GOD & PHILIP PULLMAN

by Gwyneth Evans

fter J K Rowling, Philip Pullman is probably the contemporary children's writer most widely read by adults as well as children. It wasn't too surprising when *The Amber Spyglass*, the third volume of Pullman's brilliant fantasy trilogy *His Dark Materials*, won the Whitbread Prize for the best children's book of 2001. The same year, however, it became the first children's book to win the Whitbread Book of the Year award in the adult category as well. With far more intellectual content than the *Harry Potter* books, and a more challenging, iconoclastic vision of life than Tolkien's *Lord of the Rings*, Pullman's literary fantasy offers its readers — whether younger or adult — a gripping story, an engaging central character who develops and changes through the series, and fascinating ideas about the nature of the world and the meaning of life. Among these ideas, science and the quest for knowledge through research play a prominent role.

Of contemporary children's writers, Pullman is also probably the most famous non-believer. Conservative columnist Peter Hitchens referred to him as "the most dangerous author in Britain, [the writer] the atheists would have been praying for, if atheists prayed." *The Amber Spyglass* contains an episode about the death of God — an old wizened figure known as the Authority who when freed from a cage of crystal dissolves, with relief, into the air. This is strong stuff for a children's book, but Pullman is outspoken and firm in his atheistic convictions. He has declared "I don't profess any religion; I don't think it's possible that there is a God." In *The Amber Spyglass*, a particle physicist and ex-nun named Mary Malone, tells how she "thought physics could be done to the glory of God, till I saw there wasn't any God at all and that physics was more interesting anyway. The Christian religion is a very powerful and convincing mistake, that's all."

There is no higher power in Pullman's trilogy who is going to solve people's problems and make the world right in the end — it is up to the two young characters themselves, with much help from their friends, to do what needs to be done, to create not the Kingdom but the Republic of Heaven, not in an afterlife but in the world around them. It is certainly no stretch then to claim Philip as a humanist writer. Early in the trilogy, however, the role of science is somewhat ambiguous. The scientific impulse to reach for further knowledge, through experiment and without deference to conventions and accepted belief, is in conflict with a controlling religious body known as the Magisterium. Furthermore, the scientific quest is also often in conflict with the humane values of compassion, loyalty and mercy. Whether serving the Church or operating in defiance of it, scientific pursuits are shown as sometimes heroic, but often morally ambiguous. This ambiguity is most marked in the first volume, *The Golden Compass*, and might almost lead a reader to think Pullman is anti-scientific as well as anti-religious. By the end of the trilogy, however, a deeper insight into the value and possibilities of science is powerfully conveyed.

Science fiction and its cousin literary fantasy have long been used to speculate about how changes in society might be brought about by technological development and the discoveries of experimental science. While often sounding a warning about what all this may lead to, speculative fiction generally presents scientists as problem-solvers as well as occasional troublemakers. In *The Golden Compass*, however, the pursuit of knowledge is carried out with notably arrogant inhumanity. The two major adult characters are, in opposition to each other, performing daring experiments to extend the boundaries of knowledge about human nature and human possibilities: both do so by sacrificing children. The grisly experiments performed by Mrs Coulter's research team in the far North violently separate children from their companion-souls or daemons, leaving them lost and dissociated like the victims of lobotomies or electro-shock therapy gone wrong. The other scientist, the brilliant Lord Asriel, deliberately kills his daughter's child friend to further his own quest for knowledge of the universe. Asriel's choice is Faustian: he knows he transgresses, but his desire for scientific understanding, which will give him the power to create a new, free society, overcomes all other considerations. In this he differs from Mrs Coulter, whose work is controlled by the Church or Magisterium, which Asriel defies.

Asriel: Allow it? We've gone beyond being allowed, as if we were children.

Mrs Coulter: They'll forbid it. They'll seal it off and excommunicate anyone who tries!

Asriel: Too many people will want to. They won't be able to prevent them. This will mean the end of the Church, Marisa, the end of the Magisterium, the end of all those centuries of darkness! Look at that light up there: that's the sun of another world! ... No one in the world knows better than I how strong the Church is! But it isn't strong enough for this.

Asriel's ruthless intelligence enables him to discover and travel to the other worlds which exist parallel to our own: *The Golden Compass* itself takes place in another of those worlds, which resembles our own in most respects but with some engaging differences. In this alternate world, science as we know it is called experimental theology, carried out with 'philosophical apparatus' housed in a building called the chapel; electricity is called anbaric power, and people travel by zeppelin. While much of human history has developed as ours did, the Church did not split apart at the Reformation; rather, Pope John Calvin moved the papacy to Geneva, and set up a Consistorial Court of Discipline which gave the Church absolute power over every aspect of life. At the beginning of the trilogy, scientists and explorers have posited the existence of the other worlds, material and sinful like ours (and theirs) rather than the spiritual heaven and hell of Church teaching, and the Church bitterly opposes the effort to learn more about those worlds. Lyra, the young hero, is drawn from her carefree, haphazard life into the dangerous scientific quests of both Mrs Coulter and Lord Asriel, but as she learns more about them during her dramatic adventures in the far North, she distances herself from both of them and engages in her own quest, which is motivated by loyalty and the desire to help and rescue, rather than by the longing for knowledge for its own sake.

The Subtle Knife, the second volume, begins in our own world with the pursuit of young Will by mysterious, threatening men searching for papers left by Will's father, who died while engaged in Arctic exploration. In his desperation, Will comes upon a knife which enables him to cut through to another world — a third world, in which he meets Lyra and joins with her. Prophecies, and the vicious energy with which both young people are pursued by their enemies who represent powerful institutions in both worlds, tell us that the quest of Lyra and Will for true knowledge and right action is of enormous importance to all life, but not easily discerned or achieved.

The somewhat malign image of science in *The Golden Compass* is erased in the second, and particularly the third volumes, through the character of the physicist Dr Mary Malone. Uninterested in gaining power for her own ends, Mary is a scientist who loves and is fascinated by the physical world. In several different scenes Pullman shows Mary patiently experimenting, using her scientific knowledge and experience to understand and work with things in a new, strange world. Faced with an utterly new phenomenon, Mary:

> ... laid the thing down and thought about the way this world had evolved. If her guess about these universes was right, and they were the multiple worlds predicted by quantum theory, then some of them would have split off from her own much earlier than others. And clearly in this world evolution had favoured enormous trees and large creatures with a diamond-framed skeleton.
> She was beginning to see how narrow her scientific horizons were.

> *No botany, no geology, no biology of any sort — she was as ignor-*
> *ant as a baby.*

Of course, Mary is not ignorant. Her discoveries, though less dramatic than those of Mrs Coulter and Lord Asriel in the first book, are meaningful and useful. Open-mindedness and experimentation enable her to communicate with an unfamiliar race of beings, to build an observation platform on an immensely tall tree, and to create the amber spyglass which helps to bring about the resolution of Will and Lyra's quest. Pullman shows her thinking like a scientist — putting forth different solutions to a question, thinking them through, relating the problem to something known and familiar.

Pullman's treatment of science in *His Dark Materials* trilogy is complex, and coloured by a deeply moral concern with right action towards other people and the consequences of our individual desires, particularly those for knowledge and power. Science in the first volume is misused, or irresponsibly pursued, in opposition to humane values of justice and compassion, by two prominent scientists who sacrifice other people in their own arrogant search for knowledge. Both of these characters, however, do change in the course of the trilogy, and eventually act selflessly, in a crisis resulting from their earlier dangerous experiments. Whether attained by the morally deplorable or by the admirable characters, knowledge is a value in itself, and it is through understanding as well as through courage and loyalty that the resolution is reached. In the more than one thousand pages of his trilogy, Pullman combines thrilling adventure with a sophisticated speculative approach to moral and philosophical issues, turning the traditional genre of fantasy fiction to a strongly humanist purpose. ❧

PART 7

HUMANISM AS A LIFE STANCE

Humanism is a life stance aiming at the maximum possible fulfillment through the cultivation of ethical and creative living and offers an ethical and rational means of addressing the challenges of our times. Humanism can be a way of life for everyone everywhere.

Modern Humanism

by Theo Meijer

For the last few thousand years people in the West have taken two basic approaches to explain our universe and everything in it. The prevailing proposition was and is that all of nature is so complex that there must have been an external, extra-terrestrial or supernatural entity — a God — that, for some reason, created it all. This 'dualist' concept that there must be something outside natural processes seems deeply ingrained in the human psyche. Even people who are not particularly religious sometimes express dual-istic feelings. Most major religions promote this dualist perspective.

Of course, such a perspective raises the question that if God created all, then who or what created God? The answer is generally that God is eternal and always was and will be. Another reasonable question is: why do bad things happen to good people? The answer to that generally refers to God's plan, though no one has any idea what such a plan might be and why it would have to involve undeserved suffering. Neither of these answers is very plausible or satisfying.

Consequently, concurrently with the dualist vision, the proposition persisted that nature and natural events always were and will be; hence there is no need for a supernatural intermediary. This 'monist' position has been on the margins but it has persisted all along and it is now widely held by freethinkers, agnostics and atheists. It is a foundation of modern humanism.

Inherent in the monist approach is the scientific hypothesis of evolution as the driving force of all living things. Through random mutations and natural selection all life, including human life, has evolved to its contemporary form without purposeful design and over a very long period of time.

Another basic element of the monist approach is the recognition of our unique position as human beings on this earth. Humanists are sometimes accused of being so preoccupied with this idea that they neglect other life forms and the environment. To the contrary, it is precisely because of our concern about humans that we realize how much we are a part of the web of life and how much we depend on our interaction with other life forms. Nevertheless it would seem that only the human brain has evolved to allow for introspection and the awareness of our own mortality.

This self-awareness manifests itself in a number of ways. Driven by natural curiosity we developed the scientific process to gain better insights into our environment and ourselves. Unlike knowledge through revelation, the scientific process is self-correcting. Although some scientists may falsify data or distort results, the process as a whole will ultimately correct its own deficiencies and provide us with our best understanding.

We are also capable of creating things of lasting beauty. It is true that our aggressive energy has led to massive destruction, murder and mayhem in our history to date. But that same innate energy has also been channelled into the architecture of memorable buildings, the writing of great literature, the creation of wonderful art, and the composition of stirring music.

Another aspect of our unique stature as humans is the inclination to judge our own human behaviour. We have gained a sense of morality and have indeed articulated codes of conduct to determine which actions are perceived to advance human interests and which behaviours are thought to undermine them.

There are a number of ways in which the concept of evolutionary naturalism, the recognition of our uniqueness as human beings and our sense of morality affect our daily lives as modern humanists. One concerns our attitude toward mortality. There are many people who believe that they have lived before. Under hypnosis some seem capable of remembering aspects of such previous existence. Even more people believe that our life on this earth is merely a transient experience on the way to a more exalted place after we die.

However strongly people may believe any of this, it must nevertheless be conceded that there is no credible evidence for it and it therefore remains mere speculation. As modern humanists we may find such speculation interesting but we prefer to deal with what we reasonably do know, which is that we live here and now.

Another way our lives are affected by being humanists is in our understanding of the meaning of life. For a religious person meaning presumably comes from serving God and carrying out His perceived purpose on Earth. For a modern humanist the universe and life on this Earth do not have any meaning in and of themselves. Instead, meaning derives from how we live our lives and from how we interact with others — immediate family, friends, neighbours, community and in ever widening circles to all of humanity.

When we enjoy a piece of literature or music or admire a beautiful painting created many centuries ago, we can certainly acknowledge that the lives of the originators were profoundly meaningful to us. Although most of us do not possess the exceptional talents that would allow us to leave such lasting legacies, we can all act within the scope of our given situation and make positive contributions that will infuse our lives with meaning.

A further concern is morality. Religious people sometimes claim that one cannot behave morally without belief in a supernatural being. Clearly that is wrong. There have always been bad people doing bad things and good people doing good things; some of each are religious, some of each are not. Sometimes a strong religious belief, rather than encouraging goodness, can persuade a good person to do bad things. One cannot help but wonder if the people who tortured the victims of the Inquisition or the witch hunts felt some serious misgivings about their infliction of such cruelty on their fellow humans. If they did, it must have been their religious conviction of saving souls that helped them overcome any conscientious objections.

For religious people moral behaviour may be relatively straightforward as a matter of following rigid and distinct imperatives, articulated in holy books such as the Bible or the Koran. Unfortunately such directives as the Ten Commandments originated thousands of years ago among nomads roaming the desert under circumstances that have little relation to modern life. As a result they are arguably of little real help in determining proper moral behaviour now.

Modern humanism rejects any such rules, arbitrarily derived from supernatural sources, and instead firmly supports the idea that morality must be grounded in the human experience to be valid. To arrive at a credible position in regard to any moral action, humanists take a number of matters into account. First would likely be the Golden Rule, concisely articulated as "doing as you would be done by." However that would not be sufficient, so another consideration would be the idea of utilitarianism, often defined as "the greatest good to the greatest number." A further aspect would be the careful consideration of the consequences of any action and how it may affect others.

All these considerations must then be filtered through reason, leading to the question of whether or not the contemplated action makes any sense. The result of such deliberation is more likely to enhance human well being and diminish human suffering. This is surely a much more responsible, rewarding and humanly satisfying way to behave than aligning oneself with believers in dated dogma.

The modern humanist, then, is someone who goes through life without any invisible means of support. ✿

In Defense of
Forthright Atheism

by Bryson Brown

Religion is regarded by the common as true,
by the wise as false, and by the rulers as useful.

— Lucius Annaeus Seneca

Over the past few years several widely-discussed books have criticized religious belief as irrational. Among them, Richard Dawkins' *The God Delusion,* Daniel Dennett's *Breaking the Spell: Religion as a Natural Phenomenon,* Sam Harris' *The End of Faith* and Christopher Hitchens' *God is not Great: How Religion Poisons Everything* all made the best-sellers lists. All four authors focused on the dark side of religion, including the disturbing, morally dubious and often frighteningly violent prescriptions that many religious texts present for dealing with transgressions and apostasy, the use of religious faith as a dividing principle that often helps to create and sustain confrontation between members of different faiths and the conflict between many specific religious beliefs and a scientific world view. However, reviewers have objected vigorously to the 'new atheism' movement. Its proponents are regularly accused of being strident, unfair to religion and offensive to believers. There are more critics of the new atheism than I can list here; Terry Eagleton, Christopher Hedges, Alister McGrath, Madeline Bunting, Roger Scruton, Marilynne Robinson and Julian Baggini are just a few contributors to the genre.

There is a notable bias in the treatment these issues have received in the press. Both left-leaning and centrist press outlets, including *Salon*, the *Manchester Guardian* and Canada's own *Globe & Mail*, have regularly recruited representatives of the anti-Dawkins brigade to review books by the new atheists. Oddly, however, critics of the new atheists, including Eagleton and Hedges, have regularly been reviewed by enthusiastic supporters. This unbalanced editorial policy has tilted the tables and helped produce a widespread impression that the new atheists are the secular equivalent of religious extremists and hucksters, worthy only of derision and dismissal even by humanists who agree with their atheism and their concerns about the dark side of religion.

Many negative reviews of Dawkins have also been strikingly passionate. All too often, they are downright vitriolic. Dawkins' scholarship is dismissed, his arguments distorted and mocked and his common-sense defense of a special epistemic status for science is rejected on grounds that lead, in the end, either to radical relativism or to complete scepticism. In the *London Review of Books*, Terry Eagleton opens his review with the following comparison: "Imagine someone holding forth on biology whose only knowledge of the subject is the *Book of British Birds*, and you have a rough idea of what it feels like to read Richard Dawkins on theology." This is both inaccurate — whether you agree with his arguments or not, Dawkins examines a wide range of theological arguments central to the monotheistic tradition — and ironic, since what Eagleton presents as Christian theology is a strained and paradoxical metaphysics so far removed from traditional doctrines of Christianity as to be unrecognizable to anyone but a contemporary fan of a particularly incomprehensible and often deliberately paradoxical form of theological reflection.

The uncompromising enlightenment perspective Dawkins adopts is treated as a terrible threat by these reviewers. It seems that the expression of a straightforward atheism is unacceptable unless it bows systematically to the many splendours of philosophical theology. But, to be blunt, such theologies have very little to do with the everyday beliefs of everyday believers. Those who find Dawkins' vigorous arguments threatening really should spend some time thinking about the difference between arguing against a view (the sort of activity sanctioned by the enlightenment principle of free speech) and demonizing it (as the infamous *Left Behind* series demonizes those who don't 'find Jesus' while eagerly fantasizing our extermination and condemnation to hell). Dawkins has every reason to challenge the religious on this point: though one can always privilege 'good' expressions of religion and set aside extremism and blood-thirstiness as untrue to the 'real' tradition, this quickly becomes an exercise in arbitrary picking and choosing. The contributions of central figures of the Christian tradition, notably including Augustine, to the doctrine of an eternal Hell (not to mention the ex-communication and condemnation of his more generous predecessor Origen, for whom an eternal hell could not be reconciled with God's infinite power and goodness) makes the separation of 'good, true' Christianity from all the bad things Christians and Christian theologians have done and said historically dubious at best.

What we find in these intensely hostile reviews of Dawkins is the fading echo of a long effort to suppress atheism, and especially to suppress its public expression. Throughout the enlightenment the charge of atheism was tossed about; many of the great early modern philosophers were targets of such accusations. Hobbes, Spinoza and even Leibniz (who actually applied his metaphysics to give an account of transubstantiation) were all suspect. The great 18th century Scottish philosopher David Hume was never granted a university post, largely due to (rather more justified) suspicions that he was an atheist. In the early years of the twentieth century, the greatest American writer of his day wrote of his latest work, "This book will never be published....in fact, it couldn't be, because it would be a felony." The writer was Mark Twain; the book was *Letters from the Earth*, a devastatingly funny satirical critique of religion written in 1909 and finally published only in 1962.

While homosexuality, once the 'sin that dare not speak its name', has come out of the closet to win general acceptance from the wider society (religious extremists excluded), open atheism continues to be unwelcome in polite company. I believe it's time for forthright atheists to claim their place and turn the tables on those who continue to insist they keep their inconvenient and disturbing views to themselves.

To keep the discussion here manageable, I'll be focusing on just a few of the many very negative responses to Dawkins' *The God Delusion*. But what I have to say applies, mutatis mutandis, to many similar criticisms of Dawkins, as well as Hitchens, Harris and other forthright atheists.

First, let's examine Terry Eagleton's hostile review of *The God Delusion*. After an opening rhetorical salvo against Dawkins, Eagleton sets out what he regards as the mainstream theological position: "For Judeo-Christianity, God is not a person in the sense that Al Gore arguably is. Nor is he a principle, an entity, or 'existent': in one sense of that word, it would be perfectly coherent for religious types to claim that God does not in fact exist. He is, rather, the condition of possibility of any entity whatsoever, including ourselves. He is the answer to why there is something rather than nothing." Further, this non-entity 'sustains all things in being by his love' (and, notably, bears a personal and fully traditional male pronoun). Still more opaquely, Eagleton declares, "to say that he brought it into being ex nihilo is not a measure of how very clever he is, but to suggest that he did it out of love rather than need," and, in a slight against Dawkins' own scientific cleverness, declares, "God is an artist who did it for the sheer love or hell of it, not a scientist at work on a magnificently rational design that will impress his research grant body no end."

Eagleton claims that these views are standard issue, declaring 'Dawkins… understands nothing of these traditional doctrines'. But whose Judeo-Christianity (other than Eagleton's) is this? We are a very long way from the Nicene creed here — in fact, to be honest about it, we are far off in the wooly land of pseudo-philosophical paradoxes. The entire universe is the act of a non-existent person who merely constitutes the possibility of anything at all existing? A non-existent what's-it explains why there is something rather than nothing? I'm surely not the only one who thinks we are better off with no explanation at all, or who suspects that this display of linguistic legerdemain is a transparent attempt to distract attention from the fact that in the neighbourhood of the word

'God' all the rules of sense-making and explanation have been suddenly suspended. Yet Eagleton claims that Dawkins is remiss for not making this theological mares' nest his focus. I wonder how many members of mainstream Judeo-Christian communities would recognize this list of claims as an expression of their faith.

Startlingly, Eagleton admits "it may well be that all this is no more plausible than the tooth fairy," which seems to concede Dawkins' point. But he goes on to insist that the critics of theology "have a moral obligation to confront that case at its most persuasive... the mainstream theology I have just outlined may well not be true; but anyone who holds it is in my view to be respected, whereas Dawkins considers that no religious belief... is worthy of any respect whatsoever."

What's unclear about this demand for respect is just what Eagleton wants Dawkins to respect. Is it the moral engagement Eagleton describes, when he says that "The central doctrine of Christianity... is... that if you don't love, you're dead, and if you do, they'll kill you?" As a poetic expression of the human condition, this is a bit limited but not all bad: a rich engagement with the human condition that made this doctrine central could be perfectly respectable, if a bit dark in tone. But this is not Dawkins' target; if this is what Eagleton wants Dawkins to respect, he has nothing to complain about in *The God Delusion*. So is Eagleton instead demanding respect for religion's efforts to connect the wildly metaphysical idea of an all-powerful person called 'God', who makes an essential contribution to the existence of everything around us, with the idea of a person whom we should worship? This is clearly what Dawkins has called into question. But Eagleton himself doesn't believe this. So on what grounds would Eagleton make this demand for respect? Dawkins can respect people who believe, and respect their moral engagement with important problems, without respecting such beliefs, which he rightly sees as confused and unhelpful.

Eagleton assumes that Dawkins' brief suggestion, in a book not primarily about cosmology, that the fine-tuning problem might be answered by appeal to multiple universes, is intended as a 'scientific rebuttal' of religious responses to fine-tuning. But here Dawkins is merely mentioning one simple, non-theological response to a question that some theists appeal to God to answer. There are many apparently independent features of the universe which all need to turn out in particular ways for the existence of beings like ourselves to be possible. Some theists claim God's deliberate choice of the requisite values is the best explanation of this fact. But the alternative idea of multiple universes has the virtue of positing nothing beyond the kinds of things (natural universes) we already understand how to describe. Further, the idea that there are many universes fits quite well with our understanding of physics. Eagleton prefers to invoke just one thing, i.e. God. But God is another kind of thing altogether, and, as we've seen, a very puzzling sort of thing. For now both these explanations are mere gap-fillers, but at least Dawkins' gap-filler has the potential to be empirically tested, as we refine our grasp of the foundations of physics. By contrast, it's hard to imagine how we could test the link between Eagleton's vaguely specified 'ground of possibility' and the general physical conditions required for life to exist in the universe. Of course Eagleton could simply stipulate such a link — but then his sophisticated theology would depend just as much on made-up suppositions as the fundamentalist religions he rejects.

Eagleton is sure that Dawkins has many further faults as well. He is disappointed that, while Dawkins "quite rightly detests fundamentalists," he doesn't express the same disgust for global capitalism, which "generates the hatred, anxiety, insecurity and sense of humiliation that breed fundamentalism." Of course these unattractive aspects of fundamentalism precede capitalism: just consider Martin Luther's *Of the Jews & Their Lies*. So, on reflection, other socio-political arrangements also seem able to induce fanatical and destructive forms of religious belief. Perhaps even religion itself has some tendencies that deserve examination on this point — but Eagleton, of course, will not consider this possibility; that would be to agree with one of Dawkins' main points. It's also worth pointing out that, despite Eagleton's assumption to the contrary, Dawkins has indeed criticized our current political and economic arrangements, for instance in an article written for an anti-war collection titled *Not one more death*.

Finally, with respect to proper scholarly standards, I wonder whether any serious historian would pronounce as definitely on the reasons for Jesus' execution as Eagleton does when he declares, "Jesus did not die because he was mad or masochistic, but because the Roman state and its assorted local lackeys and running dogs took fright at his message of love, mercy and justice, as well as at his enormous popularity with the poor, and did away with him to forestall a mass uprising in a highly volatile political situation." This is exactly the kind of evidentiary over-reach that makes any reasonably skeptical person dubious about religious beliefs.

Throughout his review Eagleton pretends to be speaking from a vastly superior intellectual stand; he also seems confident of having a morally superior worldview. But his treatment of Dawkins is sloppy, unfair and absurdly hostile. It's clear that Eagleton's temper has got the better of him; when confronted with a clear mind, his hectoring, moralizing tone is nothing short of comedic.

Like Eagleton, Christopher Hedges portrays Dawkins as the mirror image of a religious fundamentalist. According to Hedges, Dawkins is a 'secular utopian,' one of a group who, like religious fundamentalists, has "forgotten they are human. Both they and religious fundamentalists peddle absolutes. Those who do not see as they see, speak as they speak and act as they act are worthy only of conversion or eradication." But Hedges makes no effort to justify this charge with any quotations from Dawkins. And, though he does present a harsh citation from Sam Harris, a much more enthusiastic proponent of the 'global war on terror', even Harris' words do not come close to the absolutist view Hedges attributes to him.

Hedges' defense of faith and the monotheistic tradition insists on a historical claim that needs as much faith as any religion: Hedges credits the tradition of individualism, individual responsibility and altruism in the monotheistic religions for the separation of church and state, as well as the Kantian injunction to treat others as ends in themselves rather than as means, and for broad recognition of the need for limits on the power and authority of powerful authorities. Here Hedges seems to be ignorant of many relevant facts, including the common traditions in hunter-gatherer societies of enforced sharing and of mocking the successful and influential: efforts to limit the power of the powerful and to undermine the effects of social rank with humour and criticism are human universals, not the exclusive inventions of monotheism. Worse, this claim of Hedges demands that we set aside the long history of oppression and brutality that is also part of the monotheistic tradition, from Old Testament blood baths and genocide through witch hunts to anti-Semitism, pogroms, colonial exploitation and present-day child-abuse.

So what are the beliefs that Hedges is so concerned to defend from Dawkins' irreverent attacks? Here is what Hedges had to say about them on one occasion: "God is a human concept. God is the name we give to our belief that life has meaning, one that transcends the world's chaos, randomness and cruelty. To argue about whether God exists or does not exist is futile. The question is not whether God exists. The question is whether we concern ourselves with, or are utterly indifferent to, the sanctity and ultimate transcendence of human existence. God is that mysterious force — and you can give it many names as other religions do — which works upon us and through us to seek and achieve truth, beauty and goodness. God is perhaps best understood as our ultimate concern, that in which we should place our highest hopes, confidence and trust. In Exodus God says, by way of identification, 'I am that I am.' It is probably more accurately translated: 'I will be what I will be.' God is better understood as verb rather than a noun. God is not an asserted existence but a process accomplishing itself. And God is inescapable. It is the life force that sustains, transforms and defines all existence."

Speaking just for myself, I have no idea what this means. Concern for life and truth and beauty are things that Professor Dawkins clearly shares with Hedges, as do I. Neither Dawkins nor I associate that concern with belief in a supernatural person, and I'm not sure whether Hedges does either. The evidence seems to suggest not. As for a "life force that sustains, transforms and defines all existence," if there were some account of the kind of sustenance, transformation and definition in question, I might have some notion of what Hedges means by this phrase. Lastly, I'm not at all sure what to make of Hedge's grammatical point: after all, nouns are just as appropriate, grammatically, for processes, such as evolution, as they are for things.

Hedges has a rather dark view of human nature; he is dubious about progress, and sharply critical of anyone who dares to hope that we might improve things in this world; such hopes, for Hedges, are proof of utopianism and a denial of the human condition, of sin itself.

Nevertheless, and despite our many failings, the societies of the first world today produce and distribute enough food and clean water and have learned enough about the causes and cures of disease to ensure that the vast majority of children survive to adulthood, while receiving a basic education along the way — an accomplishment unprecedented in human history. Furthermore, the rule of law, imperfect as it is, provides both security and freedom to most members of these societies, including even freedom to oppose the party in power and to advocate fundamental social reorganization. These things seem like progress to me — and they seem more closely tied to the rationalist ideals of the enlightenment than to an ancient religious tradition with no exclusive claim to these ideals, a tradition which includes many counter-currents running against them within its own, morally dubious history.

Whether we can maintain and extend these accomplishments remains an open question — and though Dawkins is clearly an optimist, there is nothing in *The God Delusion* that says otherwise. We are already testing the limits of our resources and our planetary environment. The human condition is complex and often tragic. But Dawkins is right to say that science is the best source of answers to our questions about the world. Sources that don't meet the standards of science provide material for speculation at best, not answers we can rely on.

Modesty is required — science can go wrong, the answers it gives always need further refinement, and it certainly has limits, as Dawkins himself has explicitly acknowledged. But well-established science is as close to certainty as we can get, and the 'answers' to deep questions offered by other sources require a very different order of modesty. If we have any well-founded hope of meeting the challenges before us and improving the human condition, our choices must be guided by science, as well as careful reflection on our values and aims (which are normative matters that science simply does not address).

In the end I think the reason Eagleton, Hedges and many other reviewers object so strongly to *The God Delusion* is not that Dawkins' case isn't a good one. The book is written for a much broader audience than an academic treatment of the subject would be; by necessity, it does not focus on careful academic details and subtleties. Nevertheless,

Dawkins' challenge to religion is clear and articulate, and fair ball in the arena of public discussion. The real reason for the outrage is that an articulate and assertive atheist with a pretty big soapbox to stand on has dared to come out before the public and challenge conventional religious beliefs. The religious beliefs Dawkins has challenged aren't even held by these reviewers: what the reviewers believe is something far from the familiar tenets of Christianity or any other religion — the obscure product of a definitional retreat that has led them to a mere 'ground of possibility', or perhaps even to an apophatic God about whom one can only say what he is not (surely a desperate last resort for theology). This is a God for which worship makes no sense, a God that could not be any kind of person, let alone one born to a virgin and resurrected after a brutal execution.

It's striking that these figures are so intent on criticizing the new atheists, and Dawkins in particular. They have far more direct and clear disagreements with fundamentalist and even moderately literal-minded forms of religion, and these forms of religion dominate most public discussions of religion, especially in North America. Clearly for Eagleton and Hedges, these literalist beliefs grossly distort tenets and traditions that matter very much to them. Dawkins accepts the scientific account of the natural world, and none of these reviewers has a word to say against it; Dawkins rejects straightforward interpretations of religious assertions as false, and they reject them equally; Dawkins endorses a common sense, humanist ethics engaged with social and environmental issues, and they endorse a more mystically inclined ethics, but still one that leads them to engage with much the same set of issues.

There are serious academics who defend thoroughly conventional, literal religious beliefs — Richard Swinburne has offered an argument in support of the resurrection purporting to show that the truth of the resurrection story (though it seems to have emerged relatively late in the development of the gospels) is very highly probable. Needless to say, Swinburne's argument turns on premises only a committed Christian would accept. Worse, Swinburne relies heavily on the explanatory powers of the God hypothesis, which, as an all-purpose gap-filling 'explainer', provides us with none of the things we value in scientific explanation.

Alvin Plantinga takes a different approach. He claims that religious beliefs, including all the elements of traditional Christianity, constitute knowledge because God ensures a reliable connection between those beliefs and the metaphysical facts. On his account, the truth of Christianity implies that humans were created with a faculty, the *sensus divinitatus* (sense of the divine), through which the Holy Ghost reveals the truth of Christianity to them — but this wonderful faculty is damaged, as a result of original sin. Thus, those of us who fail to agree with Plantinga's religious convictions are simply showing the symptoms of our damaged sense of the divine. But if Plantinga's hypothesis were right, there surely ought to be some method the illuminated could use to repair this damage: the resulting, restored sense of the divine ought then to lead us all to similar conclusions, and help us correct errors on religious questions. Yet religion is closely tied to cultural authority, differs widely around the world, and is subject, even within a single faith community, to deep and apparently unresolvable schisms that, on the face of them, have more to do with struggles over power and authority than with substantive disagreements over important questions that we could actually hope to settle.

Interestingly, Swinburne and Plantinga seem to have taken less offense from the work of the new atheists than Hedges and Eagleton, despite the fact that it's Swinburne's and Plantinga's views that Dawkins directly criticizes. Already used to defending themselves against arguments, Swinburne and Plantinga seem quite happy to meet Dawkins and his academic philosopher-allies on their own terms. See, for example, the exchange between Swinburne and Adolf Grünbaum over Grünbaum's paper, *The Poverty of Theistic Cosmology* in the very respectable *British Journal for the Philosophy of Science*.

Yet it is Dawkins that Eagleton and Hedges feel impelled to attack, not these literal-minded philosophers. Why is an open challenge to religious beliefs that they don't even share so threatening to these reviewers? I think there are two reasons, one of them regrettable, but the other well worth pursuing with real patience and attention. The regrettable reason is the dependence of their abstract theological enterprise on communities of believers. Church institutions, whose ordinary believers innocently suppose that their familiar beliefs are also held by academic theologians, are the main source of support for such theologians. To the extent that Dawkins' and other atheists' arguments drive a wedge between conventional religious belief and the beliefs of academic theologians, they represent a substantial threat; the wedge must be rejected, even if these theologians largely agree with Dawkins on the status of conventional faith.

But the abstract theological enterprise is not really that important; much more important, and more interesting too, is the commitment these reviewers share with more conventionally religious people to a *moral enterprise*. They believe that shared commitment to helping others is threatened by the hard light of Dawkins' austere scientific humanism. Only 'God talk', they suspect, can sustain the allegiance, and their allies' commitment. Similarly, many humanists also worry that open criticism of religious beliefs will drive away allies in the moderate religious community who share humanist social and political concerns. From this point of view, even if the intensely hostile reviews we've been discussing are unjustified and unfair, they raise a justified concern about the consequences of openly criticizing religion.

On this score the argument is hard to settle conclusively. But I would remind my fellow humanists of something important: there is a long history of oppressed groups being encouraged to avoid notice, to be quiet about their opinions, not to protest how they are treated by the wider society but, instead, to hide who they are and blend in as unobtrusively as possible. At the individual level this can make perfect sense. Avoiding conflict is often wise for a vulnerable minority. That atheists *are* a vulnerable minority is pretty obvious; consider George Bush senior, who once said, "I don't know that atheists should be considered as citizens, nor should they be considered patriots. This is one nation under God," and the use of the phrase 'atheistic Communism' as the bogey-man of the cold war, not to mention widespread rhetorical efforts to tar evolution with the brush of atheism: atheism clearly remains a target of opprobrium and hostility today. So perhaps discretion is the better part of valour here. After all, there are worthy causes in which we can enlist alongside religious people who share many of our concerns. If we declare ourselves too openly, we may frighten our potential allies away.

However, the intensity of the attacks on Dawkins and others following the publication of *The God Delusion* worries me. Dawkins' book is no more critical of fundamentalism than Hedges and Eagleton, but Hedges is the only one among these recently prominent critics of atheism who has also written directly against fundamentalism. Dawkins is straightforward and direct about the kinds of religious ideas he rejects and the reasons why he rejects them, and his critics often seem to agree with him about those ideas. Yet the critics dismiss Dawkins' book because it fails to address the delicately balanced metaphysics of their own diaphanous theologies. They quote Dawkins out of context to make his temperate discussion sound ugly and over-bearing, and they attribute ideas and positions to him (that science has no limits, that religion should be suppressed and eliminated, that a society without religion would be a utopian ideal) that he clearly doesn't hold.

This crude over-reaction against Dawkins is reminiscent of attitudes towards other oppressed minorities: to choose a familiar example, many people feel uncomfortable or even offended when a homosexual couple walks down the street hand-in-hand. The usual complaint is that the loving couple are 'flaunting' their sexuality, but somehow the very same people just don't notice when a heterosexual couple does exactly the same thing. Similarly, Dawkins is being attacked for 'flaunting' his atheism. At one time, homosexuality was simply beyond the pale, though that is clearly changing. Outside of some very restricted circles atheism remains so, though it is easier to disguise. We can see this in the widespread demonization of atheism as a terrible threat to morality, and more subtly in the fact that anything short of explicitly, insistently assertive atheism is so regularly reinterpreted as some form of agnosticism (at worst), which is why Douglas Adams took to calling himself a "*radical* atheist." Similarly, Einstein's forthright rejection of a personal God is far too often passed over in favour of superficially religious remarks such as his wry comment contra quantum mechanics, that "God does not play dice with the universe", when a quick look at other quotes reveals clearly that Einstein's use of the word 'God' reflects only his conviction (essential to a working physicist) that the universe is orderly and comprehensible: "I do not believe in a personal God and

I have never denied this but have expressed it clearly. If something is in me which can be called religious then it is the unbounded admiration for the structure of the world so far as our science can reveal it."

It is past time for people to get over narrow arguments about religion, including crude attacks on those who have no religion. It is long past time that the possibility of 'being good without God' was accepted as a fundamental fact about human nature. Forthright atheism is not part of any plan to oppress the religious. Freedom of conscience is a central value in science, since the aim is to find evidence and arguments that really do settle questions, i.e. that *persuade* people to accept a conclusion by appeal to evidence and reason, rather than impose it on them by an appeal to authority. Any healthy form of humanism makes this a central part of its creed, and all I advocate here is that I and those who think as I do should be free to express their views openly without others feeling entitled to take offense.

Neither does forthright atheism seek the elimination of religion. The impulse to see intention when it isn't there, to *personalize* the world at large and understand it in terms of purposes and goals analogous to our own, is a strong and persistent part of human psychology, and religions give collective expression to that impulse. Misguided or not, it will persist. Further, I don't regard the effects of religion as all bad. Like any human institution it has its flaws, not least, as I see it, the flaw of making many false and misleading claims about the world. But religion tends to absorb and, at its best, even to try to think coherently about ethics. Despite the authoritarian structure of religious epistemology, the ethical thinking of religious traditions can (and happily it sometimes does) develop and improve over time. Consider the huge influence (sadly neglected by Christopher Hedges) of the ethical thinking of Greek philosophers on the Christian tradition, and the much more recent but very encouraging tolerance of homosexuality developing within many religions. The rejection of racism even amongst religions, such as Southern Baptism and Mormonism, that were once openly and explicitly racist, is another example of such positive change — though I very much suspect this was a response to broad social change in racial attitudes, rather than a result of ethical reasoning conducted within these religions.

I have no religion, and I do not believe that there is any good evidence for the sectarian beliefs about miracles and metaphysics (and many of the narrower ethical doctrines) that religions teach to their followers. I am an enthusiastic supporter of LaPlace's famous (though perhaps apocryphal) remark, "Je n'ai pas eu besoin de cette hypothèse." I call myself an atheist, not because of some unwarranted certainty over whether there is a God, but because the word frankly and economically says what I believe.

Belief is not the same thing as certainty, and scientists (like all of us) *do* form beliefs without being certain about them — for example, it was perfectly reasonable to believe in classical mechanics until roughly 1910. But there is a powerful argument against the existence of a perfect God, or even just an extremely powerful, benevolent supernatural entity who cares about us: the argument from evil, especially horrendous and seemingly unnecessary pain and suffering. Replies to this argument (especially in recent years, with the growing emphasis on 'negative theodicy' and the even more dodgy 'skeptical theism') have become exercises in *ad hoc* supposition — but such manoeuvres are purely defensive, and they cut off any positive appeal to the God hypothesis to explain anything about our world (a dubious enterprise in its own right, given the *ad hoc* and 'by fiat' character of such explanations). On the evidence, our *working hypothesis* (a more modest phrase for 'belief', when only one hypothesis on a particular topic remains promising as a guide to investigation) should be that there is no such being. More abstractly, I would urge that accepting important beliefs without strong evidence is a very bad habit — it is *bad cognitive hygiene*. It is hard enough to evaluate and correct our own attitudes and beliefs reasonably; we only make it harder when we make exceptions to this good policy and adopt some beliefs and attitudes for 'reasons' we cannot credibly explain to those who don't already agree with us (reasons, in, fact, that most believers cannot really explain to themselves, either).

Nevertheless, I am fully engaged in this world and in our country, and I value good social relations with those who do believe in God. I am no absolutist, and, unlike atheists such as Sam Harris, I am very sympathetic to those who temper their religious convictions with a generous sympathy for others and real respect for what science has to tell us about our world. Believers who reject *Leviticus'* narrow, tribal attitudes towards homosexuality (not to mention some of my favourite seafood), who accept that the use of condoms is an important way to reduce the spread of sexually transmitted diseases and who understand the powerful evidence for evolution demonstrate a far better appreciation of both evidence and humanity than those who cling to narrow, pure and absolutist forms of faith. I hope and believe that we can work together, to support each other, to help save and educate children around the world, and to protect the world on which our children and our grandchildren will depend from the many threats it faces, including those tragically posed by our own heedless wealth and consumption. ✤

CONSTRUCTIVE HUMANISM & THE HUMANIST'S WAGER

by Gary Bauslaugh

W e can probably assume that belief in the supernatural is a permanent fixture in the minds of many, perhaps most human beings. This is in spite of the obvious impossibility that all of these often conflicting beliefs could be true.

What, then, are secular humanists to do? Should we adopt a militant stance in opposition to that which we think is intellectually wrong — as some put it, issue a call to arms against this perceived delusion? Many non-believers of various sorts have advocated precisely that — at least a metaphorical call to arms. Is this wise? Is it likely to be effective?

Perhaps we could be more influential with a different approach to encouraging the development of a secular society, an approach that does not so directly challenge other belief systems. I argue this, in the following analysis, on the grounds that our ultimate goal as humanists — making a better world of this one world we have — will be better served by such an approach.

WISHFUL THINKING

Humanism remains on the fringes of society because it clashes with what is sometimes called people's 'spiritual needs'. This term is a slippery one to be sure — it means many different things to different people. But, speaking generally, it refers to the apparent need of many people to believe that this life is not all there is — there is something larger and more meaningful out there, something that gives our life some sort of higher purpose.

This need is the result of human consciousness — we know we are going to die, and since we are aware of our existence, we want to believe that it is not just the result of random chemical reactions of the material universe. This is probably one of the unintended consequences of the evolutionary development of consciousness: self-awareness has allowed the development of the logical and the abstract thought processes that have allowed humans to come to dominate the earth (apparently there are more of us now than there are rats!) But with such awareness comes concern about mortality, and the desire to find higher meaning, which may not have any particularly helpful evolutionary advantages. And it may have a significant evolutionary disadvantage if it results in, for example, the triumph of arbitrary literalism over rational thought.

Unintended or not, though, there it is. Humanist dreams that the desire to believe in an after life, with all of the attendant wishful thoughts, can be dispelled by logic and clear-thinking seem to be just another example of wishful thinking.

THE NEED FOR HARMONY

Humanists are faced either with the promethean task of overcoming a powerful inherent human proclivity, or with finding a way to contain it — most obviously to keep it in the realm of personal belief and out of the realm of public business. It seems clear that our only hope for a civilized and mature society is for it to be resolutely secular. But that can only happen with the support of people of religious faith, as has been the case in the past with formation of secular democracies. Such democracies are never the result of general acceptance of the notion that religion is superstition, but instead come from acceptance of the idea of religious freedom — that all should be able to practice their own faiths without fear of reprisal or suppression by the state.

To be a useful force in the political landscape, humanists need a strategy other than proselytizing. Trying to convert the masses to rational acceptance of mortality is hopeless, because it is not what many, probably most, people want to believe. The first rule of salesmanship is to create desire for a product. Humanists will always have difficulty making people want to believe what seems, rationally, perfectly evident — that we live in a material world, subject only to impersonal, unsympathetic, natural forces. That is a very hard idea to sell, and humanists do not seem to be making great progress in selling it. Religious fundamentalists (anti-humanists) are making far greater gains.

It is necessary, if humanism is going to be a positive force in influencing the direction of society, that some accommodation with people of faith be found.

THE HUMANIST BELIEF

Humanism is sometimes described as the belief that the only world is the natural world. Belief is an apt term because we cannot know this is true: we believe the world is a natural place because there is so much evidence for it, and there is no reliable evidence for the existence of a supernatural world. So it is a well-considered belief. But it is a belief. It is logically impossible to prove that something does not exist, so we can never prove that there is no supernatural world, and therefore we are left with the status of being believers. To be sure, our belief is much more soundly based than religious ones. But it remains a belief.

We are not, nor can we ever be, in the position of being able to claim that we have absolute knowledge to counteract the religious believers' faith. We have a belief, albeit a logically sounder one, and they have a belief, albeit a logically weaker one. This is the fundamental problem in promoting humanism — we not only have an idea that is unpalatable to many, we cannot prove it, and never will be able to prove it.

CHANGING THE FOCUS OF HUMANISM

Instead of describing humanism as a belief in a natural world, and trying to defend our belief as better than other beliefs, we should adopt the position that any speculative cosmological perspective ought to be irrelevant to the way we conduct our lives. We may as well not waste our time arguing that any one belief is better than any other, because, though we would most probably be right, we will not persuade most people that we are right.

We can, however, effectively argue that the best way for all humans to conduct their lives is on the *assumption* that there is only a natural world — not that this is necessarily the case, but that it is in the interests of all people to *assume* that it is.

The argument is this: whatever we may choose to believe about the supernatural dimensions of human life, we should conduct our interactions with others — our society — as though there is no such dimension. We may wish to believe in God, because we believe there is such an entity, and because it gives us personal comfort to do so, but we should act as though we — human beings — are in charge. We should act as though we are responsible for what we make of our world.

If there turns out to be a God after all, fine. We are not likely to be punished for accepting responsibility for and respecting the world He created. And if no God ever appears on the scene, perhaps there is no such thing, and then it is all the more important that we have behaved as though there is not.

This approach eliminates the problem of competing beliefs, and provides the basis for harmony between people of different beliefs: think whatever you want, but act secularly.

THE HUMANIST'S WAGER

Pascal's famous Wager was that he did not know if there was a God or not, but we should act as though there is one. If not, it really doesn't matter what we do, but if there is a God it is best to be on the right side of Him.

The Humanist's Wager — to act as though there is no God — is the exact opposite of Pascal's and is a much better one. For when does Pascal win? He wins only if there is a spiteful God who will punish people for failing to worship Him, even though he gives them no sensible reason for doing so. And if there is such a capricious God, how can we think that our eternal welfare will be safe in His hands? What if we happened to choose the wrong faith — can we trust such a punitive God to be forgiving of that? If there is a God such as Pascal was betting on, then our future is dubious anyway.

Pascal does not win if there is a benevolent God, for such a God would surely reward good works on earth, whether they were carried out by atheists, agnostics, or people of faith. Such a God would surely not be swayed by empty, covering-your-ass piety of the kind Pascal suggested.

But if there is no God, then Pascal and his ilk are even bigger losers. If there is no God then what we do with our lives and our world is of the utmost importance — indeed it is all that is of importance. Then what we have is the human experience, and the richness and the rewards that are possible in that experience. And the richest of those rewards are not selfish ones, but selfless ones that contribute to the health and happiness of the human community. This is true because we have evolved — there is survival value — in human compassion.

ACTING SECULARLY

If we collectively can assume there is no God, then, because we are caring creatures, there is a better chance we can work together to build a society which respects the dignity and humanity of all persons on earth. If we assume there is no God then the fate, here on earth, of each person matters and justice for all matters, because we will not be counting on some other redemption, some future bliss, some better place to go to. We will be assuming that whatever joy anyone is to get from existence must be found now.

There might be more out there, and so much the better if there is. But our role as humanists should not be to tell people there is no such thing. We should simply try to persuade people not to count on it.

The argument I have presented here does not, of course, apply to those who adopt the perverse position that what you do on earth does not matter — all that counts is faith. There can be no accommodation between humanists and people who choose to believe such things. But the argument can have appeal to more reasonable people of faith, people who should be our allies in trying to create a better world. ✤

THE WORLD
AS A HOLY PLACE,
PART 1

by Dan Overmyer

The natural world has long provided humanity with metaphors for social structure and sacred expression. Native North American myths, for instance, point to the sacredness of the earth as the basis for social life. Some Chinese traditions maintain that social order is derived from nature: the patterns of the universal life force, qi, in Yin and Yang, the four seasons, the structure of the landscape and the order of the stars and planets. The core insight of these old views is that humans are connected to all other forms of life, that we are a part of the whole of things. Modern writers such as Thoreau, Whitman, Muir and Abbey, among others, tell us that our relationship with nature is our most basic reality.

Contemporary science — biology, palaeontology, physics, astronomy — provides this idea with a factual foundation. What may once have been seen as vague nature mysticism defines, in fact, the way things really are, and provides an in-depth understanding of the truth about our own existence. It makes it possible to find the sacred and a sense of transcendence within the physical universe, to see this world as a holy place.

Most of today's dominant religious traditions, however, point beyond the natural world to a place outside our universe to define what is sacred. Ancient Indian thinkers understood that the universe was immense, but neither they nor the composers of myth and theology in other traditions could have imagined that the universe is 14 billion years old and vast, with millions of galaxies and billions of stars. Nor could they have imagined how the universe developed, how the sun and moon were formed and how life began to evolve, or how different strands of proto-humans developed with several extinctions until our own species appeared just 200,000 years ago.

Given their limited knowledge, the ancient thinkers defined a sacred dimension beyond the troubles of life and death. In Mahayana Buddhism, for example, ordinary people turned for aid and inspiration to many powerful Buddhas and *bodhisattvas*, symbols of a transcendent wisdom and peace beyond the earthly sufferings of impermanence and death, a world the pious have sought to escape.

In the monotheistic traditions of Judaism, Islam and Christianity, people have long been taught to believe in a creator God who is transcendent and all-powerful, but who still is concerned with humans and available to them in worship and prayer.

All these traditions locate the sacred, the ultimate meaning of life, in an unchanging dimension that exists beyond the physical world. They gave people hope in both life and death, and personified deities to serve as models for their own lives. They provided moral teachings, patterns of proper behaviour for long-term social justice, peace and survival. These moral teachings have been seen as rooted in the will of God or the wisdom of the Buddha, revealed in sacred texts as social expressions of a transcendent order.

Nonetheless, in the light of what we now know about the history of life and the universe, the foundations of these traditional beliefs are no longer valid. This is particularly so in their conviction that an unchanging, absolute dimension of reality — heaven, or its equivalent — exists beyond the natural universe. There is simply no scientific evidence that such an unchanging dimension could exist. In fact, from the 'big bang' 14 billion years ago to now, everything in the universe has been in a state of constant change, including the stars and galaxies themselves, which go through cycles of birth and death, coalescing from clouds of gas, burning for billions of years, then fading out or exploding in novae, to produce clouds of gas and debris from which new stars can form. Some constant principles can be found in nature, such as the speed of light, the conservation of energy and the force of gravity, but these are patterns of probability and self-organization, not imposed from outside. Within this context, natural events happen through chance and circumstance in an enormously complex way, depending on the life spans of thermonuclear reactions and collisions between stars and galaxies. The earth itself coalesced from clouds of gas, then was bombarded for millions of years by comets and asteroids to arrive at its present — and still changing — condition.

Chance and circumstance also determined the development of life on earth, beginning with the possibility that some organic molecules came here from space with the colliding asteroids and comets. Forms of life on earth have been almost wiped out several times due to volcanic eruptions, ice ages and asteroid impacts, including one 65 million years ago that threw up so much dust and debris that the dominant life form of the time, dinosaurs, could no longer survive. Among the forms of animals that survived were small primitive mammals which, freed of competition with dinosaurs, evolved into our ancient mammal ancestors and gave us the chance to exist.

Chance determines which of thousands of sperm will fertilize the egg that happens to be available at the right time to produce a particular individual; change happens constantly in the trillions of cells that make up our bodies. As the Chinese philosopher Zhuangzi understood 2,400 years ago, "everything will change of itself, that is certain."

All this means that change is how things really are. Hence, there is no point in looking for some unchanging dimension somewhere else, and no possibility of finding it. It is an illusion created by fear of our own change and death.

This is contrary to thousands of years of well-intended teachings, but it need not be a cause for despair. Acceptance of change can bring us back to our real nature and our deep connections with everything else in the universe. As some forms of Chinese Buddhist philosophy realized centuries ago, the process of change is itself the absolute, a realization that can bring a deep sense of joy. Even before that the *Yijing* put it well: "Change: that is the unchangeable."

Human societies change constantly as well. Migrations of peoples, disease, warfare, struggles for power and justice, and personal ambitions ensure that nothing stays static for long. Nevertheless, some things in nature change so slowly that they are perceived as permanent: stellar constellations, the arcs traced by the sun, moon and planets, the changes of the seasons, the locations of mountains and seas, all seem unchanging. Ancient civilizations in Egypt, Mesopotamia, India, China and elsewhere thought these things proved that order and constancy were natural conditions and applied them to human society and government. In this way social rules were understood as expressions of cosmic order. This is understandable, because it is hard to build a stable social order on a vision of constant change. We sense this same need in our own social, economic and political institutions and in our own lives and families.

There is, however, an inherent danger in this perspective. Social institutions that have been appropriate at one time may become instruments of control and oppression if carried on unchanged. We need to remember that in the long term nature just is. Our faulty perceptions of its patterns do not provide cosmic justification for our social traditions. We need to maintain some form of stable social structure without letting it become rigid and oppressive.

This same understanding applies to religious traditions, which attempt to stop time and change with claims that they are based on a self-defined, absolute and unchanging dimension of reality. But in fact there is only one world and one reality, and we are in it and part of it. These traditions of authority from beyond the world have made some useful contributions, but they have also led to a terrible self-righteousness that justifies attacks on other traditions and people. These traditions also divert attention away from preserving life and the world, and focus it on concerns produced by their own imaginations, long solidified by tradition.

We know that our universe is even more complex and beautiful than ancient seers could have possibly imagined. It was not created for us, but somehow, against all odds, we have appeared within it, which is an incomparable wonder and mystery. Though science is discovering new planets around other stars, we are, as far as we know now, the only beings in this universe capable of fully developed speech and abstract, analytical thought. This means that we are the mind of the universe. There is no other. Our responsibility is to think on behalf of the world, as the Confucian philosopher Wang Yangming realized 500 years ago:

We know then, in all that fill heaven and earth there is but this clear intelligence ... My clear intelligence is the master of heaven and earth and spiritual beings. If heaven is deprived of my clear intelligence, who is going to look into its height? If earth is deprived of my clear intelligence, who is going to look into its depth?

We do not yet understand in detail how the amazing development of human consciousness took place, but it is based on the fact that we are made, literally, of star dust. In sober reality, we are cosmic beings.

We humans have a colour-detecting pigment in our eyes called *rhodopsin*, which has also been found in algae, one of the most primitive plants. This means that we are genetically related to algae and to every other form of life that has evolved since algae appeared long ago, and reminds us that this world is the source of our lives. It is our only home. The one absolute truth we should all be able to agree on is that everything we know or can know depends on this world for its existence. It is irrelevant that the world was not created specifically for us, because the marvellous fact is that we are here anyway, to think, work and enjoy.

With this in mind, we must think again about ethics in an attempt to clarify practical rules for living in a universe of constant change, and do it without mystification, without recourse to a supposed realm of authority beyond the world. Chinese Confucian philosophers came close to doing this, but they still postulated a permanent principle of order, *li*, that is present both in the universe and in us, an idea similar to the old Greek and Hellenistic concept of *logos*, the rational principle of all things. European philosophers like Hume and Kant have tried to base ethics on reason alone.

For us, however, the place to begin is our intimate connection with the impermanent, changing universe and all its forms of life.

As the Mahayana Buddhists realized long ago, this shared impermanence provided the basis for an ethic of universal compassion through identification with the "sufferings of all beings." We are all traveling together through space; we are all genetically related and dependent on each other for survival. From this, we can build on the principle that 'good' is what protects and fosters life and earth, and 'bad' is what damages and destroys them. We can build a modern structure of ethics on this foundation, while selecting the best from the ethical traditions of the past, such as Jewish justice, Christian love, Buddhist compassion and Confucian righteousness. All human traditions are our heritage, and we have the right and obligation to learn from them.

Finally, what does all this mean for ideas about God and death? We no longer have to choose between a traditional idea of God and a completely secular point of view. We do not need to remain trapped in the false dichotomy between faith and nihilism. We can find a sacred dimension in this world itself.

Those who still want to talk about God can do so, as long as their discussion takes into account the way the world really is. Theologians such as Vancouver's Sallie McFague are already operating at this level. They might consider God as either a personified symbol of the sacred dimension in the world, or that he/she is limited in knowledge and power, struggling, making mistakes, learning as the universe unfolds, a God that is also a part of change. For Christians, the image of Jesus suffering and dying could provide a start.

A determined theist might still see God behind the beauty and complexity of life, in which case the universe would be a vast experiment. But perhaps adopting the simpler interpretation of the cosmic *Dao* or *Way* might be the better direction, humble and unobtrusive, but the source and order of all life, present in us and the universe at the same time. We need an alternative paradigm for how to live as moral persons with a new sense of what is most precious and sacred based on the way we know things really are, to make more explicit the principles by which many already live. This paradigm is based on scientific discoveries going back at least 150 years to the work of Charles Darwin and the great geologists, physicists, astronomers and biologists of the 19th and 20th centuries. The meaning of life does not come from the outside, but can be found in the human task of thinking and caring for the world. In sum, it is long past time for us to accept who we are and where we are, affirm this world as our only home, be glad we are alive, and get on with it!

As to death, it can be a terrible thing, particularly if family or friends die young, violently or unjustly. We are fortunate if we share close and loving relationships to help bear the pain. But in the larger perspective death has always been a natural part of life, and necessary for the process of evolution. Zhuangzi was way ahead of us in his statement, "Therefore, the reason why I appreciate life, is because I also appreciate death." We all want to stay alive as long as possible, but whatever immortality we have will depend on our family and friends and on what we contribute to the ongoing flow of life and knowledge. To Confucian philosophers, the options were either to "leave behind a fragrance for a hundred generations," or to "leave a stench for 10,000 years." Those are our options now as well. The choice is ours to help make this precious world a better place. ❦

THE WORLD
AS A HOLY PLACE,
PART 2

by Dan Overmyer

In September 2006 I wrote the following in response to questions concerning my views of Sam Harris' book, The End of Faith: Terror & the Future of Reason *(Norton, 2005).*

I think that his criticisms of destructive religious beliefs and actions based on them are basically correct, but that he does not give sufficient credit to teachings like Buddhist compassion for all living beings, Daoist non-interference, Jewish justice and Christian love. He also neglects the positive sense of identity, purpose and hope that aspects of some religious traditions have helped provide. In addition, he could say more than he does about the fact that much slaughter, destruction and devastation of the environment have been done out of self-centeredness, greed and stupidity not directly connected with religion.

However, my most basic reaction to his book is that it does not go far enough to suggest an alternative orientation other than a few comments about awareness. This essay evokes a larger positive picture that is just a reminder of how things really are. After all these years of studying comparative religion I have finally realized for myself what some others recognized long ago: that the whole enterprise of religion is a vast projection of human hopes, anxieties and insecurities into the world around us in a vain attempt to construct a cover of security in the face of change and death. This may have been justified in the past because people didn't know any better, but now we do, and attempts to bolster what deep down we know is not true just results in fanaticism, a desperate attempt to hang on to the old ideas by trying to force others to agree with them too; trying to use force and politics to support the outer shell of empty beliefs.

How much better it is to cut loose from all of that, accept who, what and where we really are, and find peace in what is, for which there are really no alternatives anyway! From there we can build a new ethic of deep gratitude and responsibility for all of life.

In the West "finding peace in what is" has been difficult because of 2,500 years of dualistic tradition that has sought to find peace and assurance in realms imagined to be beyond the world, beginning with such ideas as Plato's ideal forms and Hebrew belief in a transcendent God. Such beliefs have become the foundation of traditions and of institutions dedicated to preserving them, such as Judaism, Christianity and Islam. In addition, the many centuries of dominance by dualistic beliefs have so permeated Western culture that even those who do not take them literally are still profoundly influenced by them. One of the corollaries of such beliefs is that of a split between soul and body, with priority given to the soul as master of the body that it transcends after death.

Even those who prefer to talk about 'self' instead of 'soul' reflect this old belief, with mind replacing soul in a dualism of mind and body. Only in recent decades have we discovered that there is no such split, that the mind is a product of chemical and electrical activity in the brain. Without brains in living bodies there is no mind. This has been verified by experiments demonstrating the dependence of feelings, ideas and sense of identity on specific areas of the brain, but the old Chinese philosopher Wang Chong (27 – c 100 CE) realized this long ago in his own terms while discussing ideas that humans become 'spiritual beings.' He wrote:

*Man and other creatures are all creatures. When other creatures
die, they do not become spiritual beings. Why should man alone
become a spiritual being when he dies? ... Man can live because
of his vital forces. At death his vital forces are extinct. When a
person dies, his blood becomes exhausted. With this his vital forces
are extinct, and his body becomes ashes and dust. What is there to
become a spiritual being?*

— *A Sourcebook in Chinese Philosophy,*
translated and compiled by Wing-tsit Chan

Mind/body dualism becomes a basis for splits between humans and
the natural world and an exaggerated sense of selfhood that leads to
alienation between us and other people, and, by derivation, between
our culture and nation and those of others. Our bodies are intimate
parts of the natural world and completely interdependent with it; they
are nature for us. Once we try to declare the independence of our self/
mind from the body, we become alienated from our place in the midst
of things, and think that we are free to do as we wish with nature and
other people.

At a social level, old dualistic assumptions can be seen in utopian
movements, both religious and secular, that project into the future an
idealized world or state of being freed from the limitations of life in
the present. For the West, Plato held forth for an ideal society ruled by
philosopher-kings, and the ancient Hebrews believed that their God
had promised them a new land of their own where they could escape
the control of Egyptian pharaohs. Early Christians hoped for the quick
return of the Messiah, 'the Son of Man,' who would bring them eternal peace and joy. Throughout the Middle Ages there were popular
religious movements proclaiming the imminent return of the Messiah,
based on ideas of thinkers like Joachim of Fiore (c 1132–1202) who pro-
claimed a coming 'Age of the Spirit.' (For a detailed discussion of such
movements, see Frank E Manuel and Fritzie P Manuel, *Utopian Thought
in the Western World*). These utopian movements fostered a powerful
momentum of hope for a new world that transcended the old, momentum given new force by Karl Marx and Frederick Engels and all those

who followed in their wake. Of course, we need ideas and policies for improving life in the present, but many utopian movements have had the fatal flaw of diverting attention and energy away from the present toward an imagined future. It is in this sense that even the most secular-appearing of them have continued the old dualism in new forms. What we need instead is reforms free of the old illusions, reforms that focus on benefiting life and the world in specific, practical ways, such as providing better health care, education, jobs and housing, all in awareness of the need to protect the natural environment.

Another dangerous flaw in some utopian movements is the support they give for leaders who claim special wisdom and the right to tell others what to do, leaders who in some cases take over nations to foster their own power and control to build up their own egos and defeat opponents; such leaders can cause untold harm. Nations controlled by aggressive leaders with ego-centered ideologies bring terrible destruction to their own people, other countries and the natural world. There are many causes for the rise of such leaders, but one of them is the availability of dualistic justifications for creating ideal worlds in their own image. In effect, such leaders claim to be the minds that rightly control the body of society. On the basis of such assumptions, they can resort to violence to control their own people and try to impose their views and power on other nations by economic sanctions or warfare.

Dualistic views are ultimately an expression of a deep cultural immaturity, a refusal to grow up and accept who and where we are, a desire to remain protected by a cosmic surrogate parent, as Freud understood long ago. They express a preference to remain as dependent children rather than accept life and death as mature adults. One might object that rejecting such dependence might be acceptable for those with physical and social security, but what about the poor, oppressed, weak and sick; don't they need some kind of divine support? I think not. How is it compassionate to try to comfort people with ideas one knows cannot be true? Do not promises of aid based on illusions simply denigrate their suffering? Illusory hopes for life after death may be comforting to some, but they can also support destructive ideas about life and the world, and be used to justify warfare or suicide. No, the answer to poverty and suffering is practical compassion that seeks to reduce them, social programs focused on the details of peoples' lives here and now, based on the realization that we are all in this together, and so must depend entirely on ourselves and each other for aid and comfort. This is the only game in town, but it is our game, and it is up to us to play it well, because there is nowhere else to turn. The beauty of this is that the life-giving world is still here, for us to rely on, use and care for.

This world is our only hope, but what a hope it is! ✺

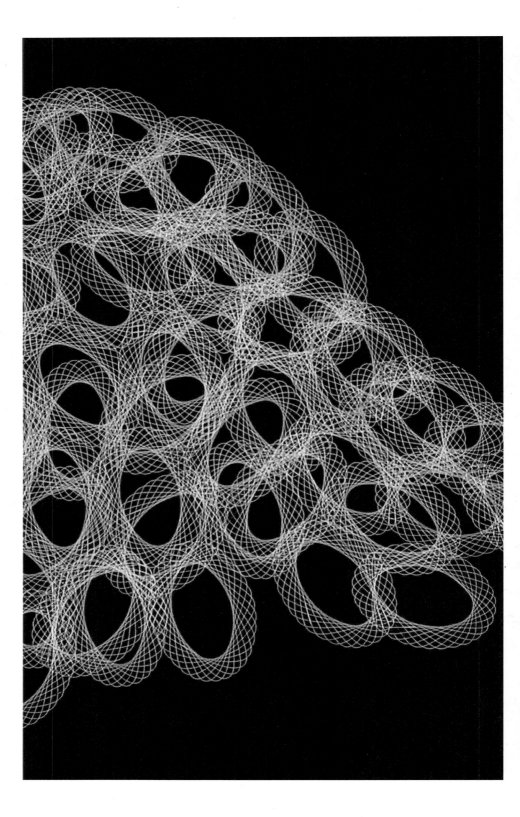

JAMES ALCOCK is Professor of Psychology at York University and is internationally known for his books and other writings on social psychology, skepticism and critical thinking. His books include the co-authored *A Textbook on Social Psychology*, 6th Ed (2005) and *Psi Wars* (2003). In 1999 he was named by a panel of skeptics as one of the outstanding skeptics of the 20th Century. He was an original member of the Executive Council of the Committee for the Scientific Investigation of Claims of the Paranormal.

MARK BATTERSBY taught philosophy for many years at Capilano University. He has many areas of particular interest including post-secondary educational reform and critical thinking, a field in which he is internationally recognized. His recent work includes a book on understanding scientific reasoning: *Is That a Fact?* published by Broadview Press, and a textbook on critical thinking entitled *Reason in the Balance*, published by McGraw Hill.

GARY BAUSLAUGH was Editor of *Humanist Perspectives* from 2003 to 2008, during which time he also served for year as President of the Humanist Association of Canada. His books *Robert Latimer: A Story of Justice & Mercy* (2010) and *The Secret Power of Juries* (2013) were published by James Lorimer & Co. Gary has a PHD in Chemistry and taught at various institutions, was VP of Instruction and Planning at Malaspina University College (now Vancouver Island University), and was CEO of a BC Provincial education agency.

BRYSON BROWN is Professor of Philosophy at the University of Lethbridge, where he has taught since 1986. His main academic interests are in logic and philosophy of science. Bryson was born in Niagara Falls, Ontario, lived in Montréal, New Jersey, Louisiana, Halifax and Mississauga while growing up, and attended Trent University before his graduate studies at the University of Pittsburgh. Although he lost his son thirteen years ago, he was already long since an atheist, for the reason Laplace is said to have given: the God hypothesis adds nothing to our understanding of ourselves or the world.

SHAWN DAWSON was raised in a small town in rural Saskatchewan and given a strong, but overbearing, evangelical religious upbringing. He had private doubts about religion as a teenager that were not fully expressed or explored until he attended the University of Regina. Here, Shawn stumbled upon Philosophy and it was this that most directly lead to his intellectual awakening. Eventually earning a MA in Philosophy, Shawn adopted humanism as the life stance most appropriate to his own, and although he is somewhat wary of labels, it is this essentially positive philosophy he hopes is expressed in his occasional writings.

JONNY DIAMOND is a writer and editor from Toronto who edited *L Magazine* in New York for about ten years. He has published many works of fiction and creative non-fiction in various publications including *Geist, Prism International, Exquisite Corpse* and *Hobart Pulp*. For four years he wrote a much-admired regular column, LETTER FROM NEW YORK, for *Humanist Perspectives*. He now lives in upstate New York with his wife Amanda and their son Lucian, and is attempting to finish a novel, a play, a screenplay, a manifesto and a libretto.

GWYNETH EVANS taught university courses and programs in English, theatre and liberal studies. She was Associate Editor of *Humanist Perspectives* (while Gary Bauslaugh was Editor). She regularly reviews children's books for the magazine *Quill & Quire*, and has done much scholarly work in Victorian Literature and other areas. She is a professional harpist and a committed environmentalist. She lives with Gary Bauslaugh, something she manages with estimable good cheer.

SHIRLEY GOLDBERG taught English and film studies for many years at Vancouver Island University (formerly Malaspina University College) in Nanaimo, BC. She is a writer, film critic and film programmer. Her column FILMS, which appeared for several years in *Humanist Perspectives*, was a rich exploration of social issues with reference to international cinema. Her work was twice nominated for *Western Magazine* awards for best regular column, winning in 2007.

TRUDY GOVIER recently retired from the Department of Philosophy at the University of Lethbridge. She is the author of many articles and books, including *Social Trust & Human Communities* (1997), *Socrates' Children* (1998) and *Forgiveness & Revenge* (2002). Her textbook *A Practical Study of Argument* is in its seventh edition and is widely used. Trudy is keenly interested in conflict resolution and has been active as a moderator and facilitator in community groups. She is a popular public speaker. In connection with her interest in reconciliation, she has traveled and worked in South Africa, East Germany and Ireland.

IAN JOHNSTON is the author of a number of justly forgotten rude satirical plays. He also taught Liberal Studies, English, and Classics for many years at Malaspina University College (now Vancouver Island University), before he retired to pursue his interest in with translating important books of the Western literary canon.

MIKE MATTHEWS was a college English and Theatre instructor whose academic work never quite quelled his need to make inflammatory exhibitions of his peculiar opinions. He has thrown those opinions up to view in assorted publications, ranging from the sublime (*Tish, True North Down Under, Pugn* and *BC Library Quarterly*) to the beautiful (*National Post, Globe & Mail, Victoria Times-Colonist* and *Malahat Review*). He was a co-author of a novel, *Piccolo Mondo,* a self-congratulating chronicle of a West Coast counter-culture coterie. He lived 22 years on a small island in the Strait of Georgia. Mike died in 2012.

THEO MEIJER was a teacher and lifelong humanist. He served as President of the BC Humanist Association (1996–99) and was for many years a member of the Victoria Secular Humanist Association. His column on humanism was a regular feature of the magazine *Humanist Perspectives.* Theo passed away in June of 2009. Because of the clarity with which he articulated a positive and constructive approach to humanism, and because of his steadfast and loyal friendship, this book is dedicated to his memory.

DAN OVERMYER is Professor Emeritus, Chinese Thought and Religion, Department of Asian Studies and Distinguished Associate Member of the Centre for Chinese Research at UBC. He is a member of the Royal Society of Canada. He was a chemistry and biology major in university, then moved on to theology and eventually to the history of religion and Chinese religion and philosophy at the University of Chicago, all of which influenced his views in his essay in this book.

JOSEPH TUSSMAN was Emeritus Professor of Philosophy at the University of California at Berkeley, and died in 2005. His book *Experiment at Berkeley,* describing an integrated liberal studies he introduced at Berkeley in the 1960s, has inspired undergraduate educational reform across North America. His first book, *Obligation & the Body Politic* (1960) was a powerful and influential analysis of the responsibilities of citizenship in a democracy.

ROBERT WEYANT is a retired Professor of Psychology and former Dean of Arts and Science at the University of Calgary. His article on Charles Darwin, reprinted in this anthology, was first published in *Humanist Perspectives*, Autumn 2004, and was a finalist for a Western Magazine Award for best science, medicine or technology article. His writings include the co-editing of *Science, Pseudo-Science & Society* (1979) and many articles and reviews.

ILLUSTRATORS

cover, Emrys Damon Miller
www.rocketday.com

introduction, Amanda Park Taylor
amandaparktaylor.tumblr.com

part 1, Marian Bantjes
www.bantjes.com

part 2, Zela Lobb
www.zelazela.com

part 3, Charlotte Campbell

part 4, Shawn Shepherd
www.shawnshepherd.com

part 5, Nathan Popp

part 6, Dushan Milic
www.dushanmilic.com

part 7, Mitsu Ikemura
www.mitsu-ikemura.com

end, Ingrid Mary Percy
www.ingridmarypercy.com

THANK YOU

We would like to thank Simon Parcher, President, and the rest of the Board of Directors of Canadian Humanist Publications, the body responsible for publishing the magazine *Humanist Perspectives*, for their support in the original publication of most of the articles in this collection. Those articles were published between 2003 and 2008 when Gary Bauslaugh was Editor and Emrys Miller was Designer of the magazine. Most of the articles were written by regular columnists for the magazine: James Alcock's THINGS THAT GO BUMP; Jonny Diamond's LETTER FROM NEW YORK; Shirley Goldberg's FILMS; Trudy Govier's PRACTICAL PHILOSOPHY; Theo Meijer's REFLECTIONS OF A HUMANIST. Ian Johnston wrote on BOOKS and contributed other articles as well. Gwyneth Evans wrote on Children's Literature.

We are indebted to this remarkable group of writers who provided the core writing of the magazine for those five years, and some of whose work we are pleased to present again here, along with some additional essays by other fine contributors to the magazine during this period. It is a pleasure also to include some new articles written for this anthology.

We acknowledge the great support each of us has received over the years from friends and family, and from members of the Canadian humanist community, who made it possible to produce the magazine and to compile this anthology.

Several others at the Rocketday studio worked beside Emrys to help design both the past magazine and this book: Jen LeMercier, Jocelyn Mandryk, Laura Gamble, Josh Nychuk and William Bull. We received much support from several illustrators and artists over the years, in particular Dushan Milic and Zela Lobb.

Lastly, we would like to extend very warm thanks to those who sponsored this book's Kickstarter campaign, providing the final boost we needed to bring this book to life.

Kickstarter Patrons ✳ Monique Gatner, Peter & Janet Hicken, Carol Hyland, Gary Miller, Lesley Marian Neilson and Nic Coopey & Karen Neilson.

Kickstarter Supporters ✳ James Alcock, Bryson Brown, Tanya Bryan, Tom Benjamin & Beverley Dondale, Mike Gower, Hemlock Printers, Sue Hughson, Robert Jeacock, Daniel & Everest Lapp, Han Lee, Stefan Lehmann, Emily MacNair, Sarah MacNeill, Trudi Margueratt, Leafe Minaker, Meredith Mitchell, Catherine Morris, Shelley Motz, Rebecca & Carl Neilson, Chris & John Neilson, Marty Shoemaker and Carmen Spagnola.

Rocketday Arts is a communications studio based in Victoria, Canada, supporting projects in education, the arts, environmental stewardship and philosophy.

Rocketday's clients have included *Humanist Perspectives* magazine (Ottawa/Victoria), the Center for Inquiry (NY), the Institute for Humanist Studies (NY), and *Skeptic* magazine (LA), each at the forefront of humanist, rational and secular explorations. The studio has also supported a multifaith art book, UVic's Centre for Studies in Religion and Society, a local community based on Bishop Desmond Tutu's concept of ubuntu, and the karma yoga magazine *Ascent*. I've intentionally set up the design studio right at the divide between theism and atheism, a place where many others have drawn battle lines, but where my personal and natural curiosity lies.

My hope in publishing this book is to stimulate further dialogue on what a vibrant and healthy collective future could look like. What is the role of religion, reason, intuition and science in our coming years? Today's civilization has inherited a complex and rich history of world beliefs, philosophy and science — and we have both the ability and responsibility to analyse our situation, and to help navigate where we go from here.

Thank you for joining us on this journey into humanist thought.

Emrys Miller, Designer & Publisher
www.rocketday.com